Method, Process, and Austrian Economics

Method, Process, and Austrian Economics

Essays in Honor of Ludwig von Mises

Edited by
Israel M. Kirzner
New York University

LexingtonBooks
D.C. Heath and Company
Lexington, Massachusetts
Toronto

Library of Congress Cataloging in Publication Data

Main entry under title:

Method, process, and Austrian economics.

Includes index.
1. Austrian school of economists—Addresses, essays, lectures. 2. Von
Mises, Ludwig, 1881–1973—Addresses, essays, lectures. I. Von Mises,
Ludwig, 1881–1973. II. Kirzner, Israel M.
HB98.M47   330.15'7   82-47573
ISBN 0-669-05545-x   AACR2

Copyright © 1982 by D.C. Heath and Company

Published simultaneously in Canada

Printed in the United States of America

International Standard Book Number: 0-669-05545-x

Library of Congress Catalog Card Number: 82-47573

Contents

Preface and
Acknowledgments

September 29, 1981 marked the one-hundredth anniversary of the birth of my teacher, Ludwig von Mises. Mises was a towering scholar in a number of fields, but it was as a world-renowned economist in the "Austrian" tradition that he did his most important work. My colleagues and I in the program in Austrian Economics at New York University undertook to organize a scholarly conference to mark this important anniversary. The conference took place September 20–22, 1981 in New York under the joint auspices of the C.V. Starr Center for Applied Economics at New York University and of Liberty Fund, Indianapolis. This book consists of revised versions of the eighteen papers and formal comments presented at the conference, together with a brief introductory chapter.

It is a great privilege to offer this book of distinguished papers to the public. I believe that there can be no more fitting memorial to our beloved mentor than this evidence of vigorous new work being done in the spirit of the Misesian approach. If we are the fortunate witnesses to a modest Austrian revival, this must certainly be attributed to the powerful influence of Mises's immensely persuasive teaching and writing. Together with the continuing flow of work from Mises's most brilliant follower, F.A. Hayek, the Misesian influence has nourished a new generation of younger Austrians, the impact of whose work undoubtedly will be felt in the years to come. It is with exceptional pleasure that their written contributions to the conference are included in this collection.

It is my pleasant obligation to acknowledge gratefully the help, cooperation, and wise counsel of a number of good friends. We are grateful indeed to Margit von Mises for her gracious presence during part of the first day of our conference. Her warm words of encouragement were memorable and poignant. Her own boundless energy and initiative in the posthumous dissemination of her husband's works and ideas have been an inspiration to us all.

The generosity of Liberty Fund made the conference possible; I owe an incalculable debt to Kenneth S. Templeton, Jr., for his wisdom and encouragement in planning this conference—from the very first leisurely discussion in the garden at Graz, Austria, in the summer of 1980 to its successful completion in New York some fourteen months later. Others who contributed advice during the planning and execution of the conference and/or of this book are: Ludwig Lachmann, Richard Ebeling, George Pearson, Don Lavoie, Richard Langlois, and Lawrence H. White. My colleagues at

New York University, Gerald P. O'Driscoll, Jr. and Mario J. Rizzo, have been generously supportive throughout the project. R. Robert Russell and Eliana Covacich of New York University's C.V. Starr Center for Applied Economics were helpful in every possible way. Finally, I owe a special debt of gratitude to all the chapter authors for their patience and good humor in graciously meeting the demands of what must at times have appeared a cantankerously inflexible conference director and editor.

New York, February 1982   *Israel M. Kirzner*

1

Introduction

Israel M. Kirzner

Mises and the Austrian Tradition

We are witnessing what appears to be at least a modest revival of interest in the Austrian tradition on the part of the economics profession. There can be no doubt that this revival is to be attributed to the tenacity with which Mises continued to pursue his writing and teaching when it appeared that the profession had decisively turned its collective back on that tradition.[1] Much, perhaps most, of Mises's substantive contributions to economics had been completed before Mises arrived in the United States early in World War II. But the decades that followed witnessed an explosion of work in economics along lines that Mises considered profoundly mistaken. Instead of developing theory informed by subjectivist insights, the profession was turning toward a mindless and spuriously quantitative empiricism; instead of pursuing the subtle social processes set in motion by interacting, purposeful human individuals, the profession was entranced by the "hydraulics" of dubious models constructed from crude aggregative components. The Austrian-trained economists who had sought the intellectual leadership of Mises in Vienna during the twenties and thirties became, as a result of the imminent conflagration in Europe, geographically scattered and disorganized. During the lonely decades that followed, undeterred by thinly disguised disparagement on the part of his professional colleagues, and without the suitable academic base to which his stature and contributions entitled him, Mises continued to publish prolifically and to teach and lecture to whomever would listen.

In the 1960s and 1970s it appeared that economists were retreating, to a degree, from some of the aggregative excesses that had marked the immediate postwar era. There has been a return, in the professional mainstream, to a theoretical perspective aware of the importance of the microfoundations of the discipline. There has been a return to the neoclassical theory developed during the half-century following the marginalist revolution of the 1870s—a milieu in which the Austrian tradition in economics originated and flourished.

Yet the mainstream neoclassical revival of the past two decades has by no means constituted a return to the perspectives of the Austrian tradition.

1

This may, at first glance, appear paradoxical. For many historians of thought, after all, the Austrian school is considered simply one of the intellectual tributaries from which the neoclassical mainstream took its source. Yet the truth is that the body of thought that developed in Vienna from Menger to Mises embodied insights that never were absorbed into the neoclassical tradition that drew from the confluence of Marshallian and Walrasian doctrine. A persuasive case can be made that the cracks and strains developing recently within the structure of contemporary economic theory, can be attributed precisely to the absence, in the dominant neoclassical tradition, of those Austrian insights.[2] It is no accident, therefore, that at this time of dilemma within economics, the ideas of the Austrians, and of Mises in particular, are being rediscovered. The perspective that Mises steadfastly pursued during the inhospitable forties and fifties has come to be seen as offering for the eighties a remarkably sensitive understanding of the operation of modern economic systems.

Mises and the Modern Austrian Revival

The chapters in this book reflect, in many ways and in different degrees, this recognition. There have been occasions in the past when admirers of the economic contributions of Ludwig von Mises have been accused, not entirely without grounds, of according his views the unswerving acceptance ordinarily reserved for incontrovertible truth. There are, no doubt, altogether understandable sociological forces inducing such uncritical attitudes toward a great but neglected thinker on the part of admirers dismayed by contemptuous treatment of him. Fortunately, the rediscovery in recent years of the brilliance, power, and depth of Mises's work has substantially eliminated the forces that might induce such unswerving acceptance. Mises's ideas are being treated with the respect they so richly deserve: they are discussed extensively, seriously, and critically. The reader of this book will, therefore, encounter lively and uninhibited discussion of a number of fundamental Misesian ideas as well as innovative attempts to reappraise such ideas in the light of recent work by leading contributors to other traditions within the modern literature. But whether these chapters represent departures from Misesian orthodoxy, or revised assessment of the role of Mises in the history of economic thought, or measured reaffirmation of Misesian insights, they share an awareness of the subtle and profound aspects of the Misesian economic system that set it apart from the contemporary mainstream and that account for the thoroughly Misesian character and outlook of the modern Austrian revival. The various issues in Misesian economics raised in this book may be grouped under four headings: (1) the choice of economic method; (2) the nature of human action; (3) the character of the market process; and (4) the Misesian system as a framework for applied economic theory. It may be useful to show how thoroughly interrelated these groups of issues are within the Misesian system.

The Misesian System

For Mises the *market* constitutes a social process made up of the systematic sequences of decisions of interacting purposeful individual human beings continually discovering what they believe to be better ways of improving their respective situations. From this overall vision of the market process flow a number of the characteristically Misesian insights. We note immediately, of course, that the emphasis on social processes of discovery at once demotes the concept of market equilibrium from any position of centrality (as it enjoys, for example, in neoclassical orthodoxy). On the other hand the perceived systematic character of the social-discovery process renders it far away indeed from any conception of the market as sheer, unorganized chaos. (As Roger Garrison points out in chapter 11, the Austrians occupy, on more than one theoretical issue, a comfortable middle ground!) Several chapters grapple with the problems faced in demonstrating the systematic character of the market process.

The Misesian view of the market is peopled by purposeful individuals—human beings continually making discoveries. This feature of the Misesian view entails an unorthodox view of the analytical unit in economic theory—the individual decision, as expressed in human action. At the same time, because this view of the analytical basis for economic theory places so much emphasis on an unobservable—the purposefulness held to actuate human behavior—it follows that the epistemological character of the discipline, and hence the method appropriate to it, differs sharply from those relating to the physical sciences. In this, too, Mises found himself in disagreement with his fellow economists. In these regards (as well as in regard to Mises's well-known dismissal of the use of mathematics in economics) several chapters subject the Misesian position to searching and critical analysis.

The Misesian notion of purposeful human action bears resemblance in many respects, of course, to the concept of the individual decision in standard neoclassical microeconomic theory. But it is by now fairly well recognized that for Mises human action embraced far more than the simple economizing decision of neoclassical theory. The difference between the two concepts draws attention, in turn, to different levels of subjectivism identified in chapters of this book. Methodological individualism, although insisting on tracing market phenomena back to their roots in individual action, is consistent, in principle, with a variety of levels at which the subjectivity of action may be recognized. At the lowest level, perhaps, the individual is viewed as merely reacting in programmed, maximizing fashion to the environment that confronts him. Subjectivism is here confined to recognizing the given configuration of tastes and expectations with which the individual is somehow viewed as being endowed. At higher levels, on the other hand, the individual decision may be recognized as incorporating in an essential way the *discovery* of what that environment is or is likely to be. Or again, it may be held as *creating* that environment in devising feasible courses of action that were hitherto nonexistent. In discussions of these higher levels of subjectivism, Mises's vision of the entrepreneurial character of individual action has been compared or contrasted with the view of the decision extensively developed by George Shackle. In view of the radical indeterminacy emphasized by Shackle in his discussions of human decisions, these comparisons raise issues that extend, in turn, once again to the very possibility of systematic market processes. If the human decision is as spontaneous, creative, and dynamically subjective as both Mises and Shackle appear to maintain, is it still possible to speak meaningfully of systematic processes of discovery? From such themes it is but a short distance to explicit consideration of the role of uncertainty in the Misesian system. To what extent is the concept of human action inseparable from that of continuous, kaleidic change in the environment? The exploration of these delicate themes, along lines both more and less sympathetic to Mises's views, occupies much of several chapters in this book.

Mises was not merely an abstract theorist. He viewed his theories as providing the analytical framework within which to assess real-world problems and policies. Thus his view of the market as a process called for a sharp departure from the orthodox neoclassical perception of both the meaning and virtues of competition. Moreover, Mises's view of the market as a process of discovery entails rather definite implications for the analysis and assessment of monopoly resource ownership and of government intervention in markets—without, it must be emphasized, departing, he believed, one iota from the valuefree stance of the detached scientist. His views on these and related matters are critically examined in this book.

Mises and the Future of Austrian Economics

The chapters in this book, as well as the conference discussions that they generated, reveal modern Austrians to be far from unanimity on numerous fundamental issues. At times it may even appear legitimate to question the very existence of a clearly defined, generally accepted body of Austrian doctrine. Yet I believe that, on reflection, it can be maintained fairly that: (1)

despite their disagreements Austrian economists do by and large share an overall perspective on the nature and tasks of economic science that permits their designation as a distinct school of thought; (2) this shared overall perspective, when understood against the sweep of the developments in twentieth-century thought, is unquestionably the heir of the earlier Austrian tradition; and (3) the strains and stresses evident at the frontiers of the present Austrian revival are the healthy products of attempts to reconcile Austrian insight with intellectual developments elsewhere in social science.

To the development of this shared overall Austrian perspective, and to the ferment and sense of excitement now evident in the resurgence of interest in this Austrian perspective, Mises's contributions have been crucial and decisive. The true memorial to Ludwig von Mises will be the future work within the Austrian tradition that these contributions continue to generate.

Notes

1. Because of the focus on the Misesian contributions to current ferment at the frontiers of economics, no attempt has been made here to provide an appraisal of Mises in broader terms. We are fortunate in that a significant literature exists that provides excellent material on Mises, including a wealth of biographical and bibliographical detail. Readers may obtain a perspective on Mises's greatness as man and as social scientist from the following works: M. Sennholz, ed., *On Freedom and Free Enterprise* (Princeton, N.J.: D. Van Nostrand, 1956), a *Festschrift* (festival writing) on the fiftieth anniversary of Mises's doctorate from the University of Vienna; Mont Pelerin Society, *Tribute to Mises, 1881–1973* (Chislehurst, Kent: Quadrangle Publications, n.d.); Margit von Mises, *My Years with Ludwig von Mises* (New Rochelle, N.Y.: Arlington House, 1976); L.S. Moss, ed., *The Economics of Ludwig von Mises, toward a Critical Reappraisal,* (Kansas City: Sheed and Ward, 1976); Ludwig von Mises, *Notes and Recollections* (South Holland, Ill.: Libertarian Press, 1978), including postscript by Hans F. Sennholz; Percy L. Greaves, Jr., introduction to Ludwig von Mises, *On the Manipulation of Money and Credit* (Dobbs Ferry, N.Y.: Free Market Books, 1978); J.K. Andrews, ed., *Homage to Mises, the First Hundred Years* (Hillsdale, Mich.: Hillsdale College Press, 1981). For a comprehensive bibliography of Mises's writings the reader is referred to Bettina Bien [Greaves], *The Works of Ludwig von Mises* (Irvington-on-Hudson, N.Y.: Foundation for Economic Education, 1969).

2. See, for example, D. Bell and I. Kristol, eds., *The Crisis in Economic Theory* (New York: Basic Books, 1981).

2

The Domain of Subjective Economics: Between Predictive Science and Moral Philosophy

James M. Buchanan

We . . . are in part living in a world the constituents of which we can discover, classify and act upon by rational, scientific . . . methods; but in part . . . we are immersed in a medium that . . . we do not and cannot observe as if from the outside; cannot identify, measure, and seek to manipulate; cannot even be wholly aware of, inasmuch as it . . . is itself too closely interwoven with all that we are and do to be lifted out . . . and observed with scientific detachment, as an object.   —Isaiah Berlin

Introduction

Any discussion of the methodology of subjective economics must at once confront an elementary fact along with a necessary hypothesis. That fact is that, in any science of human behavior, the observer is himself among the observed. The hypothesis is that human beings *choose*. Without this hypothesis the activity of the observer becomes meaningless exercise. The fact and the accompanying hypothesis impose constraints or limits on any "positive economics," if the model is taken from those sciences within which these attributes are missing. The natural scientist remains separate from the objects of his observation, and, despite the acknowledgment of the possibility of mutual influence between observer and observed, there remains the basic category differentiation. Furthermore, the simple ability to put these words together in a meaningful sentence distinguishes me, as a man, from those objects of science that most resemble me, the higher animals. By the process of writing a sentence, I am choosing what I create; I am not merely reacting to external stimuli, at least in a sense readily amenable to prediction.

I am indebted to Pamela Brown and Karen Vaughn for helpful comments. Precursory ideas to those developed in this chapter are present in my essays, "General Implications of Subjectivism in Economics," and "Natural and Artifactual Man," in my book *What Should Economists Do?* (Indianapolis: Liberty Press, 1979).

In summary terms, the *subjective* elements of our discipline are defined precisely within the boundaries between the positive, predictive science of the orthodox model on the one hand and the speculative thinking of moral philosophy on the other—hence, the chapter's title. For our purposes, I define *moral philosophy* as discourse that embodies an explicit denial of the relevance of scientific explanation. Note that this approach does not require a categorical rejection of the relevance of empirically testable, positive hypotheses concerning certain aspects of human behavior commonly labeled "economic." Nor does the approach rule out the relevance of normative moral philosophy. The approach emphasizes, instead, the existence and the importance of the area between empirical science and moral philosophy. It denies that these categories of thought span the universe of relevance. On this point, I think that my own professor, Frank Knight, and Ludwig von Mises would have been in substantial agreement. Both would have been extremely critical of the modern economists who seek to rule out any nonempirical economics as nonscientific and, by inference, normative. Both these seminal thinkers would have been comfortable with a science of subjective economics, although they might have differed somewhat on the relevance of any other part of our discipline.

Adam Smith and Classical Economics

Classical economics has been almost universally interpreted as an attempted, and ultimately failed, effort to derive an objective and predictive theory of the relative values of commodities. The central features are perhaps best exemplified in Adam Smith's famous deer-beaver illustration, which I shall use here. Smith's hypothesis was that one beaver would "naturally" exchange for two deer in that setting where two days of labor are required to kill a beaver and one day of labor to kill a deer. I want to ask the following question: Even if we grant all the required presuppositions of the Smith model, do we then derive a genuinely predictive theory of the relative values of beaver and deer? Or do there remain necessarily subjective elements in the inclusive explanatory model, even within such an extremely restricted setting?

The required presuppositions are familiar. Deer and beaver must be "goods" to all potential consumers and producers: labor must be a "bad." Labor is the only productive resource, and units of labor are completely homogeneous. Further, each commodity must be producible at constant returns. But we must recall that Adam Smith was seeking to explain *exchange* values. The restrictions of the model, even if fully realized, do not explain the emergence of exchange, and, in the strict sense, no exchange would take place in the setting postulated. If the input ratio is two for one, precepts for rationality suggest that each behaving unit will attain an equilibrium adjustment when the two-for-one ratio is equated to a two-for-one valuation ratio for the two goods. There is no subjective element in the analysis, as I have deliberately limited the scope for the term *subjective* here.

Adam Smith and classical economics were not, however, interested in explaining individual behavioral adjustment. Smith was interested in explaining *exchange* values. And, to explain these, he had to explain the emergence of exchange itself. To do so, he must have incorporated an additional presupposition not listed. The productivity of labor when specialized must be higher than when unspecialized. Smith's emphasis on the importance of the division of labor suggests, of course, that this presupposition was indeed central to his explanatory model. But why would exchange emerge in the first place? Here Smith resorted to man's "propensity to truck, barter, and exchange one thing for another."[1] The critical role of this propensity in Smith's analysis has been too much neglected in interpretations of his work. But with this propensity, Smith places a subjective element at the heart of the whole explanatory model. He quite explicitly contrasts the actions of man with the animals in this respect when he says that "nobody ever saw a dog make a fair and deliberate exchange of one bone for another with another dog."[2]

In some preexchange setting, the exercise of the "propensity to truck"—behavior that must necessarily have been different in kind from that which had been reflected in established patterns (and, hence, predictable scientifically, at least within stochastic limits)—allowed man to discover the advantages of specialization and to create the institutions of exchange within which relative values of commodities come to be settled. The person who initially imagines some postspecialization, postexchange state and who acts to bring such a state into existence must engage in what I shall here call "active" choice. He must do more than respond predictably to shifts in the constraints that are exogenously imposed on him.

An economy (if indeed it could be called such) in which all persons respond to constraints passively and in which no one engages in active choice could never organize itself through exchange institutions. Such an economy would require that the constraints be imposed either by nature or by beings external to the community of those participants who are the passive responders. In either case, such an economy would be comparable in kind to those whose participants are the "animal consumers" examined by John Kagel and Raymond Battalio, and their coworkers.[3]

Even at the level of Adam Smith's most elementary discourse, there are two interpretations that may be placed on his analysis. If Smith is read as relatively unconcerned about the emergence of exchange institutions, and if he is assumed simply to have postulated the existence of specialization, it may be argued that his aim was to present a positive, predictive theory of the relative values of commodities. On the other hand, if Smith is read as primarily or centrally concerned with explaining how exchange institutions emerge, he becomes a thoroughgoing subjectivist in that he resorts to that particular propensity that distinguishes man from other animals. There could be no predictive science concerning the exercise of this propensity, since to predict here would imply that the direction of all future exchanges would be conceptually knowable at any point in time.

The two interpretations of Smith's basic analysis differ in their *explananda*. The first involves an explanation, or attempted explanation, of relative exchange values of commodities. The second involves an explanation of exchange institutions themselves. That which can be predicted (conceptually) can be explained with an objective or scientific theory. That which cannot be predicted can be explained (understood) only by a subjective theory. If this basic methodological duality had been accepted at the outset, much confusion in the history of economic doctrine, then and now, might have been avoided. Subjective economics, properly, even if strictly, defined, occupies an explanatory realm that is mutually exclusive with that properly occupied by positive economics. If this much is granted, however, the relative significance of the two realms of discourse for the inclusive understanding of human interaction becomes clear. Positive or predictive economics becomes largely exercise in triturating the obvious; subjective economics can offer insights into the dynamics through which a society of persons who remain free to choose in a genuine sense develops and prospers.

In subsequent parts of this chapter I shall illustrate this basic argument by reference to somewhat misguided and at least partially confused efforts to emphasize the subjective elements in economic theory, broadly defined. I shall discuss the so-called subjective-value revolution and its transformation into the modern neoclassical synthesis. I shall discuss also the dimensionality of economic theory to show that the dimensionality problem should be considered separately from that of operationality of theory. A discussion of the particular Austrian variant of neoclassical economics, as exemplified notably in the works of Mises, follows with particular emphasis on his insistence of the praxeological foundations of the discipline. The following section discusses the potential applicability of subjective and objective economic theory, and I shall offer a provisional explanation for the relative dominance of the latter in the postclassical century. Finally, I shall summarize the argument and draw some inferences for the direction of research.

The Subjective-Value Revolution of the 1870s and the Subsequent Neoclassical Synthesis

As noted previously, classical economic theory was widely interpreted as an attempt to derive a predictive theory of the relative values of commodities.[4]

Classical economics was acknowledged to have failed in such an attempt. Emphasis came to be placed on the specific difficulties that could not be satisfactorily met with the classical models. The diamond-water paradox remained; the classical effort to explain relative exchange value by objectively measurable costs of production could not survive.

The so-called subjective-value revolution, presented in various ways in the early 1870s by Jevons, Menger, and Walras, was explicitly aimed at resolution of the prevailing difficulties in the classical explanation of exchange values. The early contributions here demonstrated that relative values depend on schedules of evaluation on both sides of the markets for goods, on demand and supply. But we must ask a question here that has not, to my knowledge, been frequently posed. To what extent does the economic theory of Jevons, Menger, and Walras, or their neoclassical successors, embody genuine subjective economics as I have defined this term? Despite its label as the subjective-value revolution in economic theory, are there any necessarily subjective elements in the inclusive explanatory models that were offered in place of the discarded classical edifice?

I suggest that the label *subjective* may be misleading in application to this theory of exchange values, notably so as the initial contributions were redeveloped and refined into the neoclassical synthesis of the twentieth century. The marginal-utility theory of the 1870s embodied the central notion that values are determined at the appropriate margins of evaluation and that the locations of the margins are relevant. The diamond-water paradox was thereby resolved satisfactorily. But there is nothing in the whole analytical framework here to suggest that the evaluation schedules (those of demand and supply), which simultaneously interact to determine the location of the margins and hence exchange values, are not, themselves, *objectively determinate,* at least in a conceptual sense. There is nothing in neoclassical economic theory that precludes the universalized existence of simple reaction patterns of behavior on the part of all persons in the economy, reaction patterns that, even if more complex, are still analogous to those that might empirically describe the behavior of rats. Once individual-utility functions are formally specified, individuals whose behavior is thereby depicted cannot choose differently. Choice, as such, cannot remain in any such formulation.

I am not suggesting here that the objectification of the solution to the problem of determining relative exchange values of goods (and bads) was necessarily central to neoclassical theory. It was not. The earlier classical effort was aimed to provide a single, and simplistic, objective measure of relative exchange values that might be both readily understood and empirically estimated. The neoclassical effort, in contrast, was primarily aimed at resolving difficulties at the level of logical coherence and rigor. There was a shift of emphasis from attempts to provide empirical bases for measurement toward attempts to offer understanding of the whole logical structure of economic interaction. For the latter purpose, the issues involved in making empirical estimates or predictions about relative exchange values do not take on critical significance. These issues tend to be overshadowed by those concerning the derivations of proofs of the existence of solutions to the complex interdependencies that the economy embodies. That the empirical measurability or predictability of exchange values does not occupy center stage in orthodox neoclassical theory should not, however, be taken as evidence that, conceptually, such measurability is categorically impossible. The focus of neoclassical economic theory, in comparison with classical, is shifted from empirical estimates to analyses of structures, but there is nothing directly in neoclassical theory that implies the absence of conceptual predictability. If utility and production relationships are ascertainable, solutions exist and are determinate. It is meaningful in this context to make an attempt to compute equilibrium prices.

The Dimensionality and Data of Economic Theory

My purpose in this section is to clarify possible confusion and ambiguity that may arise from my somewhat restricted definition of subjective economics and from my claim that the term subjective-value revolution as applied to the contribution of the 1870s, may be, in this context, misleading.

It is necessary to distinguish carefully between the definition of the dimensions of the space within which the operations of economic theory are performed and the operationality of the theory itself. My narrowly restricted definition of subjective economic theory is relevant only to the second of these subjects. As I have limited the term here, subjective economic theory embodies those elements of explanation of the economic process that cannot be operationalized in the orthodox sense of predictive science. For those elements of economic theory that can be operationalized, however, I have advanced no presumption whatever about the dimensionality of the space.

Confusion necessarily arises at this point between the claim that any economic theorizing must take place within a subjective-value dimension and the totally different claim that, because of the subjective dimensionality, an operational theory is not possible. The first of these claims must be accepted. Economic theory is surely concerned with evaluations, with values. It is totally misleading to think of physical dimensionality here. Goodness and badness are qualities that are assigned to physical things, to commodities or services, by personal evaluations.

The naive and simplistic efforts by the classical economists to derive a predictive theory of relative exchange values tended to obscure the value dimension and generated the absurdity that commodities may be produced by commodities, somehow independently of the evaluation put on these by persons. In the sense that it emphasized and brought to full realization the essential value dimension, it is appropriate to label the 1870s effort as a subjective-value revolution. But, as I have noted, this corrective shift in implied dimensionality of the space for the application of economic theory carries with it no direct implication for the potential operationality of the theory itself. Indirectly, of course, there is the obvious implication that only if economic theory applies within a value dimension could there arise any issue of nonoperationality. Subjective economics could hardly be discussed in any analysis of variables in pure-commodity space. On the other hand, however, there is nothing in the value dimension itself that logically prohibits the derivation of a fully operational science. Whether or not such analysis is possible depends not on dimensionality but instead on the possible uniformity of valuations over persons.

A related source of confusion involves the informational requirements that a thoroughgoing recognition of the value dimensionality of economics places on any putative scientist who seeks to derive empirically testable hypotheses. F.A. Hayek, in particular, has emphasized the value dimensionality of economic theory and the informational implications of this attribute for the organization of society.[5] Markets utilize information efficiently; they do not require extensive centralization of information about individual evaluations. And, indeed, the informational requirements for a centrally planned economy may be practically insurmountable. There is nothing in the basic Hayekian insight, however, that precludes the possible derivation of a set of conceptually refutable hypotheses about the evaluations of all persons over all goods and services.

In earlier works I have stressed the subjectivity of costs, and I have tried to show how errors arise in applications of economic theory when this basic dimensionality is overlooked.[6] In the restricted classification scheme that I have suggested in this chapter, however, there is nothing in my analysis of cost, as such, that precludes the derivation of a set of conceptually refutable hypotheses, which is, of course, the criterion of a predictive theory. Costs are, of course, related to choices, but if there are sufficient data on the environment of a past choice and if the chooser's behavior is, in some sense, predictable on the basis of observed uniformities, choices may be judged ex post. Practically, the subjective-value dimension of economic behavior may make enforcement of any cost-price rule impossible, but such application of the predictive science cannot be deemed conceptually impossible.

Mises and Praxeology

Mises explicitly denied that economic theory can be operational in the orthodox meaning of this term. Economic theory was, for Mises, necessarily a priori; it offered a pure logic of choice. In taking this extreme position methodologically, Mises seemed to be aware that attempts to force economic theory into the straitjacket imposed by the requirements for predictive science must, at the same time, deny to persons who act the possibility of making genuine choices.

I shall confess here that I have never been able to appreciate fully the Misesian emphasis on praxeology or "the science of human action."[7] Central to this conception is the purposefulness of all human action. Man acts always with a purpose; he seeks to replace a state of relative dissatisfaction with one of relative satisfaction. However, an observer can never get inside anyone else; he can never know what a person's purpose is. Hence, there is no way, even conceptually, to predict what action will be taken in any particular circumstance. A person chooses that which he chooses, and when he so chooses, he must anticipate that the chosen course of action will yield a net increment to his satisfaction. Although he may err, we can never infer, ex post, that he acted irrationally.

At its most general, this Misesian theory of choice is totally nonoperational. It can "explain" any conceivable course of action that a person might be observed to take; the obverse is, of course, that the theory can really "explain" nothing at all. Mises himself did not worry about nonoperationality as such, presumably because his reliance on introspection provided him with a basis for sorting out meaningful from meaningless explanations. To return to the Adam Smith illustration, Mises could claim to have explained why exchange institutions emerged from the vision of some person who imagined the mutual advantages of specialization and exchange. Mises could also explain the relative values of deer and beaver quite simply as those exchange ratios that emerge from the purposeful choice behavior of participants in the exchange process, whose acts of participation or nonparticipation are themselves purposeful.

Misesian economic theory becomes strictly subjective economics in my earlier definition of the term. But my basic criticism of Mises is that he claimed far too much for the subjective-economics domain. He seemed to want to preempt the whole territory when he totally rejected the existence of any relevant domain for what I have called positive or predictive objective economic theory. This somewhat overzealous extension of methodological frontiers may be at least partially responsible for the relatively limited reception that the ideas of Mises have had among economists, catholically classified.

The basic Mises conception of praxeology seems flawed in that it appears to incorporate two quite distinct sorts of human action, one of which may be analyzed scientifically and empirically in the orthodox sense. Consider two examples: (1) A man is walking along a road; he sees a car approaching; he jumps to the side of the road to avoid being run down. His action here is purposeful. It is surely aimed at removing a potential state dissatisfaction and replacing it by one that is preferred. (2) A man is walking along a road barefooted. His feet are sore. He sees some cowhide and he imagines the possibility of shoes. He acts to make the shoes from cowhide. (My thanks to Israel Kirzner for this exmple.) This action is purposeful, and it, like the first, is surely aimed at replacing a state of dissatisfaction (sore feet) with one that is preferred.

But Misesian praxeology, as I understand it, would seem to include both examples within the realm of human action that theory seeks to analyze and to explain. I submit, however, that they are categorically distinct. The first action need not reflect conscious, active, or creative choice; it can be interpreted as an animal-like response to a change in the external environment. It is reflective of behavior that might have been scientifically predicted. It is the sort of action that could describe the behavior of rats as well as men. By evident and sharp contrast, an animal could never take the second sort of creative action, which becomes uniquely human.[8] The Misesian praxeological umbrella that seems to encompass both sorts of action does not allow the sophisticated discrimination that must be made between the two. Indeed the Misesian emphasis on treating all human action as if it were like the second example tends to foster a critical response that involves the danger of neglect of the very type of action that subjective economics properly emphasizes.[9]

The Mutually Exclusive Domains for Economic Theory

There are patterns of human behavior in economic interaction that are subject to conceptual prediction about which empirically testable hypotheses may be derived. There is a legitimate domain for predictive economic theory. Or, to put my point differently but somewhat more dramatically, in some aspects of their economic behavior, with appropriate qualifications, men are indeed like rats.[10] They are essentially passive responders to economic stimuli; they react; they do not choose. They are programmed, whether genetically or culturally, to behave in potentially predictable ways to specific modifications in the constraints that they face. The scope for this predictive theory of economic behavior is enormously extended when it is acknowledged that it is the behavior of some average or representative member of a group that is to be predicted here, not the particularized behavior of an individual.

The recognition of the domain of an operationally meaningful economic theory does not carry with it any implication concerning the practical usefulness of this theory in making predictions in the real world and/or in using such predictions to control man's behavior in that reality. There remains the awesome gap between the science that embodies conceptually refutable hypotheses and that science that embodies definitive refutation or corroboration. The familiar distinctions between the human and the nonhuman sciences involving controls on experiments arise here, along with the informational problems noted briefly earlier. Nonetheless, ultimate empirical content remains in the theory, regardless of actual testability, and the elaboration of the structure of relationships can add to our understanding of economic reality.

There are also aspects of human action that cannot be subjected to explanation in an operationally meaningful theory of economics. Any attempt to derive even conceptually refutable hypotheses about such action would amount to epistemological confusion. I have labeled this domain that of subjective economics or subjective economic theory. The objects for analysis are the *choices* of persons, which cannot be genuine choices and at the same time subject to prediction. Theory or analysis can be of explanatory value in this domain without the attribute of operationality in the standard sense. Theory can add to our understanding (*verstehen*) of the process through which the economic world of values is created and transformed. Subjective economics offers a way of thinking about economic process, a means of imposing an intellectual order on apparent chaos without inferentially reducing the status of man, as a scientific object, to something that is not, in kind, different from that of animals.[11]

The limits of this vision of economic process must be recognized, however, along with its advantageous insights. Subjective economic theory can be of little assistance in an explanation or understanding of the allocation of values or in predicting general responses to changes in constraints imposed on actors. Since this theory advances no claim to prediction, it can, at best, suggest that any predictions made will likely prove to be wrong, indeed must be wrong to the extent that its own domain of choice is allowed operative range.

The purpose of the explanatory exercise determines the appropriate domain of economic theory to be employed. If this purpose is that of control of the economy through some manipulation of the constraints within which persons respond, the first domain of positive, predictive economic theory is the only one that holds out any scope for assistance. To the extent that this theory can isolate predicted response patterns to shifts in imposed constraints (to an increase or decrease in taxes, for example), those persons who participate in making political decisions (who may, of course, also be members of the group whose reaction behavior is being predicted by the economists) make their choices among alternative constraints on the basis of better information. The predictions of the economists have value, and this value commands a price. It is, therefore, not at all surprising that the efforts of economists shifted toward the predictive-science domain during the century-long period of increasing controls over national economies. Faith in the efficacy of such predictive science for assistance in controlling the economy perhaps reached its apogee in the 1960s, after which skepticism emerged from its dormacy. The very failures of the predictive science of economics suggests the necessity of allowing for the existence of that domain of human action not amenable to scientistic explanation.

As the purpose of inquiry shifts toward understanding the sources of value creation with some ultimate objective of encouraging the establishment and maintenance of an environment within which human choices are allowed to take place relatively free of imposed constraints, we should expect economists to direct more of their attention to the domain of subjective economic theory.

Of Rats and Men

I have found a discussion of the methodology of subjective economics impossible without first defining what I have called the "domain," and my discussion in the chapter has been almost exclusively limited to definitional issues. After considerable intellectual floundering, my proposed classification of the two domains of economic theory emerged from a consideration of the very interesting laboratory experiments of rats and pigeons that have been conducted by Kagel, Battalio, and their colleagues. It seemed evident to me that this experimental work was scientific in a sense fully analogous with that carried out by our noneconomist peers in the natural sciences. And yet, as this work has revealed, rats have been shown to choose rationally, to respond predictably to stimuli, to react to "prices," and in many respects to behave as true (even if simple) "economic men." It is possible to derive demand and supply schedules for rats. That part of economic theory, therefore, that analyzes human behavior of the sort that is also evidently descriptive of rat behavior must be categorized as a genuinely predictive science.

The residual aspects of human action that are not reducible to ratlike responses to stimuli, even in the much more complex human variants, define the domain for a wholly different, and uniquely human, science—one that cannot, by its nature, be made analogous to the positive-predictive sciences of the orthodox paradigm.

There is surely room for both sciences to exist in the more inclusive rubric that we call economic theory. We must acknowledge that in many aspects of their behavior, men conform to laws of behavior such that such behavior becomes subject to scientifically testable prediction and control through the external manipulation of constraints. But we must also acknowledge that men can choose courses of action that emerge only in the choice process itself. Men create value by the imagination of alternatives that do not exist followed by the action that implements the possibilities imagined.[12]

Perhaps the methodology of subjective economics, once the definition of its domain is accepted, can best be advanced by a deliberate attempt to sweep out thought patterns that are carried over from its positivist counterpart. I cannot, in this concluding section, discuss such steps in particular, but one example indicates my meaning. It has been suggested that subjective economic theory necessarily draws attention to the elementary fact that choices are made under conditions of uncertainty. Any attempt, however, to carry over the modern analysis of individual choice under uncertainty to the genuine choice making that is the subject of subjective economic theory reflects intellectual confusion. How can anything remotely resembling a probabilistic calculus be applied to choices that are among alternatives that only come into being through the act of choice itself? The human beings whose choices occupy the thoughts of G.L.S. Shackle could never be reduced to the status of rats, even superintelligent ones.[13] In my view, no economist other than Shackle works exclusively within the domain of subjective economic theory, as I have defined it here.

Any methodological advance must build on the work of Shackle. But as many scholars have already found, the next steps are not easy. The advances themselves will, of course, be genuine choices in the full Shackleian sense. They cannot be predicted. But there is surely some relationship between the objects of attention and the imaginative results that emerge. So long as modern economists devote their considerable intellectual energies, and imaginative skills, to the search for empirically testable regularities in human conduct, they will succeed in extending the scope of applicability for the man-as-rat metaphor to describe economic theory. To the extent that modern economists use their own imagination in efforts to understand more fully those aspects of human action that reflect man's own distinctive imaginative ability to choose his own reality, we can expect new insights about the process of economic interaction to emerge.

Notes

1. Adam Smith, *Wealth of Nations,* Modern Library Edition (New York: 1937), p. 13.

2. Ibid.

3. See John. H. Kagel et al., "Demand Curves for Animal Consumers," *Quarterly Journal of Economics* 96 (February 1981):1–16.

4. This statement should be qualified to limit its relevance to the core problem of economic theory, that of explaining how an economy allocates resources and distributes product. Classical economics has been differently interpreted as offering a theory of economic development or growth.

5. F.A. Hayek, "Economics and Knowledge," *Economica* 4 (1937):33–54.

6. *Cost and Choice* (Chicago: Markham, 1969).

7. Thomas Nagel's fascinating review of Brian O'Shaughnessy's recently published, two-volume book suggests that at least some of the attention of modern analytic philosophers is turning to what seems to be a Miseslike a priori conception of human action. See Thomas Nagel, "The Self from Within," review of Brian O'Shaughnessy, *The Will: A Dual Aspect Theory,* vols. 1 and 2 (Cambrigde: Cambridge University Press, 1980), in *London Times Literary Supplement,* 27 March 1981, pp. 327–328.

8. I ignore the tool-using action of some primates. My purpose is conceptual classification rather than ethology.

9. My criticism of the Mises-Austrian position in this section (although it was developed independently before I knew about Nozick's paper) closely parallels that taken by Robert Nozick in part 2 of his paper, "On Austrian Methodology," *Synthese* 36 (1977):353–392, especially pp. 361–369. For an informative critique that is somewhat differently directed, see, Willy Meyer, "Erkenntnistheoretische Orientierungen und der Charakter des ökonomischen Denken," in *Zur Theorie marktwirtschaftliches Ordnungen,* E. Streissler and C. Watrin, eds. (Tubingen: Mohr, 1980), especially pp. 82–91.

10. The qualifications refer to the obvious differences in the complexity of response patterns as between man and rat. I am not saying that men are like rats in any descriptive sense. My purpose, to repeat, is conceptual classification, not accuracy in description.

11. The work of Israel Kirzner exemplifies subjective economic theory in the sense defined here. Few critics could argue that Kirzner's discussion of entrepreneurship and the role of the entrepreneur in the competitive economic process is not explanatory in the ordinary meaning of the term. See Israel Kirzner, *Competition and Entrepreneurship* (Chicago: University of Chicago Press, 1973).

12. Methodologically, it is important to insist that the two domains be treated as mutually exclusive. Unless this precept is strictly adhered to, the operational status of the predictive theory may become meaningless. Suppose that an hypothesis derived from this theory is empirically refuted. The theorist cannot be allowed to fall back on an essentially subjective-economics explanation to the effect that utility functions have shifted, that persons have exercised genuine choice. He should, instead, be forced to acknowledge the falsification of his hypothesis about behavioral reality. To resort to presumed shifts in the reality itself while holding to the central hypothesis is methodologically illegitimate.

For a fascinating discussion of a related problem that arises in the relationship between moral and predictive theory, see David Levy, "Rational Choice and Morality: Economics and Classical Philosophy," December 1979, mimeo.

13. Among Shackle's many books, see, in particular, *Epistemics and Economics* (Cambridge: Cambridge University Press, 1972) and *Imagination and the Nature of Choice* (Edinburgh: Edinburgh University Press, 1979).

3

Subjectivism, Predictability, and Creativity: Comment on Buchanan

Karen I. Vaughn

James Buchanan has presented us with a stimulating chapter that raises a crucial but so far underexplored issue: the relationship between positive economics and subjectivism. He need not apologize for writing a chapter that is primarily definitional. On the contrary, the definitions he attempts are necessary before any real progress can be made in exploring the implications of subjectivism for economic theory. One simply cannot write about subjectivist methodology without first understanding what subjectivism is and what it can and cannot say or do. I agree with many of the individual pieces of Buchanan's argument and indeed have found these pieces very helpful in arriving at my own understanding of subjectivism. But I also find that the individual pieces as Buchanan presents them do not fit together into a complete argument. In chapter 3 I will attempt to locate some of the missing links in the argument and point to some sources of confusion about the methodological basis of positive economics and subjectivism that underlie not only Buchanan's chapter but also much of the existing literature on subjectivism. Second, I will briefly sketch a reconstruction of the argument that avoids some of the confusions and points up the fruitful areas of study indicated by subjectivist insights.

The gist of Buchanan's argument is that predictive, positive economics applies to those situations where humans respond passively to shifts in constraints and that subjectivism applies to situations where humans actively seek to alter their constraints. Early in chapter 2 Buchanan illustrates the distinction by contrasting Smith's beaver-deer example, a good predictive, scientific hypothesis about relative prices, with Smith's further need to supply an explanation of why there would be a division of labor and exchange in human society in the first place. If all people ever do is consume such that the ratio of the marginal utilities between all goods matched their relative prices, as the beaver-deer hypothesis requires, there would be no explanation for the emergence of markets, economic institutions—no change and no innovation. Clearly we need some explanation, as did Adam Smith, of those phenomena that reflect what Buchanan calls "active choice"; choices that involve creative, innovative thinking—what some Austrians might call entrepreneurial choice.

Although Buchanan particularly identifies the conventional, orthodox neoclassical theory as the predictive theory he means—the predictive theory that only applies to reactive behavior—he does not limit his comments to neoclassical economics. That is, Buchanan is not here talking about neoclassical economics versus Austrian economics, despite recent attempts to identify Austrian economics with subjectivism. Buchanan is distinguishing any even conceptually predictive theory, including many Austrian theories, from a Shacklesque subjectivism that denies even the possibility of theory. In chapter 2, Buchanan is trying to reconcile the possibility of theorizing about human behavior with the problem of undetermined choice. If human choice is undetermined, without cause in Shackle's sense, how can we have determinate theories about their choices? And on the other hand if we can formulate in principle testable theories about human action, does this necessarily mean that the actions are in some sense not free? Buchanan's way out of this dilemma is extreme. He argues that there are two kinds of human behavior that are conceptually different: Reactive, in some aspects almost instinctive, behavior that is predictable because it is not genuinely free—it is animal-like and somehow caused by changes in constraints—and truly free, creative behavior that is by its nature unpredictable because of its freedom.

On the Alleged Conflict between Predictability and Freedom

My first comment has to do with the relationship between scientific prediction and human predictability and freedom. At the risk of sounding trite, I would point out that any theory is necessarily predictive at some level of generality. A theory is a set of hypothesized causal relationships that we use to organize and understand our world of sense experience. The tacit assumption with all theory is that if the initial conditions are met, the predicted consequences will follow. To speak of a realm of human action that is not amenable to even conceptual prediction at some level of generality is to deny the possibility of theorizing about that action. There might in fact be such a realm of human action, but that realm would have little interest for the social scientist.

Given that there is a realm about which we can theorize, to make conceptually refutable predictive statements within that realm is not to deny human freedom. That our predictions are sometimes or even often correct does not mean that human action is in any philosophical sense predetermined or genetically programmed or in any sense necessary in such a way that humans could not have chosen otherwise. (Mises, as we remember, did not rule out the possibility of determinism but only argued that if our actions are determined, we do not know or cannot know that that is the case. Certainly, there is no evidence at present for making that assumption.) It is true that action in the Misesian sense is necessary, but no specific action is ever certain. As scientists, we start from the assumption that human beings have choices, and our theories are attempts to make sense out of the choices they do make. Because we are human, we can conceptualize the problems faced by human actors, and we can theorize about the kinds of solutions they will produce. (The framework of constrained maximization is one such attempt at theorizing about the solutions at which humans will arrive. In so far as humans attempt to get the most for the least, constrained maximization is a way of anticipating the solution—a technique that requires us to see the world as the subject himself sees it). When we are successful in predicting the actions of human beings, as scientists we have simply demonstrated our understanding of the actors' ends and the way they perceive the means possible. They are free; we must understand how they use their freedom.

The basic insight of social science, it seems to me, is that human action may be free, but it is not random. As Mises told us repeatedly, human beings act purposefully by using means to achieve ends. However, the consequences of their actions are not always what they intend. Economic science is primarily about the systematic nature of the unintended consequences of human purposeful action. Were there no predictable (or observable) regularities in the consequences of human actions, there could be no science at all. The real question Buchanan is addressing is in the nature of these regularities. He seems to want to argue that they exist only because in some aspects of life, humans are repetitive, reactive, unthinking, bordering on automata. There is an element of truth here, but it has nothing to do with the problem of undetermined action or free choice. It is much more fruitful to think of humans as willfully and rationally limiting their choices in some areas. Human beings establish habits, customs, usual methods of business dealings, and institutions, all of which limit their creative actions. They can always choose not to act within the given modes, but the fact that they do not so choose has important implications. I would argue that there are predictable aspects of human action because people, when allowed to experiment and learn from one another, often come up with similar solutions to a common problem. Once the solution is arrived at, it is repeated until some reason to change presents itself. Humans may also choose to limit their responses to minor variations in the problem they face simply because they rightfully assume that a new solution is more likely to be worse than a tried-and-true pattern of action. This does not in any way deny their freedom to make that decision.

Of Rats and Men: A Revisionist Interpretation

The issue of determinism versus freedom aside, the real heart of Buchanan's view of the domains of positive and subjectivist economics is his claim that there are two conceptually different kinds of action, reactive and active choice. Reactive behavior might be the result of a prior active choice but still can be categorically different from active choice. He presents support for this view by making brief reference to the recent experimental work of John Kagel et al., who have used economic theory to model the behavior of laboratory rats.[1] Buchanan observes that conventional economic theory predicts rat behavior at least as well as some aspects of human behavior and concludes that humans and rats have a lot in common, an observation that is not calculated to flatter the humans. His chain of reasoning is something like this: Rat behavior is instinctive and reactive. Instinctive, reactive behavior is modeled successfully using conventional consumer-demand theory. Conventional consumer-demand theory also applies to human action. Hence, at least in some areas, humans are instinctive and reactive in their behavior. After looking carefully at the structure and results of the rat experiments, I come to the conclusion that Buchanan's argument is demeaning to the rats. It is worth looking more closely at those rat experiments, since the implications we can draw from them are useful for understanding the uses of economic theory.

For the benefit of those who are unfamiliar with the design of these experiments, I offer a brief description. Rats were placed in laboratory cages where they could only obtain food and water by depressing levers, one for each. Prices were represented by the number of presses it took to obtain the food and water; for example, one press for a food pellet and two for a measured amount of water made water twice as expensive as food. Each rat had a budget constraint of only so many presses per day. After an initial learning period, each rat settled down into some consumption pattern that became predictable and stable. When the relative prices were changed, the rats generally substituted the cheaper for the more expensive reward and once again settled down into a predictable consumption pattern. After many of these relative-price changes were imposed on the rats, downward-sloping demand curves could be estimated for the rats.[2]

I call your attention to a few aspects of these experiments that may escape notice. First, the rats, without the aid of arithmetic or verbal information, had to discover their constraints. They did so through several days of experimentation on their part, during which time their behavior was not predictable in any sense. Only after they learned the best consumption bundle for the given set of constraints did they repeat the bundle. Generally, they would experiment up to three or four days before they settled on a new pattern of consumption. The second interesting aspect is that each rat had a different demand curve for food and water. Their tastes were not uniform across individuals, suggesting that they are not predestined or genetically programmed for any particular level of consumption. Certainly their tastes and actions are not nearly as simplistic and reactive as that of frogs, for example, who are said to follow a very simple decision rule: If it moves and you can catch it, mate with it. If you cannot mate with it, eat it. By contrast, the rats were actively intelligent. They perceived changes in their environment and searched out new responses to those changes to improve their well-being. What is more pertinent, the rat behavior only became predictable in a quantitative sense after their search was complete and they had established a new consumption pattern. For those experimental rats, each point on the estimated-demand curve was an equilibrium solution to a new problem, and their repetition of the same equilibrium solution was an example of the Evenly Rotating Economy (ERE) in miniature. It should be no surprise that action in the ERE is predictable. Note, however, that this particular ERE was the result of a process of experimentation and learning about the constraints and tastes engaged in by each individual rat—an unpredictable disequilibrium process. The best the experimenter could do was to predict an inverse price-quantity relationship between equilibrium points—a qualitative prediction. Only when an equilibrium point was reached could they quantitatively predict the amount the rat would continue to consume. I conclude that the rats were indeed like people in that they were displaying a high level of intelligent, choosing behavior in what for them was a complex and unknown environment. At least in these experiments, what we might legitimately call reactive behavior was only evident once an equilibrium was reached. During the disequilibrium search, the rats were actively intelligent.

Professor Buchanan may concede my point about the rats' intelligent behavior but still argue that there are two kinds of intelligent behavior important for economics, only one of which is displayed by rats. The rats did not seek to change their constraints by their own ability to imagine an alternative future.[3] And remember, Adam Smith never saw a dog (or a rat) exchange bone for bone. Although they may not be reactive versus active choices, whatever you call them, are there still two different kinds of behavior that are conceptually or categorically different only one of which characterizes rat or animal behavior? And does positive economics apply to one and subjectivist economics to the other? I argue that it is not scientifically useful to distinguish sharply between reactive and active choices as if they were categorically different behaviors. I will agree, however, that there are two different kinds of conceptual problems for the economic theorist that closely parallel the distinction Buchanan wants to make between reactive and active choice.

To illustrate, assume a state government imposes an excise tax on hard liquor sold in that state (the human equivalent of changing the number of lever presses in the laboratory). Humans quite quickly react to the change in prices by buying less liquor. As time goes on even less liquor is purchased at higher prices as they predictably start driving across the state line to import cheaper liquor from a neighboring county and as local producers start firing up their illegal stills. And as even more time goes on, some people search for a legal alternative to alcohol that is not taxed and they find it. In each case, the action taken by the individuals in our story was a reaction to the change in relative prices, and, in each case, it was predictable by economists in some sense. Yet does this mean it was all uncreative, all nonactive choice? Certainly the discovery of the legal alternative to alcoholic beverages must be considered an act of creation despite the motivation for the discovery. But if we grant the creativity of that action, do we also grant the case where the formula was already known to someone who only decided to exploit it commercially after the change in the relative price of liquor? And is not driving to the next county a manifestation of imagining an alternative future? But if that is so, so is substituting beer for liquor when the tax is imposed—one had to actively figure out that beer was an acceptable substitute and at what rate it was subjectively acceptable. What I have described is a continuum of actions all reactive in the sense of being inspired by a change in relative prices but all displaying some degree of creativity and imagination. Where are the categorical differences here?

Of the Dangers One Encounters While Walking Along a Road

Although I do not think there are categorically different behaviors, I do believe there are distinct theoretical problems for economists captured by Buchanan's reference to Adam Smith. To see this, let us turn to the now familiar Buchanan-Kirzner man who walks along dusty highways barefoot. Buchanan mentions him to draw the distinction he wants to make between reactive and active choice. I will try to use him to draw a distinction between two kinds of scientific problems faced by economists. Buchanan argues that the man who jumps out of the way of an oncoming truck is being reactive and predictable, but the man who walks along the road barefooted and suddenly gets the idea to fashion a pair of shoes out of some cowhide resting on the side of the road is an example of a person engaging in active, unpredictable choice.

At the risk of straying a bit from my argument, I cannot resist pointing out that the first case is not as clear cut as it seems. Suppose the man facing the oncoming truck is despondent about his failing career and wants to end it all and alertly grasps the opportunity that presents itself to accomplish the deed while still permitting his beneficiaries to collect his insurance money. He does not jump and our predictions fail because we do not know his utility function. But, even if we did, we cannot even predict that he will not jump with complete confidence, since we do not know that he will choose this instance to accomplish his goal. He may judge that the benefit of getting it all over with right then and there is not worth the cost of the possibility of surviving and living on in protracted and expensive pain, in which case he will deliberately jump out of the path of the oncoming truck and leave his suicide for another day. The moral seems to be that what seems like reactive behavior may well be deliberative behavior, and we cannot be too confident of our predictions about any one individual choice. This seems to be a good, subjectivist critique, although I concede it has very little to do with Buchanan's argument. My more important comment is that the two examples presented do not capture the distinction important for economic theorizing.

I believe a more useful contrast could be made between the following: In the first case, the barefoot man is walking along the road on his way to the marketplace to buy himself a pair of shoes. He thought he could get by without them, but his feet have been killing him lately and he decides to forgo repairing the pig trough and to use his limited money to acquire shoes. This man lives in a culture where shoes are worn, he knows about them, they are elements in his utility function (or his scale of values), a market for shoes exists to which he has access. This man engages in deliberative, purposeful action, weighs alternatives, and decides to acquire a pair of shoes. As economists, we can talk about the alternatives he perceives, what his eventual decision implies about his relative values, what the market price is likely to be on that particular day, how his actions will affect the market price of shoes and pig troughs, and a myriad of related consequences to his simple action. This is what neoclassical economics— including Austrian economics—has primarily concerned itself with.

Let us consider the second man, Kirzner's pure entrepreneur who walks along the rocky road and discovers shoes for the first time. What can we say about that as economists? Once he makes the discovery, we can talk about shifts in tastes and marginal rates of transformation for the individual and how he may substitute shoes for woven baskets at the margin. And, once he offers his hand-crafted shoes in the marketplace, we can talk about profits and loss and the consequences of imitation and competition. But we can say very little about the discovery process itself. Why are shoes invented when they are? If someone does invent them, will he notice their commercial potential? If he imagines their potential profitability, how does he establish or create a market for something about which other people know nothing? It seems to me that these questions are of a very different nature from those we asked in the first case. In the first case, we try to explain a set of choices and their consequences within an established culture and an established market—within a set of given institutions. Because there are established institutional parameters, we can make informed theoretical predictions about the outcome of any action. In the second case, we are asking questions about the process of market creation and institutional change brought about by the discovery of new knowledge or the perception of previously unimagined opportunities. With changing institutional parameters brought about by discovery or changing perceptions, we can predict very little even in principle, since we cannot know in advance what is going to be learned or perceived. Hence, the problem for economic theory is not so much one of the differences between reactive and active behavior as it is the difference between action without new learning and action where learning takes place. (Brian Loasby discusses this issue in chapter 10.)

The Domain of Subjectivist Economics

The final question is whether, by describing these two theoretical problems, we have successfully located the respective domains of positive and subjectivist economics. I must confess I found this the most troubling aspect of my reconstruction of Buchanan's argument. In private correspondence, I accused Buchanan of veering sharply away from the schema he presented in his 1968 article, "Is Economics a Science of Choice?"[4] His reply, that his chapter was entirely consistent with the earlier article, I found incomprehensible until I sorted out the above problems to my satisfaction. Now I think I see better what he was trying to get at.

In the earlier article, Buchanan argued that praxeology was pure logic of choice, where wants are completely unspecified and means can be described only in the most general sense. Hence, it is a framework for making sense out of people's actions, but it is totally nonpredictive in any concrete manner. Although very important, its usefulness was tautological. Predictive science, however, is a subset of praxeology where wants and constraints are specified. Hence, it is a set of, in principle, empirically testable hypotheses about real-world events, and, because positive economics attempts to say something specific about real-world events, it must be falsifiable. Given these distinctions, we can then argue that positive economics is only likely to be possible where institutional parameters are set, because it is only in that situation that we as scientists have a stable environment about which to theorize. Where institutional parameters are changing because of real learning, we cannot even theorize about outcomes except in the tautological sense of praxeology. Hence, if we take subjectivism to be synonymous with praxeology, Buchanan's argument is sustained. That is not precisely my understanding of subjectivism, but it is certainly a reasonable one in a world where there is no consensus on the meaning of the word. To me, any definition of subjectivism should include its function of serving to point out the limitations of positive economics in all circumstances, even when there is no new learning taking place; but certainly Buchanan's thought-provoking chapter requires that we open up a dialogue on the meaning of subjectivist economics.

Notes

1. John Kagel et al., "Demand Curves for Animal Consumers," *The Quarterly Journal of Economics* 96 (February 1981):1–15. See the bibliography in this article for a list of further experiments conducted in the same vein.

2. The experiments were really far more detailed and complex. The rats were tested for income-compensated demand curves as well as regular demand curves, luxury goods as well as necessities, and product variation (in the size of the food pellet). Ibid.

3. Even here, we must not be too hard on the rats. In the particular laboratory setting, they had very little opportunity to do anything but press levers. They were isolated from each other, so social interaction was precluded. About the best any rat might have accomplished would be to have escaped from his cage to eat the experimenter's sandwich.

4. Streissler, ed. *Roads to Freedom: Essays in Honor of Friedrich Hayek.* London: Routledge and Kegan Paul, 1969.

4 Ludwig von Mises and the Extension of Subjectivism

Ludwig M. Lachmann

The fact that we are celebrating the centenary of the birth of Ludwig von Mises means that the time has come to assess him and his work, viewed in the perspective of history. That "the time has come" must mean that enough time has passed, providing us with enough new knowledge, to render possible such a new assessment. If so, the circumstances in which we celebrate the Mises centenary impose a duty upon us while they afford us fresh insight and a new and wider perspective. Austrians, of all people, who subscribe to the view that "as soon as we permit time to elapse we must permit knowledge to change," cannot eschew the task of making use of such knowledge once it has come within their grasp. Such a reassessment, then, becomes imperative, not merely possible.

To many of us who knew Mises, and in particular to those who knew him as a teacher and friend, to have to look at him and his work once again in the cold and glaring light of history will be an irksome duty. To some of us it may be a painful one. The fact remains that we have no right to congregate for the centenary of one who was a thinker of merit unless we are ready to shoulder the duties and responsibilities of a historian of thought. We may be sure that Mises himself, with his acute sense of history and stern view of the duties of a historian, so prominent in the early chapters of his *Recollections,* would not have wanted it otherwise.

Mises was a rationalist and a conservative. The first part of this statement is unlikely to give rise to controversy, but the second requires a little comment and interpretation. Mises, very much a man of the Enlightenment, regarded as his foremost task the defense of the precious inheritance we owe to the eighteenth century against all comers and, in particular, against positivism, which, in its various forms, threatened to engulf it for most of our century (having only recently abated). To Mises, that men will apply reason to their circumstances was apparently something of a self-evident axiom: "Action and reason are congeneric and homogeneous" (Mises 1949, p. 39). It is evident that his views on the methodology of the social sciences, for instance, cannot be appreciated except in the light of this circumstance.

Mises was a liberal in the classical European tradition, not of course in the sense this term has acquired in current American usage. It may therefore seem odd to call him a conservative, and perhaps he would have resented it. The fact remains, however, that in our twentieth-century world the values of individualism and classical liberalism are continuously under threat from a variety of forces. On the other hand, these values undoubtedly form the basis of Western civilization. Are we, then, not entitled to call the defenders of this tradition conservatives? As matters stand today in Western society, defenders of classical liberalism and its values, whether they like this terminology or not, are conservatives. No purpose is served by denying facts.

We also have to remember that Austrian liberalism, owing to circumstances peculiar to the Hapsburg Empire, gained ascendancy for a very short period only, much shorter than in other parts of Central and Western Europe. Only for the thirty years between the *Ausgleich* (treaties between Austria and Hungary) of 1867, following two lost wars, and the turn of the century, when the extension of the franchise led to the rise of the two mass parties of Social Democrats and Christian Socials, can Austrian liberals be said to have been in power. When Mises joined the secretariat of the Chamber of Commerce and Trade for Lower Austria in 1909 liberalism was already on the defensive. Most of his economic and political views reflect this fact.

We now must turn to consider Mises's position as an economist, both within the Austrian school and within the world community of economic theorists. It is clear that he regarded himself very much as Carl Menger's heir.

Menger retired from his chair in 1903. As we learn from Erich Streissler and Wilhelm Weber in their article "The Menger Tradition," "it is clear that in his later years Menger slipped into the background. Böhm-Bawerk and later Wieser took over" (Hicks and Weber 1973, p. 227). Mises had a low opinion of Friedrich von Wieser. "He had the good fortune to get to know Menger's work earlier than others, and he deserves credit for having at once realized its significance. He enriched the doctrine in some respects, but he was no creative thinker and has, on the whole, done more harm than good. He never really grasped the essence of subjectivism, and from this there arose a number of fatal mistakes. His theory of imputation is untenable" (our translation) (Mises 1978, p. 21).

Mises's attitude to Eugen von Böhm-Bawerk was quite different, and in the same chapter of his *Recollections* he pays him a warm tribute. Böhm, however, had no talent for, or inclination toward, philosophy and took no interest in methodology, while to Mises, as a rationalist, every part of economics was inextricably linked to a common basis in philosophy. He saw in Menger's distinction between "exact laws" and empirical regularities the pivot of Austrian methodology, but few of his contemporaries shared his view, if they took any interest in such abstruse matters. After Menger's retirement the climate of academic Austria did not favor the discussion of fundamental issues. So Mises had to work out his own position on such matters in some solitude.

However, toward the end of the first decade of this century, a new development in economic thought began to impinge on the intellectual ambient of the *Ringstrasse*. It proved to be hostile to the Austrian school. Here Mises's *grand moment* came when almost the whole of the Austrian tradition was threatened by a new brand of positivism. We, first of all, have to look at the historical background of these events.

For about a generation, from the early 1870s to the first decade of this century, the combination of forces that had jointly brought about the subjective revolution remained in rather loose contact, and what differences there were between the leaders did not lead to any notable conflict. At first one could hardly speak of "schools of thought," but by the end of the period Menger and Leon Walras had succeeded in founding such schools. In England the early death of Stanley Jevons soon enabled Alfred Marshall to occupy a similar position. There were currents and crosscurrents. Menger disapproved of Walras, who, on his part, took no notice of the Austrians. Marshall felt that Walras had given the notion of general equilibrium so wide a scope as to render it virtually useless. He thought that Jevons had assigned to himself a position of originality to which he had no claim. Böhm-Bawerk borrowed one of his most significant ideas, the higher productivity of roundabout production, from Jevons. These were the contacts characteristic of a rather loose form of coalition.

All those committed to the idea of marginal utility as the basis of economic value had several common tasks to solve in this period. Since utility as such is a property of consumer goods and services only, it was necessary to show that the new principle indirectly also applied to the value of capital goods and factor services. J.B. Clark, Marshall, and the Austrians, with their various theories of imputation, all contributed to the solution of this task, which, by the end of the century, had been more or less accomplished. But there was another task that confronted the coalition partners in our period. Classical economics was concerned with wealth and surpluses, with growth and the accumulation of capital. It was an economics of production that had no place for the consumer. In the new economics promoted by the subjective revolution, by contrast, the consumer became, for the first time, not merely an economic agent. He became the primary economic agent on whose choices all economic values ultimately came to rest. And since, with division of labor, most such choices have to be expressed in markets, it now become necessary to evolve a theory of the market that in classical economics was not needed and did not exist. In the terminology suggested by Sir John Hicks, classical economics was *plutology,* and post-1870 economics became *catallactics* (Hicks 1976, pp. 212–216). [Mises used the word frequently, (Mises 1949, p. 3)]. By the turn of the century a rudimentary theory of markets, not, to be sure, without its open problems (Edgeworthian recontract), had been brought into existence. The second task, if not solved, had at least been tackled. After the turn of the century, however, a new issue arose that divided the partners of our loose coalition and eventually drove the Austrians into isolation.

So far the word *utility* had been used rather loosely, and everybody seemed entitled to assume that he and his readers or listeners knew very well what was meant by it. Now, reflecting the rise of the new philosophy of science, its meaning began to be questioned. What precisely did it mean? Did it have any scientific status? If so, how was it to be measured? If men could not measure it, should economists not substitute for it something else more in conformity with the canon of the new behaviorism? In 1906, in his *Manuale,* Vilfredo Pareto, the protagonist of these new ideas, replaced *utility* with *ophelimity,* supposedly measurable, and treated preferences as human dispositions, directly observable and recorded in the graphic form of indifference curves. Two years later the young Joseph Schumpeter, the brightest hope of the Austrian school and cherished pupil of Böhm-Bawerk, achieved sudden fame by publishing a book that presented Pareto's new methodological views in German (Schumpeter 1908). He also stressed, as Pareto had not, that economics is not concerned with men and their actions but solely with relationships between measurable quantities such as, typically, prices. Most Austrians were shocked by these new ideas, quite apart from Pareto's varied animadversions about "literary economists," but they seemed strangely helpless against them. If all our knowledge is derived from experience alone, the new epistemology of positivism was hard to resist.

This was the situation in which Mises had to find his orientation. Most of his teaching, certainly the fundamental part of it, has to be seen as a reaction to it. His diagnosis was that the real cause of the Austrian calamity lay in a failure to distinguish between what is rational and what is empirical in economic knowledge. His contemporaries had ignored Menger's emphasis, which had played such an important part in the *Methodenstreit,* that "exact laws" that are of universal validity require no testing, and that the search for them is the prime task of all sciences. They were now paying the price for their neglect of the heritage Menger had left them. Salvation lay in the realization that at least the fundamental parts of economics were of an a priori character.

What we have just presented is to be understood as a somewhat stylized account of the origin and character of the Misesian methodology of the social sciences. In appraising it we must not ignore the time factor, which in the transformation of human knowledge and the rise of new ideas always plays its part. While the crises we have referred to hit Austrian economics after 1908, it was not until the late 1920s that Mises began to present his thought on the methodology of the social sciences.

In this period of gestation, quite apart from the time and effort absorbed by his activity at the Chamber of Commerce and the political upheavals of the times, two events appear to have been of major significance to him—the publication in 1914 of Wieser's *Theorie der gesellschaftlichen Wirtschaft* and his acquaintance with Max Weber and his work. The former, we have to remember, was that volume of the prestigious *Grundriss der Sozialökonomik* that was explicitly devoted to the presentation of the (then) current state of economic theory. Certainly in Germany it was, at its publication, widely regarded as the definitive account of the teachings of the Austrian school.

We know already what Mises thought of Wieser. It seems legitimate, therefore, to infer that the book served him largely as a warning lesson: Here was to be seen what would become of Austrian economics unless there was a genuine return to Menger and if Menger's official successor and his disciples were permitted to continue to misunderstand and misrepresent his teachings. The inspiration of Wieser's work to Mises was thus largely negative in that it prompted him to concentrate his critical energies on its weakest spots.

Mises's relationship to Max Weber is a far more complex matter and naturally calls for more detailed investigation than is possible here. Like everybody else, Mises was struck by Weber's genius and admired his work. Their personal acquaintance was brief, though, confined to the few summer months Weber spent at the University of Vienna in 1918. Both men shared an interest in neoKantian philosophy and an aversion to the cruder brands of positivism and behaviorism. Beyond this it is clear that *Economy and Society,* Weber's *magnum opus* left unfinished at his death in 1920, provided the main focus of orientation for the methodological essays Mises began to publish in the German journals in the second half of the 1920s. Even where he disagrees with Weber, as, for example, on the need to distinguish analytical theory from historiography, it is clear that, throughout, his thought reflects the impact of Weber's work.

We have attempted to adumbrate the circumstances in which Mises took the field as Menger's heir and had to substantiate this claim. In doing so, however, he faced a strange dilemma. Most scholars appear to agree today that Menger was an Aristotelian and an essentialist (Hutchison 1973, p. 18). The reason the "exact laws" do not require empirical testing is that they reflect essential as well as necessary relationships between phenomena.

In this respect Mises was unable to follow his master. He was no essentialist. To him reason was inherent in human action, to be sure, but by no means in the nature of things in general. Indeed, few of what are usually regarded as typical manifestations of the Aristotelian tradition in European thought he found to his taste. As Murray Rothbard recently saw reason to remind us, Mises was strongly opposed to the Natural Law tradition in all its forms (Rothbard 1980). A good deal of the thought of Aristotle has reached modern Europe through channels provided by Thomas Aquinas. Such channels of course were anathema to Mises.

In his quest for a reputable philosophical position that would supply him with enough intellectual armor to withstand the onslaughts of positivism and to espouse the cause of rationalism in human affairs, he was driven to seek refuge in neoKantianism, the dominant school of thought in the German universities in the first quarter of this century. How far this endeavor was successful is a matter of debate. Some have held that no epistemology that fails to grant major status to experience is entitled to claim affinity to Kant. Be this as it may, this is not the occasion on which to pursue such weighty issues of epistemology.

We now turn to a problem that has puzzled us for many years. Mises was a subjectivist and regarded subjectivism as an essential ingredient of Austrian economics. He saw that this view entailed a commitment on the part of all Austrians to bring their thought (as well as the application of thought to practical problems) into consistency with subjectivism. In *Epistemological Problems* he reproaches even Menger and Böhm-Bawerk for having, on occasion, neglected this task. Hayek has said of Mises that "in the consistent development of the subjectivist approach he has for a long time moved ahead of his contemporaries. Probably all the characteristic features of his theories . . . follow directly (although, perhaps, not all with the same necessity) from this central position" (Hayek 1955, p. 210, n. 24).

How, then, do we explain the fact that, when the problem of expectations came to the fore in economic theory in the 1930s, Mises and most Austrians took no interest in it? Here was a golden opportunity to extend the scope of subjectivism from preferences to expectations and to widen the range of phenomena that subjectivism could help explain by showing that what men will do in a period depends on what they expect to happen in the future periods, more or less distant. Over time a man's expectations change, at any point different men's expectations differ. In a capitalistic market economy the divergence of expectations is a fact of fundamental significance. Why, then, was the golden opportunity, when it presented itself, not grasped with both hands?

This is the more puzzling because Mises was well aware of the importance of uncertainty for a market economy. Chapter 6 of *Human Action* is devoted to it, although it is mostly taken up by a discussion of probability. We are told "every investment is a form of speculation. There is in the course of human events no stability and consequently no safety. . . . Gambling, engineering and speculating are three different modes of dealing with the future" (1949, pp. 112–113). For Mises, then, the kaleidic nature of our world is not in doubt. Why did he choose to ignore one of the most important corollaries of this fact?

In seeking an answer we may have to take into account some peculiar features of Misesian rationalism. Menger had distinguished between the realm of necessary phenomena governed by exact laws, the search for which was the primary task of science, and the rest of the world in which we might happen to find some empirical regularities. Interesting as these latter may be, the search for them and their testing can be no more than a secondary task of science. It is plausible to interpret Mises as consigning expectations and uncertainty to Menger's second category, the realm of the merely empirical, as distinct from the realm of the necessary and essential. These phenomena may be interesting, but to Mises they were not interesting enough to engage his attention, which properly belonged to more fundamental matters. If so, we cannot but ask whether the same reasoning would not apply to all phenomena of the business cycle. Yet Mises took considerable interest in it.

On the other hand, it is possible for us in 1982 to view Mises's neglect of expectations from a Shackleian perspective and find it justified. "Time is a denial of the omnipotence of reason" (Shackle 1972, p. 27). Who could blame a stout rationalist for ignoring phenomena concomitant to elusive Time?

A second reason for the neglect may be harder to detect as it involves a shift in the meaning of *subjectivism*. The radical subjectivism that inspired the Austrian revival of the 1970s is a subjectivism of active minds. The mental activity of ordering and formulating ends, allocating means to them, making and revising plans, determining when action has been successful, all these are its forms of expression.

To Mises subjectivism had a more restricted meaning. It meant to him no more than that different men pursue different ends. The modes of interaction entailed by this fact constitute the subject matter of economics. The ends themselves, he insisted, we have to regard as "given." His definition of subjectivism we find in the following passage of *Human Action:*

> The ultimate judgments of value and the ultimate ends of human action are given for any kind of scientific inquiry, they are not open to any further analysis. Praxeology deals with the ways and means chosen for the attainment of such ultimate ends. Its object is means, not ends.

> In this sense we speak of the subjectivism of the general science of human action. It takes the ultimate ends chosen by acting man as data, it is entirely neutral with regard to them, and if refrains from passing any value judgments. The only standard which it applies is whether or not the means chosen are fit for the attainment of the ends aimed at. . . .

> At the same time it is in this subjectivism that the objectivity of our science lies. Because it is subjectivistic and takes the value judgments of acting man as ultimate data not open to any further critical examination . . . it is free from valuations and preconceived ideas and judgments, it is universally valid and absolutely and plainly human (1949, p. 21).

Later it appears that the range of discussion to which subjectivism lends itself is subject to even further restriction. We are warned that "however, one must not forget that the scale of values or wants manifests itself only in the reality of action. These scales have no independent existence apart from the actual behavior of individuals. The only source from which our knowledge concerning these scales is derived is the observation of a man's action" (Mises 1949, p. 95).

It is hardly surprising that this rather narrow definition of subjectivism has given rise to a host of problems. Even faithful Misesians see in the passage quoted last a regrettable concession to behaviorism, if not an actual lapse into it. How do expectations and plans fit into the framework of this definition? Since ends always lie in the unknowable future, and our ability to attain them is thus problematical, how can they be "given" to us?

Here, however, we are not concerned with such matters. Our task is to explain why Mises neglected expectations. We are inclined to find at least part of the explanation in the fact that he adopted a definition of subjectivism that did not permit him to see the extension of subjectivism from preferences to expectations as a great step forward. Every student of the history of ideas knows that gradual shifting in the meaning of words may have a number of awkward consequences. We can never be sure that for different authors using the same word in successive epochs it retains the same connotations. There are many traps awaiting the unwary. We are all aware of what happened to *value* between the middle and the end of the nineteenth century or to *equilibrium* in recent decades.

What too often we are inclined to overlook is that here there are opportunities to be exploited, sources of knowledge to be tapped, as well as traps to be avoided. In our case what clearly emerges from the facts recorded is the extent to which our own notions of subjectivism and problems related to this term have been shaped by Shackle, the master subjectivist.

It was he who elucidated for us the difference between the unknowable future, which our imagination may picture but cannot grasp, and the dilemma of the decision maker, who, forever a captive of the "solitary moment," has to turn his mind to a whole stretch of future over which his decision may have consequences, but who cannot know what they will be.

It was from him that we learnt so much about the nature of the problem-solving activity that has to accompany, guide, and direct observable action, about the "creative" acts of our minds that enable us to choose ends that lie in the future as well as those other acts embodied in the making and revision of plans.

Having learned so much, it seems almost inconceivable how we could find our way back to a position in which we should be compelled to assert that all we can observe, and thus take account of, are (courses of?) actions and that whatever different meanings these may have to different people, we must ignore all of them. Our inability to look at the social world again as we did before we became acquainted with his work is the true measure of Shackle's achievement.

What matters here is not just that subjectivism has come to mean different things to thinkers of successive generations (that is obvious indeed) nor that the term has gradually acquired a wider and wider meaning. As we saw, Mises said as much in his criticism of certain statements by Menger and Böhm-Bawerk. What in our view matters most is that the ever-wider meaning acquired by the term has enabled us to see, and gain an understanding of, features of our world and our minds that formerly had no place in our field of vision. We may describe the evolution of subjectivism from Menger through Mises to Shackle as an evolution from a subjectivism of given wants through one of given ends to that of active minds.

In this process of the widening of meaning of subjectivism the work of Mises has a prominent and honorable place. His claim to it is in no way impaired by the fact that his perspective is no longer ours. In the true spirit of subjectivism a future generation of historians whose perspective is no longer ours will, in its turn, reappraise the work of Mises as well as our own and perhaps reach very different conclusions.

References

Hayek, F.A. 1955. *The Counter-Revolution of Science.* Glencoe, Ill.: Free Press.

Hicks, J.R. 1976. Revolutions in economics. In *Method and appraisal in economics,* ed. S.P. Latsis. Cambridge: Cambridge University Press.

Hicks, J.R., and Weber, W., eds. 1973. *Carl Menger and the Austrian school of economics.*

Hutchison, T.W. 1973. Some themes from *Investigations into method.* In *Carl Menger and the Austrian school of economics,* ed. J.R. Hicks and W. Weber. Oxford: Oxford University Press.

Lachmann, L.M. 1977. Methodological individualism and the market economy. In *Capital, expectations and the market process,* ed. with an introduction by Walter Grinder. Kansas City: Sheed Andrews and McMeel.

Menger, Carl. 1883. *Untersuchungen über die Methode der Socialwissenschaften.* Leipzig.

Mises, Ludwig von. 1978. *Erinnerungen.* Tübingen: J.C.B. Mohr.

————. 1960. *Epistemological problems of economics.* New York: Van Nostrand.

————. 1949. *Human Action.* New Haven, Conn.: Yale University Press.

Rothbard, Murray N. 1980. Ludwig von Mises and natural law: A comment on Professor Gonce. *Journal of Libertarian Studies* 4:289–297.

Schumpeter, Joseph A. 1908. *Wesen und Hauptinhalt der theoretischen Nationalökonomie,* Leipzig.

Shackle, G.L.S. 1972. *Epistemics and economics: A critique of economic doctrines.* Cambridge: Cambridge University Press.

Weber, Max. 1921–1922. *Wirtschaft und Gesellschaft.* Tübingen: J.C.B. Mohr.

Wieser, Friedrich von. 1924. *Theorie der gesellschaftlichen Wirtschaft.* Tübingen: J.C.B. Mohr.

5

The Ambiguous Notion Of Subjectivism: Comment on Lachmann

Stephan Boehm

And unless economics is content to remain for ever in the age of Alchemy it must resolutely turn its back on the pursuit of gold, however precious it may be to human welfare, and embark upon the path of an austere and disinterested search, not "for the Truth," but for a single self-consistent system of ideas.

Objection is sometimes raised to the emphasis on expectations as introducing an unduly subjective element into analysis. But if we cannot mention expectations, we cannot say anything at all. Any economic action, say, buying a bus ticket, is made with a view to its future consequences and is influenced by beliefs about what the outcome will be. Expectations are revealed in intentions and intentions are revealed in actions. However, a businessman is not a black box. You can ask him about his intentions. You will not necessarily believe what he says, but you are bound to learn a lot from how he answers.
—Joan Robinson

Taking up a familiar theme of his oeuvre, we find Ludwig Lachmann once again indefatigably "in pursuit of the subjectivist paradigm." We are indebted to him for addressing himself to a topic of special interest and fundamental importance for anyone who is at all attracted to the methodology of Austrian economics. More specifically, the scope of Mises's subjectivism is under consideration.

Lachmann's chapter is clearly a sequel to and a substantial elaboration of his stimulating essay "From Mises to Shackle," in which he first noted with dismay the "curious fact that, when around 1930 (in Keynes's *Treatise on Money*), expectations made their appearance in the economic thought of the Anglo-Saxon world, the Austrians failed to grasp with both hands this golden opportunity to enlarge the basis of their approach, and, by and large, treated the subject rather gingerly."[1]

Material quoted in epigraph is from the following works, respectively: *Economics Is a Serious Subject* (Cambridge: Heffer, 1932), p. 4, and "Misunderstandings in the Theory of Production," *Greek Economic Review* 1 (August 1979):5.

In chapter 4 Lachmann is exploring why Mises neglected the problem of expectations, and he comes up with some far-reaching suggestions. Although it seems, at first sight, as if only one, albeit important, aspect of Mises's methodological framework was touched on, one should recognize that the issue is, I am afraid, a much broader one, encompassing the whole conception of apriorist social theory. Although the writings of Israel Kirzner and Murray Rothbard have certainly helped to rescue Mises's work on the foundations of economic science from oblivion and to clarify in many respects "what Mises really meant," it may be surmised that the overwhelming majority of economists today is not familiar with praxeology.[2] But there are encouraging symptoms of change.[3] That Mises's iconoclastic epistemological views are once again at the center of controversy after having been buried for many years is indicative of the change that has occurred.[4] To be sure, Mark Blaug's recent trenchant dismissal of Mises's methodological writings as "so cranky and idiosyncratic that we can only wonder that they have been taken seriously by anyone," is most unlikely to enhance the proliferation of praxeology, let alone the reputation of its foremost representative.[5]

The present conference affords us the opportunity to take a fresh look at Mises's foundation of economic science about which Blaug would perhaps feel less uneasy. Like Lachmann I feel no desire whatsoever to pursue "weighty issues of epistemology," or "to meddle with philosophy," as Frank Hahn scornfully put it.[6] For instance, I do not wish to inquire into the eternal issue whether Mises's position is correctly characterized as Kantian or whether his fundamental propositions are synthetic a priori propositions, and so forth.[7] Rather than taking up an awkward topic that I cannot adequately tackle, I suggest that we focus our attention on such mundane matters as the concept of subjectivism, or "radical subjectivism," as Lachmann is fond of putting it, one of the twin pillars, aside from methodological individualism, on which the edifice of Austrian economics methodology has come to rest.

There are many ambiguities surrounding the notion of subjectivism. In the last section of chapter 4, Lachmann hinted at some of them. My discussion will be arranged as follows: First, I shall present different notions of subjectivism that have been entertained in the literature by economists of very different persuasions. A few examples may suffice. Second, I shall briefly outline the issues involved in the eternal subjectivism-objectivism controversy. Finally, I shall consider specifically some of the points raised by Lachmann and indicate my reservations about the use which Mises makes of the term *subjectivism*. But before I proceed, let me add that it is of the utmost importance that advocates of Austrian economics are perfectly clear when they are talking about concepts such as "methodological individualism," "subjectivism," "*Verstehen*," "reductionism," and so on and the relationships that are to obtain between them. At the risk of being stamped on for heresy I venture to propose that there are some important obscurities in the thesis that Austrians adhere to the principle of subjectivism.

Different Notions of Subjectivism

In many of the early reactions to the writings of the Austrian school the term subjectivism has acquired the status of a catchword, or rather an invective, to denote the hallmark of the Austrian style of theorizing as contrasted with the Marxian approach to economics. This was the line of criticism taken, for example, by Nikolai Bukharin, to mention one of the most prominent critics of the Austrian school. He draws the distinction between the fundamental tenets of Marxism and the Austrian school as follows: According to Bukharin, Marxism is characterized by "recognition of the priority of society over the individual; recognition of the historical, temporary nature of any social structure; and finally, recognition of the dominant part played by production. The Austrian School, on the other hand, is characterized by extreme individualism in methodology, by an unhistorical point of view, and by its taking consumption as its point of departure."[8] It turns out what Bukharin really has in mind when speaking of subjectivism is individualism, the Austrian economists' fondness for constructing their theories in terms of "isolated atoms," or "economic Robinson Crusoes." The subjectivism of the Austrian school is delineated as emanating from "the intentional isolation of the "economic subject," the ignoring of the social relations."[9]

In a similar vein, Oskar Lange identifies a Marxist, a subjectivist, and a historical trend in modern political economy. According to Lange, it is the hallmark of subjectivism, as epitomized by the Austrian school, to focus on "the study of the relation of man to the objects satisfying his needs, to the goods the possession of which causes pleasure or constitutes wealth," in marked contrast to classical political economy, which is "the study of the social relations arising in the process of production and distribution, i.e., the study of economic relations between men."[10] In Lange's reading, Mises's praxeological conception of economics is the culmination of the subjectivist trend leading to the "liquidation" of political economy as a social science and transforming it into a purely formal logic of choice. Following Lange's lead, the late Ronald L. Meek insisted that from a Marxist perspective the term subjectivism is much more appropriate than marginalism to denote the changes in the *content* of economic theory since the 1870s.[11]

There is still another usage of subjectivism that has gained wide currency, meaning essentially that economics could and should be reduced to psychological concepts. This view reflects a once widely shared view to the effect that marginal-utility theory is nothing but psychology.[12]

Let me now turn to the notion of subjectivism Professor Hayek subscribes to. According to F.A. Hayek, the social sciences are concerned with human actions, that is, conscious or reflected behavior in which a person can be said to choose between various courses open to him.[13] The purposefulness of human actions implies that in their analysis the social scientist has to proceed from the thoughts and intentions of the actors. This procedure involves that the data informing choice have to be taken into account as perceived and experienced by acting man.

In his early discussions of methodology Hayek emphasized the notion of introspection in the interpretation of human action. To my knowledge, he does not use the term *Verstehen* but this is what he has in mind. The meaning that acting man attaches to his action can be intuitively grasped by introspection because everybody has an idea of how he would act given similar circumstances, that is, we interpret other people's actions by analogy of our own mind. This is, *in a nutshell,* Hayek's position with respect to the special epistemological status of the social sciences.

Subjectivism versus Objectivism

The issue of subjectivism versus objectivism has been a constant source of controversy for many years among philosophers and social scientists.[14] It has appeared and reappeared in many disguises, as in the dualisms of introspectionism(psychologism)-behaviorism, rationalism-empiricism, materialism-idealism, deductive-inductive, and so on. Although this may sound very trivial, it is very important to distinguish carefully two sets of problems that are not always kept apart in discussions of subjectivism. First we have to consider the question whether the *subject matter* of the social sciences is constituted of subjective or objective phenomena. Second, there is the problem of how to obtain knowledge of these phenomena. Should the *method of obtaining knowledge* be subjective or objective?[15]

With respect to the subject matter, Hayek has provided us with a frequently quoted answer: "So far as human actions are concerned the things *are* what the acting people think they are."[16] Putting it another way, according to Hayek, the subject matter of the social sciences consists of people's goals, attitudes, expectations, beliefs, opinions, and so forth. Thus stated, the thesis of subjectivism will hardly provoke heated disputes among social scientists. On the other hand, a social science construed as concerned with subjective phenomena only does not imply its subjectivity. As one commentator on Hayek has aptly observed: "If Social Science is subjective because its subject matter is, then by the same argument Ornithology would have to be considered a bird-like science and Archaeology an archaic one. At most, what such considerations seem to show is that the results of social science thus construed are distinguishable from the results of any other science. This is hardly a unique property of social science.''[19]

The second question, however, is the crucial one. It is a *methodological* question, that is, it refers to the *context of justification* (logic of validation) as opposed to the *context of discovery* of a scientific statement. It is at this juncture that the issue of a methodological distinction between the social and the natural sciences has to be settled. Very crudely stated, the issue is between advocates of some sort of introspectionism and behaviorism. Hayek's former arguments in favor of the indispensability of introspection in the justification of hypotheses, that is, *methodological subjectivism,* are well known. The counter arguments centering chiefly on the issue of inter-subjective confirmation are also familiar.[18] Suffice it to say that Hayek himself expressed some doubts:

> There can be no doubt that we all constantly act on the assumption that we can in this way interpret other people's actions on the analogy of our own mind and that in the great majority of instances this procedure *works*. The trouble is that we can never be sure. . . .

> If what we do when we speak about understanding a person's action is to fit what we actually observe into patterns we find ready in our mind, it follows, of course, that we can understand less and less as we turn to beings more and more different from ourselves.[19]

Some Problems with Mises's Notion of Subjectivism

Before I proceed to discuss Mises's notion of subjectivism I shall sketch his general position in regard to the epistemological status of the social sciences as far as it is relevant to what follows.

All characteristic features of Mises's approach to the social sciences can be traced to his espousal of *methodological dualism:*

> Methodological dualism refrains from any proposition concerning essences and metaphysical constructs. It merely takes into account the fact that we do not know how external events—physical, chemical, and physiological—affect human thoughts, ideas, and judgments of value. This ignorance splits the realm of knowledge into two separate fields, the realm of external events, commonly called nature and the realm of human thought and action.[20]

Nature reacts according to regular pattern; man chooses. The natural sciences cannot tell us anything about the relationship that exists between the physical and psychical.

The fundamental categories of action (which is defined as purposeful behavior) are derived not from experience but from within. The a priori science of human action, praxeology, "conveys exact and precise knowledge of real things."[21]

The upshot of all this is the claim that real action can be explained without resort to (empirical) hypotheses concerning human behavior, that is, Mises emphatically holds that it is possible for a theory to be both a priori valid and empirically rich. Throughout his work one can detect many instances where Mises draws a sharp line between praxeology and psychology, defending the autonomy of the former. In the vigor of this endeavor only young Schumpeter could compete with Mises.[22] In this connection it is worth recalling Hayek's caution that it is a serious "misunderstanding" that the social sciences are concerned with the explanation of individual action: "The social sciences do in fact nothing of the sort. If conscious action can be "explained," this is a task for psychology but not for economics."[23]

Mises points out that, in the comprehension of the meaning that the actor has attached to his action, two components are involved: first, the desire to attain a definite end, and, second, a theory connecting cause and effect.[24]

Although Mises was aware that the ends chosen and the theories underlying actions—that is, assumptions concerning the results of alternative courses of action—are clearly dependent on the actor's past experience, his environment, and descent, he does not see any problems for praxeology, because its propositions "are valid for every human action without regard to its underlying motives, causes, and goals.[25] In fact, Mises often referred to motives, causes, and goals as "data," the explanation of which is not the task of economics but of psychology. In this connection the term *data* is meant to serve as a demarcation criterion separating the domains of economics and psychology. So far, so good. However, in his definition of subjectivism (see chapter 4) he referred to something completely different, namely the perennial problem whether value judgments could be scientifically established. But again Mises stumbles; he fails to discriminate between the valuations of the actors whose actions are being analyzed and the valuations of the social scientist *about* his subject matter.[26]

Finally, let me turn to the "puzzle" of Mises's neglect of expectations. Lachmann seems to suggest that expectations cannot be properly accommodated by praxeology.[27] I can only agree with him: a type of explanation that purports to explain human actions by reconstructing the situation in which the actor found himself and by then stating that the overt purposeful behavior was as prescribed by the logic of choice cannot adequately handle expectations.

The framework of the logic of choice does not allow for considerations of *time*. Lachmann writes: "To Mises, that men will apply reason to their circumstances was apparently something of a self-evident axiom." And with respect to Mises's neglect of expectations he writes: "Who could blame a stout rationalist for ignoring phenomena concomitant to elusive time?" This is precisely the issue that George Shackle's *Epistemics and Economics* is concerned with.[28] The book is an elaboration of the thesis that the categories of reason and time are fundamentally antagonistic. Problems of what can be known and how it can come to be known in regard to the circumstances in which action takes place—problems of ignorance, risk, uncertainty, perception, and learning—occupy center stage in Shackle's work. The acquisition and dissemination of knowledge are also, of course, a recurrent theme in the works of Hayek, Kirzner, and Lachmann. In fact, concern with these problems can be traced back to Carl Menger. However, these questions are not *central* to Mises's work. In his *structural, formal,* and *rationalist* theory of action there is no room for these questions, save for the introduction of *ad hoc* assumptions. The familiar rejoinder that expectations are implied in the concept of action because action is necessarily future oriented is trivially true, but it does not help us in the theoretical explanation of the market phenomena of the real world.[29]

Lachmann draws our attention to an instance of Mises's "regrettable concession to behaviorism, if not an actual lapse into it." I am inclined to argue that this is "an unintended consequence" of his whole approach! Lachmann is alluding to a general problem of Mises's theory of action, but I do not think that he is aware of it.

The facts of the social sciences—valuations, beliefs, opinions—are not directly observable in the minds of other people, but "we can recognize them from what they do and say because we have ourselves a mind similar to theirs."[30] However, if there are no standards of reference that are independent of the action to be explained, any inference from actions to valuations, beliefs, and opinions is prone to *circular reasoning*.[31] The intentions governing actions are deduced from the actions and then used as an explanation of the action! If one is particularly interested in the *unintended consequences* of individual actions, that is, the difference between actions and results, as Hayek and Karl Popper are, one should always be aware of that danger. The real problem seems to be how subjective factors can be integrated into explanations. The alternative approach, which Mises should not be prepared to accept from his praxeological point of view, is to link observable phenomena with subjective factors, such as expectations, via (testable) hypotheses. Its advocates claim that the Misesian approach simply begs the question that needs to be explained, that is, why somebody acts in the way he does.

Lachmann often describes the evolution of subjectivism during the last century as an extension from preferences to expectations. This statement may give rise to misunderstandings—that expectations are an important element of the *subject matter* of the social sciences cannot be denied even by a staunch positivist. As we all know, however, Lachmann is a vigorous advocate of *methodological* subjectivism.

For many years Lachmann, along with Shackle, has been engaged in devising and cultivating a language for imprecision in economics, allowing for the kaleidic nature of the world, as opposed to the adherents of the neoclassical faith, who "in aiming to be precise, end up being precisely wrong."[32]

In a telling passage of *History of Economic Analysis* Schumpeter writes: "Actually, the 'subjective' theory must always appeal to 'objective' facts (data) if it is to produce concrete results. . . ."[33] Lachmann has always insisted that he is not interested in obtaining "concrete results" because in economics one is concerned with many concepts that are characterized by an irreducible degree of imprecision and vagueness.[34]

Notes

1. L.M. Lachmann, "From Mises to Shackle: An Essay on Austrian Economics and the Kaleidic Society," *Journal of Economic Literature* 14 (March 1976):58.

2. I am referring particularly to I.M. Kirzner, *The Economic Point of View: An Essay in the History of Economic Thought* (Kansas City: Sheed and Ward, 1976); M.N. Rothbard, "In Defense of 'Extreme Apriorism,'" *Southern Economic Journal* 23 (January 1957):314–320; M.N. Rothbard, "Praxeology as the Method of Economics," in *Phenomenology and the Social Sciences,* ed. M. Natanson, vol. 2 (Evanston, Ill.: Northwestern University Press, 1973).

3. In recent years a number of very thoughtful assessments of Mises's contributions to epistemology and methodology have appeared in the German literature. See, for example, V. Vanberg, *Die zwei Soziologien: Individualismus und Kollektivismus in der Sozialtheorie* (Tübingen: Mohr, 1975); W. Meyer, "Erkenntnistheoretische Orientierungen und der Charakter des ökonomischen Denkens, "in *Zur Theorie marktwirtschaftlicher Ordnungen,* ed. E. Streissler and Ch. Watrin (Tübingen: Mohr, 1980), with comment by Hans Albert, and, most recently, W. Mayer, "Ludwig von Mises und das subjektivistische Erkenntnisprogramm," *Wirtschaftspolitische Blätter,* no. 4 (1981):35–50. It is interesting to note that Professor Albert has changed his views on Mises considerably over the years, although he still cannot accept Mises's apriorism.

4. It is worth recalling that among the first critical reactions to Mises's

praxeology were: A.W. Stonier, *Der logische Charakter der Wirtschafts-wissenschaft* (Heidelberg: C. Winter, 1935); F. Kaufmann, *Methodenlehre der Sozialwissenschaften* (Vienna: J. Springer, 1936), and T.W. Hutchison, *The Significance and Basic Postulates of Economic Theory* (London: Macmillan, 1938), whose principal target was clearly Mises. For today's controversies compare R. Nozick, "On Austrian Methodology," *Synthese* 36 (1977):353–392; W. Block, "On Robert Nozick's 'On Austrian Methodology,' " *Inquiry* 23 (December 1980):397–444; C. Gutierrez, "The Extraordinary Claim of Praxeology," *Theory and Decision* 1 (1971):327–336; W. Block, "A Comment on 'The Extraordinary Claim of Praxeology' by Professor Gutierrez," *Theory and Decision* 3 (1973):377–387.

    5. M. Blaug, *The Methodology of Economics* (Cambridge: Cambridge University Press, 1980), p. 93. Elsewhere, in a "potted version" of this book we read: "This school of so-called 'modern Austrian economics' has interesting things to say about the study of competitive processes, as distinct from the properties of final equilibrium states, but its methodological ideas are a throwback to the Neanderthal 'essentialism' of yesterday." M. Blaug, "Economic Methodology in One Easy Lesson," *British Review of Economic Issues* 2 (May 1980):10.

    6. It is somewhat ironical that Hahn, together with Martin Hollis, has edited a book on *Philosophy and Economic Theory* (Oxford: Oxford University Press, 1979).

    7. Compare with A. Martin, "Empirical and A Priori in Economics," *British Journal for the Philosophy of Science* 15 (1964):123–136. According to Mises, however, the whole controversy over the existence of synthetic a priori propositions is "meaningless when applied to praxeology," because "the starting point of praxeology is a self-evident truth, the cognition of action, that is, the cognition of the fact that there is such a thing as consciously aiming at ends." *The Ultimate Foundation of Economic Science* (Kansas City: Sheed Andrews, 1978), p. 5.

    8. N. Bukharin, *The Economic Theory of the Leisure Class,* 1927, reprint (New York: Kelley, 1970), p. 36.

    9. Ibid., p. 43.

    10. O. Lange, *Political Economy,* vol. 1 (Oxford: Pergamon Press, 1963), p. 234.

    11. Compare with R.L. Meek, *Smith, Marx, and after: Ten Essays in the Development of Economic Thought* (London: Chapman and Hall, 1977), p. 166n. This is a position that is particularly emphasized in Maurice Dobb's work. See, for example, "The Trend of Modern Economics" in his *Political Economy and Capitalism: Some Essays in Economic Tradition,* 1940, reprint (London: Routledge, 1980).

    12. See, for example, W. Sombart, *Die Drei Nationalökonomien,* 1930, reprint (Berlin: Duncker & Humblot, 1967) p. 120. The term is also

used in this way by N. Moszkowska, "Methodologischer Subjectivismus in der Nationalökonomie," *Schmollers Jahrbuch* 85 (1965):513–524.

13. F.A. Hayek, *The Counter-Revolution of Science: Studies on the Abuse of Reason*, 1952, reprint (Indianapolis: Liberty Press, 1979), pp. 41ff; F.A. Hayek, "The Facts of the Social Sciences," reprinted in his *Individualism and Economic Order* (Chicago: Chicago University Press, 1948). It is important to note that Hayek's views on methodology have changed drastically since the late thirties and early forties when he first pronounced on these matters, crudely put, in a direction away from Mises toward Popper. See N.P. Barry, *Hayek's Social and Economic Philosophy* (London: Macmillan, 1979); H.-G. Graf, *"Muster-Voraussagen" und "Erklärungen des Prinzips" bei F.A. von Hayek* (Tübingen: Mohr, 1978); and T.W. Hutchison "Austrians on Philosophy and Method (since Menger)," in his recent book *The Politics and Philosophy of Economics: Marxians, Keynesians and Austrians* (Oxford: Blackwell, 1981).

14. Unfortunately the recent monograph of Alex H. Shand *Subjectivist Economics: The New Austrian School* (Oxford, 1981), despite its title, does not shed any new light on these issues. I understand that at the recent meetings of section F of the British Association at York, the proceedings of which will be edited by J. Wiseman, several papers were delivered to clarify the notion of subjectivism in economics.

15. See the illuminating paper by A. Gewirth, "Subjectivism and Objectivism in the Social Sciences," *Philosophy of Science* 21 (1954):157–163, P. Diesing, "Objectivism vs. Subjectivism in the Social Sciences," *Philosophy of Science* 33 (1966):124–133.

16. Hayek, *Counter-Revolution,* p. 44 (Hayek's italics).

17. R.S. Rudner, "Philosophy and Social Science," *Philosophy of Science* 21 (1954):164–168, reprinted in J. O'Neill, ed., *Modes of Individualism and Collectivism* (London: Heinemann, 1973), p. 120.

18. For a typical critique see E. Nagel's review of *Counter-Revolution,* reprinted as chapter 10 in his *Logic without Metaphysics* (Glencoe, Ill.: Free Press, 1956).

19. Hayek, *Individualism,* pp. 64, 66 (Hayek's italics).

20. L. von Mises, *Theory and History: An Interpretation of Social and Economic Evolution*, 1957, reprint (New Rochelle, N.Y.: Arlington House, 1978), p. 1.

21. L. von Mises, *Human Action: A Treatise on Economics* (London: Hodge, 1949), p. 39.

22. J. Schumpeter, *Das Wesen und der Hauptinhalt der theoretischen Nationalökonomie* (Berlin: Duncker & Humblot, 1908), pp. 541ff. There are more analogies between Mises and Schumpeter than Lachmann would be prepared to accept. For instance, it is obvious that Mises's conception of human action as exchange can be traced to Schumpeter, *Wesen and Haupt-*

inhalt, pp. 49ff. See also H. Albert, *Marktsoziologie und Ent-scheidungslogik* (Neuwied: Luchterhand, 1967), pp. 258f. I also disagree with Lachmann's harsh verdict on Wieser. In fact, Mises pays tribute to Wieser as the one economist who comes closest to his praxeological conception of economic science [*Epistemological Problems of Economics* (New York: New York University Press, 1981), p. 21]. What separates them is Wieser's adherence to what Mises calls "understanding" (*Verstehen*), that is, the identification of the meaning of actions by way of some cozy introspection, as opposed to Mises's espousal of "conception" (*Begreifen*), that is, the identification of the meaning of actions by way of discursive reasoning. For a more detailed analysis of Wieser's methodology see my paper, "The Later Work of Friedrich Freiherr von Wieser," delivered at the 1981 Meetings of the History of Economics Society at East Lansing, Michigan, June 1981.

23. Hayek, *Individualism,* p. 67.

24. Mises, *Epistemological Problems,* p. 131.

25. Mises, *Human Action,* p. 21.

26. See Vanberg, *Die Zwei Sociologien,* p. 94n. The following quotation illustrates the confusion: "For the science of human action, the valuations and goals of the final order at which men aim constitute the ultimate given, which it is unable to explain any further. Science can record and classify values, but it can no more explain them than it can prescribe the values that are to be acknowledged as correct or condemned as perverted." (Mises, *Epistemological Problems,* p. 135.) Obviously Mises intermingles three sets of problems here: the delimitation of the respective domains of praxeology and psychology, the questions whether adherence to specific values could be explained scientifically at all, and the problem of the scientific establishment of value judgments.

27. As a matter of fact, he had done so before: ". . . in a dynamic world there are economic problems that the logic of choice by itself cannot master. While it explains the designing of economic plans under given conditions, the revision of economic plans in the course of time, as well as the entire range of the problems of expectations, are outside the realm of logic." L.M. Lachmann, *Capital, Expectations, and the Market Process* (Kansas City: Sheed Andrews, 1977), p. 59.

28. For an appraisal of Shackle's views see the incisive review by A. Coddington, "Creaking Semaphore and beyond: A Consideration of Shackle's 'Epistemics and Economics,' " *The British Journal for the Philosophy of Science* 26 (1975):151–163.

29. In discussion Rothbard vigorously pointed out that Mises's theories of the market process, the business cycle, and inflation virtually bristle with expectations. I entirely agree. But this is emphatically not the question I wish to address. My contention is rather that Mises's vivid pic-

ture of the market process could only emerge to the extent that he left his apriorism behind and formulated (empirical) hypotheses about the expectations of the actors involved. Whereas I have great difficulty in reconciling Mises, the praxeologist, with Mises, the economist, such problems do not exist for Rothbard. My claim is (and I interpret Lachmann as saying the same, at least implicitly), that praxeology cannot accommodate expectations in any *meaningful* way. For a more detailed analysis along similar lines see Professor Meyer's recent paper, "Ludwig von Mises und das subjektivistische Erkenntnisprogramm."

30. Hayek, *Counter-Revolution,* p. 47.

31. The charge of circular reasoning has already been raised by A.R. Sweezy, "The Interpretation of Subjective Value Theory in the Writings of the Austrian Economists," *The Review of Economics Studies* 1 (1933–1934):179.

32. P. Davidson, "Post Keynesian Economics: Solving the Crisis in Economic Theory," *The Public Interest,* special issue (1980):162.

33. J.A. Schumpeter, *History of Economic Analysis* (London: Allen & Unwin, 1954), p. 919n.

34. In this enterprise he has been joined by forceful allies from the Postkeynesian camp. See D. Vickers, "Uncertainty, Choice, and the Marginal Efficiencies," *Journal of Post Keynesian Economics* 2 (Winter 1979–1980):240–254, and D. Vickers, "Real Time and the Choice-Decision Point," *Journal of Post Keynesian Economics* 3 (Summer 1981):545–551. It is precisely the issue of expectations that is at the heart of a controversy that has been raging for some years now within the Cambridge School between a Keynesian and a Ricardian wing. A flavor of the issues involved may be tasted in P. Garegnani, "Notes on Consumption, Investment and Effective Demand: A Reply to Joan Robinson," *Cambridge Journal of Economics* 3 (June 1979):181–187.

6 Mises and Lakatos: A Reformulation of Austrian Methodology

Mario J. Rizzo

Complex phenomena in the production of which various causal chains are interlaced cannot test any theory. Such phenomena, on the contrary, become intelligible only through interpretation in terms of theories previously developed from other sources. —Ludwig von Mises

It is not that we propose a theory and Nature may shout NO; rather, we propose a maze of theories and Nature may shout INCONSISTENT . . . Nature's actual "INCONSISTENCY" in a pluralistic methodology takes the form of a "factual" statement couched in the light of one of the theories involved, which we claim Nature had uttered and which, if added to our proposed theories, yields an inconsistent system. —Imre Lakatos

The methodological writings of Austrian economists have rarely been properly understood. This communication failure has in part been due to the somewhat eccentric terminology of the Austrians and in part to the almost universal sway that naive falsificationism has had among some economic methodologists. One noted methodologist and historian of thought has recently said of Ludwig von Mises that "he made important contributions to monetary economics, business cycle theory and of course socialist economics, but his later writings on the foundations of economic science are so cranky and idiosyncratic that we can only wonder that they have been taken seriously by anyone."[1]

The purpose of this chapter is to reconstruct rationally the Austrian methodological framework along lines delineated by Imre Lakatos's methodology of scientific research programs (MSRP).[2] By so doing, we shall demonstrate both the seriousness and profundity of Austrian methodological work as well as the grave mistake made by methodologists in ignoring this tradition. Rational reconstruction of an area is not the same thing as

I am indebted to Israel Kirzner and Gerald O'Driscoll for helpful discussions. Responsibility for errors remains mine alone. Material quoted in epigraphs comes from the following sources: Ludwig von Mises, *Human Action: A Treatise on Economics,* 3d ed. (Chicago: Henry Regnery, 1966), p. 31, and Imre Lakatos, "Falsification and the Methodology of Scientific Research Programmes," in *Criticism and the Growth of Knowledge,* ed. Imre Lakatos and Alan Musgrave (Cambridge: Cambridge University Press, 1970), p. 130 and p.130, n.2.

rendering a body of ideas more or less as expounded by its leading thinkers. Instead, rational reconstruction involves showing the interconnection of ideas even where their originators had not perceived them and creating new analytical categories or distinctions where that seems implicit in the original treatment. Most importantly, however, rational reconstruction sometimes involves departure from the original ideas where they cannot be made consistent with the central insight or core of the theoretical system. In fact, such deviation is required if our task is to have any importance other than as a footnote in the history of thought. Rational reconstruction is the first, albeit necessary, step in rendering a previously dormant research program viable and fit for continued development in the modern community of scientists.

There are two distinct advantages in rationally reconstructing Austrian methodology in terms of the MSRP. First, Lakatos's system enables us to specify clearly the sense in which economic statements are nonfalsifiable or *a priori,* as well as to understand the proper role of observational or historical evidence.[3] Second, the MSRP emphasizes the logical unity of both the natural and social sciences.[4] Although the content of the abstract categories in the MSRP differs from discipline to discipline, they perform virtually the same logical functions in all areas.[5] This should dispel the widely held view that Austrian methodology is eccentric and based on antiquated and incoherent logical foundations.[6]

This chapter is divided into three parts. The first section briefly outlines Lakatos's MSRP, emphasizing the major categories of hard core, protective belt, and positive heuristic. The second section shows how the Austrian framework can be reconstructed along these lines. Here we shall stress the senses in which economic statements are a priori or untestable. In the third section a proposal is made that Austrians in their applied work adopt Lakatos's criteria for progressive and degenerating problemshifts. In the final part of this section, we address the question of under what circumstances might the Austrian research program be abandoned. In answering this question we hope to throw some light on the a priori nature of the program's research policy.

The Methodology of Scientific Research Programs

The unit of analysis in most philosophies of science is the theory; in Lakatos's framework, however, the relative unit is a set of theories bound together by a common logical foundation. This foundation is characterized by three major features: a theoretical hard core, a protective belt of auxiliary assumptions and observational theories, and a positive heuristic or set of instructions on how to carry out the research program.[7] Each theory within a program bears a logical relationship to the others in terms of these analytical categories. As a consequence, no single theory stands alone when confronted by complex experience. Inconsistencies between the theory and experience will, sometimes, bring about changes in the former. However, these changes will not adversely affect the research program in the least as long as revisions are made in certain specified directions. In fact, inconsistencies constitute the dynamic whereby the program as a whole ultimately gains ever-increasing applicability.

The theoretical hard core of a research program consists of one or more statements that are rendered irrefutable by the methodological decision of the scientists working within the program. Hard cores frequently make use of purely nonobservable or metaphysical entities like force or gravity. However, the elements of a hard core need not be totally foreign to observation. They can be features of reality that are so general and so pervasive that they are capable of almost infinite variation or manifestation. One such feature is rationality. The pure form of ratiocination is a highly abstract "entity" that is never really seen or perceived. What is perceived, instead, at least in an indirect way, is specific goal-directed behavior such as profit or sales maximization. A research program that includes rationality in its hard core will admit evidence that argues against one of its specific manifestations but will not hear "evidence" that denies the existence of rationality altogether.[8] Thus, a hard core consists of those basic presuppositions to which the scientist clings tenaciously and which he refuses to change whenever mere observation is inconsistent with his theory.

The protective belt, on the other hand, is the part of a theory that is subject to modification when observations are inconsistent. The impact of recalcitrant facts on a theory is never unambiguous. Any part of the theory may be at fault, and it is impossible to test each part separately. The negative heuristic of the program forbids us from directing the refutations at the hard core itself.[9] Instead, the components of the protective belt are altered, stretched, and manipulated to accommodate observational inconsistencies. These components consist of two closely related parts: the auxiliary statements and background observational theories.

Auxiliary statements include the initial conditions, the boundary conditions, and the closure clause. The term *initial* conditions is perhaps unfortunate since it appears to limit consideration to those conditions existing prior to the explanandum event. In fact, a better term would be *logically antecedent,* since it is possible to infer an earlier state from later initial conditions.[10] The term is therefore one of logical and not temporal relation.[11] Initial conditions accordingly form the logical context of relevant factors in which the system's general laws operate. The second type of auxiliary statement is the boundary conditions that specify the values of the relevant factors that exist between the time of the initial conditions and the explanandum event. In economics boundary conditions are usually incorporated in the status of the ceteris paribus clause. Finally, the closure clause consists of a statement of the types of variables that are relevant in both the initial and boundary conditions and, at least implicitly, a statement of those that can be ignored.

Any auxiliary statement, if properly altered, can save a "refuted" theory. The inconsistency between observation and theory may be because of an improper ascertainment of the initial conditions, some disturbing boundary variable, or premature closure of the system (an important variable may have been left out of consideration).[12]

The second major component of the protective belt is the background observational theories. These are the interpretative schemes that act as a filter through which we perceive (1) the initial and boundary conditions and (2) the explananda data or observations. Observational theories are generally part of the accepted intellectual environment in which testing takes place. For example, the theory of optics is a necessary, although perhaps implicit, prerequisite for the corroboration of astronomical theories. Nevertheless, in cases of inconsistency between the "facts" and a theory, the observational theory itself may be challenged. As Lakatos put it, "[We] may reject the 'facts' as 'monsters.' "[13] The rejection or alteration of an observational theory is also subject to the general features of the MSRP. This theory also will have an irrefutable hard core, and change will occur only through its protective belt.[14]

The third major feature of the MSRP is the positive heuristic. In the first instance, this tells the scientist where to direct the potential explanatory power of the theories deriving from the program. What kinds of problems are within the potential range of applicability? What is the appropriate subject matter of the discipline? In this light one can see the older controversies over the proper subject matter of economics as attempts to formalize a positive heuristic rather than mere disputes over nominal definitions. Economics evolved from the science of wealth to a more general science of human action.[15] The research program expanded to include all manner of subjects undreamt of by Ricardo or Mill. In addition to formulating a general research domain, the positive heuristic also "consists of a partially articulated set of suggestions or hints on how to change, develop the 'refutable variants' of the research programme, how to modify [or] sophisticate, the 'refutable' protective belt."[16] There are proper and improper, fruitful and unfruitful ways of modifying the auxiliary hypotheses. The positive heuristic shows the way.

Austrian Economics as a Scientific Research Program

The Hard Core

The fundamental presupposition of Austrian economics is that man acts or, equivalently, that he engages in purposeful behavior.[17] This is not to say that he never does anything else or that reactive stimulus-response is foreign to our conception of man. It is to argue, at least implicitly, however, that action is of primary importance in a significant domain of social phenomena. This is not obvious a priori, and ultimately the action presupposition must validate itself by bringing forth a fruitful research program.[18] From the simple statement that man acts several important corollaries can be derived, and these constitute a more detailed picture of the hard core. We shall examine each of these corollaries in turn.

Individuals Perceive a Decision-making Environment. Without some idea of the relevant context, no action at all would be possible, because individuals could not then formulate a plan to achieve their ends (assuming they could even formulate ends in such chaos).[19] Planning requires knowledge of technological relationships, the availability of resources, the alternatives sacrificed, and so on. Since all action is oriented toward the future, only the imagined or projected state of these variables matters. In addition, the objective future state is prima facie unimportant, because all action is a mental balancing of alternatives.[20] In this sense, then, economics is about thoughts and not about things.[21]

Perceptions Take Place in a World of Uncertainty. The concept of action logically implies the existence of uncertainty. To see this, consider first a world in which everything except an individual's actions is certain. Under such conditions, why would anyone ever act? By assumption, men could affect nothing, and hence, strictly speaking, action would be impossible. There could be no such thing as a means to an end.[22] Consider now a world in which everything including human action is certain. In such an environment action could not exist as we normally understand it. Instead we would see merely automatic or reflexlike behavior similar to "the involuntary responses of the body's cells and nerves to stimuli."[23] Part of what we mean by human action is its lack of deterministic nature and consequent imperfect predictability.[24] Hence action in a world of complete certainty is strictly a logical impossibility.

That action logically entails uncertainty does not mean that it is not sometimes useful to imagine it in a world of certainty. Here action would take the form of an equilibrium adaptation to the environment: the set of actions that, if performed, would result in the complete compatibility of individual plans. Action, under these circumstances, is a description of certain end-states rather than of a process of achievement. Although the logical incompatibility of genuine action and certainty should give us pause to reflect, it need not be a complete obstacle to the heuristic use of a certainty model.[25] Indeed, "some of the most important research programmes in the history of science were grafted on to older programmes with which they were blatantly inconsistent."[26] In effect, this is the grafting of a general human-action program on to the older determinist maximizing program. Although they are not strictly compatible, each can illuminate some different aspect of complex reality.

Individuals' Perceptions Are Not Always Correct. The possibility that individuals will act in a mistaken fashion in no way compromises the assumption of rationality. Rationality is a purely formal relationship between means and ends and does not depend on the accuracy of the individuals' information. A decision can be optimal or rational relative to incorrectly perceived data.[27] Such a decision could be called inefficient but never irrational.[28] On the contrary, the concepts of perception and uncertainty, which were derived from the rationality postulate, would have no importance if perceptions were always correct. For then we could ignore these filters, and the relevant conditions would be the objective circumstances themselves. This would mark a return to the simple neoclassical research program.

The importance of error in the Austrian research program does not demonstrate the dichotomous nature of the subjectivist method. Although for a perception to be incorrect it must be incorrect relative to some "objective" state of affairs, the latter is always perceived in terms of a background observational theory. Hence error really involves the conflict or inconsistency among two or more theories. To the extent that we regard the observational theory as completely noncontroversial, we can predict the revision of agents' perceptions in the direction of objective reality. However, there is nothing automatic about this, since events can be interpreted differently by different people. The road to equilibrium is thus much rougher than that portrayed in simple neoclassical parables.

Action Is Coordinating.[29] The tendency toward coordination follows directly from the action postulate itself.[30] Discoordination opens up the opportunity for profit. A would like to buy X at any price below \$75 and B would like to sell it at any price above \$70. There is thus a potential arbitrage profit of \$5 to be gained by bringing them together or coordinating their plans. The purposeful pursuit of profit sets in motion a tendency toward elimination of this discoordination.

The coordination presumption may appear to be in conflict with the statement that perceptions are not always correct. If a profit opportunity exists but is not perceived, then coordination will not result. Furthermore, if entrepreneurs are not purely profit maximizers, then striving for other goals may interfere with complete coordination of plans. This is undoubtedly true, but it is beside the point. Our claim is only that there is a tendency toward coordination, not that there will be actual coordination (as the simple neoclassical hard core requires). To assert that there is such a tendency is to make no claim about the frequency with which coordination comes about. A tendency law says merely that a specified state of affairs will come about, but only under certain circumstances.[31] Our attention is then directed to the variables that can interfere with the attainment of coordination. If these variables turn out to be important factors in understanding *observed* market phenomena, then the tendency law has proven its worth. The presumption that action is coordinating does not have direct empirical applicability. Nevertheless, it can still be a useful tool in identifying important features of actual markets.[32]

The Protective Belt

Initial Conditions. In economics, initial conditions are typically those factors existing at the time of an assumed disturbance (for example, an increase in demand) that are logically antecedent to the explanandum statement.[33] These include such things as the agent's motivation (for example, profit maximization), the state of knowledge, the condition of expectations, and so on. When observations are inconsistent with the implications of a theory, the problem may be that the initial conditions have been misspecified. For example, suppose that the demand for a commodity has permanently increased. Because suppliers mistakenly think that the shift in demand is only temporary, they decide not to raise prices.[34] A hypothesis that assumes perfect foresight, on the other hand, would predict a rise in the price of the commodity, and this would be in conflict with the observed stable price. The inconsistency between our theory and observation could be eliminated, however, by changing the assumption regarding the initial state of expectations.

The key question here is: Must the initial conditions (sometimes referred to as "the assumption") be independently testable, at least in principle? Alternatively, is the corroboration of the entire theory's implications sufficient to justify use of a particular set of assumptions? To anticipate the argument of the subsequent paragraphs, we claim that if initial conditions are not subject to independent tests, at least three important problems will emerge.

Consider, for example, the proffered motivational assumption of profit maximization. What can it mean to say that individuals act as if they maximize profits instead of acting in order to maximize profits?[35] It can only mean that, although sometimes this motivational assumption is false, predicted market outcomes are nevertheless consistent with profit maximization.

This creates a paradox. It is asserted that individuals who do not maximize profits behave in the same way as those who do. Here we obviously have a puzzle. To say that the motivational assumption is unimportant or irrelevant to the explanation will not suffice. If that were true, then the hypothesis would have been misspecified in the first place. Presumably, if the content of individuals' motivation is unimportant, then it should be possible to invent an explanation that makes no use of the rationality postulate at all.

When a statement constituting the explanans[36] is false, we do not have genuinely scientific explanation.[37] If the profit-maximization premise of an explanation is false, then the deductions or implications can only be true by accident. Hence such premises are not really involved in the explanation.

Suppose, finally, that we assert that the motivational assumption is true, but, by a methodological decision, we choose to test it only through the success or failure of the central hypothesis. Since the assumed motivation is part of the central hypothesis, the whole idea of the latter's success or failure becomes ambiguous.[38] If the model predicts Y, and X occurs instead, what went wrong? There is more than one initial condition that could be inaccurate. It is also possible that the ceteris paribus clause was inapplicable. Or that the range of important variables (closure clause) was defined too narrowly. Finally, the general law may be wrong or, more exactly, inapplicable to this class of phenomena. We have no guidance to the improvement of the hypothesis.

If the foregoing arguments are correct, then initial conditions ought to be independently testable, at least in principle.[39] The performance of these tests, however, requires an implicit or explicit observational theory. Such a theory enables us to interpret the data that bear on the initial conditions or assumptions. Consider, once again, the motivational hypothesis of profit maximization. Before we can say that individuals are maximizing profits, we must be able to understand or interpret their actions. The theory that permits us to do so will have much in common with the overall hypothesis. Both will have a hard core consisting of the action or rationality postulate and a set of auxiliary hypotheses. In the case of the observational theory, all the tentative hypotheses about the motivation of certain individuals presuppose rationality. Therefore, we need merely vary the content of the rationality assumption (that is, the auxiliary hypotheses) until we understand the relevant behavior.[40]

From the perspective of testing the central hypothesis, the hard core of the observational theory is part of the accepted background knowledge. Although the hard cores of both theories are substantively the same, acceptance of the latter does not imply that we *must* choose to insulate the rationality postulate in the major hypothesis from refutation. The decision to render it nonfalsifiable is still merely a methodological decision. It is important to keep in mind the different functions of the postulate in each context. In the observational case its acceptance means that it has been found useful in describing patterns of relatively simple behavior.[41] However, it does not logically follow that such an assumption will be useful in explaining the causes of more complex phenomena like overall market outcomes (for example, the nature of oligopolistic markets). The question is whether presuppositions that are useful in simpler situations are also useful or applicable in more complex situations.[42]

The decision to regard the action assumption as an irrefutable part of the Austrian research program is thus quite different from the decision to accept it in an observational context. The former decision does not admit the possibility that rationality is inapplicable to understanding complex market outcomes. We could allow this possibility (if we were to go outside the program) and yet believe that individual behavior in simpler settings (everyday life, for example) is best explained on rational grounds. The relevant choice is whether, for a certain class of explananda, the rationality component of the explanans shall be irrefutable. Acceptance of that postulate for one class of (simpler) phenomena need not imply acceptance for another class.

Boundary Conditions and the Closure Clause. Suppose we want to infer an event at t_1 from the state of the system at t_0. Then knowledge of the initial conditions at t_0 will not be enough. It is also necessary to know something of the conditions prevailing between t_0 and t_1 (the boundary conditions).[43] When the conditions at t_0 are unchanged between t_0 and t_1, we can say that some appropriately specified ceteris paribus clause is applicable. If conditions do not remain unchanged, then, of course, the predictions of the hypothesis may be inconsistent with observed outcomes. Any such inconsistency can potentially be attributed to the inapplicability of some aspect of the ceteris paribus clause. A decrease in prices following an increase in demand, for example, might be explained by changes in technology.

There are two ways of stating ceteris paribus clauses: either they can remain general and their contents left vague, or else they can be explicitly specified (that is, $x_1 \ldots x_n$ are held constant). In the former case, they merely insulate the hard core from refutation and provide no guidance as to how the hypothesis might be improved. Since nothing is ever completely unchanged, it is always possible to attribute inconsistencies to changes in some boundary condition. When, on the other hand, those conditions are specified, we have clues as to where a particular change must be made.[44]

If a prediction is falsified but the values of the initial and boundary conditions are accurately ascertained, the problem may then be with the closure clause.[45] It is no simple task to determine what are the relevant variables to be included in the auxiliary statements. For example, the requirement that other factors must be held constant does not tell us what or how many these factors are.[46] Even if $x_1 \ldots x_n$ have been held constant, the relevance of an additional factor, x_{n+1}, may have been overlooked. When that is taken into account, it is possible that the theory-observation inconsistency may be resolved.

Background Interpretation of the Explananda Events. The explananda, as well as the auxiliary statements, associated with all theories must be interpreted within the context of an observational theory. There are two levels on which this occurs: (1) interpretation of the observational categories themselves (for example, prices and money); and (2) interpretation of the accuracy of the operational counterparts to the theoretical categories (for example, the accuracy with which rents are reported).

The explananda of economics are overall market outcomes rather than merely the behavior of particular individuals. Nevertheless, these market phenomena are often described in terms that imply purposeful orientation or purposeful-interaction patterns.[47] For example, economics seeks to explain why rents in the unregulated sector of the New York housing market have risen rapidly or whether the oil embargo of several years ago caused a decrease in the purchasing power of money. Merely to understand these questions, however, it is necessary to comprehend the subjective-meaning content of the theoretical terms. A price, for example, is not just a number written on the tag of an item. It refers to the terms on which an exchange is made. Further, money is not merely a piece of paper with some writing on it that happens to change hands when goods change hands. It is a medium of exchange, that is, something that is generally desired or bargained for.[48]

Although the terms of the explananda are viewed as embodying purpose-oriented functions (that is, they are Mengerian institutions), it does not logically follow that causal explanations must incorporate reference to the purposes. There is an important distinction between the purposes that define an institution, like money, and those that may be involved in bringing it about, changing, or maintaining it (that is, the causal factors).[49] A theory is necessary to demonstrate the connection between the function of an institution and its causal genesis. No one need have been aware of the ultimate function of an institution when his behavior brought it about. It is logically possible to design a causal explanation of market phenomena without reference to their function-associated purposes, or any purposes whatever. Teleological explanations are required not by the nature of the explananda but by the positive heuristic of the research program.

Theoretical consideration can be brought to bear on the accuracy with which individuals report economic data. If, for example, landlords are taxed more heavily the higher the rents they charge, and if tenant taxes are invariant with respect to the level of rents, we would expect tenants to be more accurate in reporting than landlords. As in the discussion of initial conditions, the observational theories here also rest on a hard core of rationality. Unless some background theory of data accuracy is accepted, there will be a highly ambiguous relationship between actual collected data and the theory under test. If quantity X, alleged to be the price of A, rises, this does not mean that the prediction of a fall in the price of A is thereby falsified. For that to be so, we must be confident that X indeed measures, within tolerable levels of accuracy, the price of A.

The Positive Heuristic

The positive heuristic specifies the fundamental research policy of the scientific program.[50] This includes both the basic problem to which work undertaken within the program is addressed and a set of instructions on how to modify auxiliary statements to deflect falsification from the hard core.

The Fundamental Problem. The central research goal of Austrian economics has been stated in two, not altogether compatible, ways. First, Carl Menger believed that the problem of the social sciences is: "How can it be that institutions which serve the common welfare and are extremely significant for its development came into being without a *common will* directed toward establishing them?"[51] Menger thought that the recognition of certain institutions as "organic" or spontaneous in origin did not exclude "striving for the exact (the atomistic) understanding of them."[52] In more familiar terminology, he believed that they were the unintended outcomes of individual human action.

The Mengerian statement unduly restricts the scope of economics. First, the basic question is directed toward "institutions which serve the common welfare" and not those that may be inimical to it. Second, an institution is an equilibrium phenomenon—it exhibits a certain constant and coordinated pattern of individual behavior.[53] It is equally important, however, to understand "noninstitutions," or failures to achieve coordinated activity. Although Menger cannot be fairly characterized as an equilibrium theorist, his formulation of the positive heuristic may restrict our thinking to equilibrium terms.

In Hayek's view, on the other hand, the central problem is "to explain the unintended or undesigned results of the actions of many men.''[54] This statement is broader insofar as it makes reference to ''results'' and not to ''institutions.'' Furthermore, there is no attempt to evaluate these results as beneficial or not. Therefore, the Hayekian research policy is to recompose or reconstitute either equilibrium or disequilibrium phenomena from the purposeful activity of individuals. Whether these phenomena ''serve the common welfare'' can be the subject of a separate, auxiliary investigation, but the central research problem is not restricted to beneficial developments.

The Set of Instructions. As we have seen, when observations are inconsistent with the implications of a theory, the protective belt must be altered. The positive heuristic offers a set of very general instructions on how this ought to be done. It is not possible to set these out in explicit detail. The treatment of anomalies involves scientific creativity rather than mechanical surveying of a checklist. Nevertheless, two broad, and partially overlapping, strategems suggest themselves:

1. Reconsider the expectational component of an explanation. Perhaps observations are inconsistent because inadequate attention has been paid to the content of expectations.

2. Search for the relevant communication breakdown among economic agents. When phenomena appear discoordinative despite the equilibrating tendency, the Austrian economist first asks why information has failed to be transmitted correctly. Perhaps, as in the Austrian business-cycle theory, price signals have been seriously distorted. The neoclassical economist, on the other hand, is more likely to search for changes in the underlying data, because the hard core of his theory presupposes the effective communication between economic agents.[55]

Summary: Apriorism

The previous two sections of this chapter have elucidated Lakatos's concept of a research program and applied it to Austrian economics. From this perspective, the role of nonfalsifiable or aprioristic statements in economics can be greatly clarified. Much of the confusion that has plagued discussions of Austrian apriorism arises from a failure to distinguish four senses in which economic theory is ''logically and temporally antecedent to any comprehension of historical facts.''[56] First, the postulate of rationality is immune to falsification as part of the research program's hard core. Second, since the laws of economic theory are of the deductive variety—arising out of implications from the action postulate and a few generally accepted empirical assumptions,[57]—the irrefutability of the hard core is thus passed on to the theoretical structure. Third, the rationality principle is part of the accepted background theory underlying the interpretation of both auxiliary statements and the explananda themselves. Hence, ". . . any conceivable experiment must use hard-core concepts of that very theory to structure the observations to be utilized."[58] Finally, the positive heuristic presupposes purposefulness by requiring social phenomena to be recomposed from individual human action. This research policy must obviously be logically prior to any concrete application of it.

The Method of Appraisal

We have previously discussed the general directions in which Austrian economists will strive to change specific theories when they are inconsistent with observations. However, nothing has been said about the method of appraisal or the standard against which these revised theories are to be judged. Unfortunately, since Austrians have been traditionally more concerned with the logical development of economics than with application, there is little in their work to suggest such a standard. In this section, however, we propose that Austrians adopt Lakatos's criterion for the revision of theories: "[W]e must require that each step of a research programme . . . *constitute a consistently progressive theoretical problemshift. . . .* [T]he programme as a whole should also display an *intermittently progressive empirical shift*. We do not demand that each step produce *immediately* an *observed* new fact."[59]

Before we can examine this proposal more fully, it is necessary to define some terms. By a "progressive theoretical problemshift" Lakatos means that each new theory in the series under consideration predicts, in addition to all that predicted by its predecessor, some novel fact inconsistent with the previous theory.[60] A "progressive empirical shift" means that "some of this excess empirical content is corroborated."[61] The novel facts that ought to be predicted by progressive problemshifts need not be future events. Consistent with standard scientific usage, the word *prediction* includes postdiction or retrodiction.[62] Therefore, the inferrence of past events from a theoretical model satisfies the criterion. In addition, novel facts need not be those that are unknown to the observer before testing the theory. Facts known to everyone are as much candidates for scientific investigation as those previously unknown. A fact is novel with respect to a given theory if it does not constitute part of the evidence corroborating the auxiliary hypotheses or background observational theories.[63] If a fact, a, is used as evidence that the auxiliary assumptions should be changed from $y_1 . . . y_n$ to $z_1 . . . z_n$, and then this revision is used in conjunction with a general law to explain the *same* fact, we have partly explained a by a.

An example should make all this clearer. Suppose at t_0 individuals each buy three units of Y and then at t_1 buy five units. If we can explain the outcome at t_0 but not that at t_1, then the outcome at t_1 is an anomaly within our theory. The Austrian seeking to eliminate this inconsistency should keep at least two things in mind. First, he should never challenge the consistency of preferences: this is part of the program's hard core.[64] Second, he ought to ask whether the cause to which he attributes the changed behavior is observable independent of the behavior itself. Suppose, for example, the economist tries to explain the altered consumption pattern by claiming the individuals' tastes had changed. If this statement is merely imputed from the observed behavior and not independently ascertainable, then the shift in theories is "degenerating." Instead of predicting additional facts, the new theory merely patches up the prior inconsistency. Since we do not observe independently the auxiliary assumption about tastes, we have no way of knowing whether the assumption is true or whether we have merely explained a by a.

If, on the other hand, the economist revises his previous assumption of static expectations and claims that in the second period consumers believed the price was about to rise dramatically, this may be a progressive problemshift. To the extent that the change in expectations is independently ascertainable, the new theory will predict some novel facts. For example, it may predict in a host of other situations that, although current prices have risen, the quantity demanded will nevertheless increase. The independent testability of the expectations assumption assures us that we can genuinely explain both the anomalous fact and other phenomena previously thought to be inexplicable.

This method of appraising shifts in theories outlined is intimately related to the question of when a research program ought to be abandoned. Even Mises believed that the praxeological or purpose-oriented program could be surpassed. Although the laws of economics are, in a certain sense, nonfalsifiable, the usefulness or applicability range of economics is not beyond question. He left open the possibility that what we today call action may someday be explicable in terms of "physical, chemical, and physiological phenomena." "We may or may not believe," Mises concedes, "that the natural sciences will succeed one day in explaining the production of definite ideas, judgments of value, and actions in the same way they explain the production of a chemical compound."[65] Although he did not think this was likely, it was at least logically conceivable. Unfortunately, Mises did not pursue the implications of this point and therefore did not specify the conditions under which his research program ought to be abandoned. Lakatos, on the other hand, did give serious attention to this issue. He suggested a criterion that follows immediately from the method of appraising theory revisions: "A research programme is successful if all this [adjustment of auxiliary hypotheses] leads to a progressive problemshift; unsuccessful if it leads to a degenerating problemshift.''[66] This criterion is not without its ambiguities and difficulties in application. Hard cores do not suddenly arrive ready-made.[67] Their development can easily be confused with the degeneration of a research program.[68] To a great extent, these two developments can only be identified ex post, as we see how the insulation of hypotheses is utilized. If ultimately there is an expansion of the program's novel predictions, then it is at least theoretically progressive. Similarly, the corroboration of additional empirical content may not occur immediately. The length of time we should wait, the toleration or patience we accord a research program, is not something for which we can lay down hard and fast rules. Nevertheless, the MSRP provides an anchor or center of gravity in the appraisal of research frameworks. To put matters another way, good scientists exhibit a *tendency* to abandon a program when it has become degenerative. How quickly or how often they are actually observed to abandon such programs is another matter. It is sufficient that they be required to justify their continued adherence to the program in the terms of the MSRP, that is, in terms of the program's expected potential for ever-increasing explanatory power.

Conclusion

This chapter has rationally reconstructed Austrian methodology within the framework of Imre Lakatos's methodology of scientific research programs. We have clarified the several different senses in which economics can be considered a priori as well as clarified the proper role of testing and observation. As interest in Austrian economics continues to grow, and increasing numbers of economists seek to apply its insights to concrete problems, Lakatos's methodological ideas ought to become the solid basis on which we build our science.

Notes

1. Mark Blaug, *The Methodology of Economics* (Cambridge: Cambridge University Press, 1980), p. 93.

2. For a collection of the relevant articles see Imre Lakatos, ''The Methodology of Scientific Research Programmes,'' in *Philosophical Papers,* vol. 1., ed. John Worrall and Gregory Currie (Cambridge: Cambridge University Press, 1978).

3. Mises uses these terms in several senses, see discussion of a priorism in second section of this chapter.

4. Alfred Schutz, "Concept and Theory Formation in the Social Sciences," in *Philosophy of the Social Sciences,* ed. Maurice Natanson (New York: Random House, 1963), p. 235.

5. On the application of the MSRP to non-Austrian economics see Spiro Latsis, ed., *Method and Appraisal in Economics* (Cambridge: Cambridge University Press, 1976). The application to the natural sciences is discussed in Collin Howson, ed., *Method and Appraisal in Physical Sciences* (Cambridge: Cambridge University Press, 1975).

6. See, for example, Blaug's inclusion of the modern Austrians in the chapter on the nineteenth-century methodology. Blaug, *Methodology of Economics,* pp. 91–93.

7. See, generally, Imre Lakatos, "Falsification and the Methodology of Scientific Research Programmes," in *Criticism and the Growth of Knowledge,* ed. Imre Lakatos and Alan Musgrave (Cambridge: Cambridge University Press, 1970), pp. 132–134.

8. Such evidence can, of course, be heard outside of the research program.

9. Lakatos, "Falsification," p. 133.

10. Israel Scheffler, "Explanation, Prediction and Abstraction," *British Journal for the Philosophy of Science* 7 (1956–1957):293–304.

11. In teleological explanations it is not possible for initial conditions to be later than the explanandum event. An image or projection of the goal to be achieved must precede the explained action. It is, however, possible that the initial condition motives may be inferred after the explanandum event. Thus, we may infer the existence of certain motives at t_0 from the evidence at t_2 which, in conjunction with general laws, produces an effect at t_1.

12. Whether these factors must be independently observable will be discussed later in chapter.

13. Lakatos, "Falsification," p. 130.

14. This is a point that Lakatos does not pursue, but see the second section of this chapter.

15. Israel M. Kirzner, *The Economic Point of View,* 1960, reprint (Kansas City: Sheed, Andrews and McMeel, 1977).

16. Lakatos, "Falsification," p. 135.

17. Ludwig von Mises, *Human Action: A Treatise on Economics,* 3d ed. (Chicago: Henry Regnery, 1966), pp. 11–13.

18. The meaning of a "fruitful research program" will be discussed later in chapter.

19. See, generally, Mises, *Human Action,* p. 22 and G.L.S. Shackle, *Epistemics and Economics* (Cambridge: Cambridge University Press, 1972), p. 351.

20. "So far as human actions are concerned the things *are* what the acting people thing they are." Friedrich A. Hayek, *The Counter-Revolution of*

Science (New York: Free Press, 1955), p. 27. This is not to imply that the ex post mistakes are unimportant. This is the reason for the prima facie qualification.

21. Shackle, *Epistemics and Economics,* p. 66.

22. Mises, *Human Action,* p. 105.

23. Ibid, p. 11.

24. See, generally, G.L.S. Shackle, "Imagination, Formalism, and Choice," in *Time, Uncertainty and Disequilibrium: Exploration of Austrian Themes,* ed. Mario J. Rizzo (Lexington, Mass.: Lexington Books, D.C. Heath, 1979), pp. 19-31.

Explanation and prediction are logically symmetrical operations. "If E [the explanandum statement] is given, that is, if we know that the phenomenon described by E has occurred, and a suitable set of statements $C_1, C_2 \ldots C_k$ [initial conditions], $L_1, L_2 \ldots L_r$ [laws] is provided afterwards, we speak of explanation of the phenomenon in question. If the latter statements are given and E is derived prior to the occurrence of the phenomenon it describes, we speak of prediction. It may be said, therefore, that an explanation of a particular event is not fully adequate unless its explanans, if taken account of in time, could have served as a basis for predicting the event in question." Carl Hempel and Paul Oppenheim, "Studies in the Logic of Explanation," in *Aspects of Scientific Explanation,* ed. Carl Hempel (New York: Free Press, 1965), p. 249. (Hempel and Oppenheim use *prediction* in the literal sense—see both discussion of prediction later in chapter and Lakatos, "Falsification," p. 118.) See also the endorsement of this view by an Austrian economist in Friedrich A. Hayek, "Degrees of Explanation," in *Studies in Philosophy, Politics and Economics,* ed. F.A Hayek (Chicago: University of Chicago Press, 1967), p. 9, n. 4.

The reason that prediction is usually more difficult than explanation is that *ex ante* not all the initial conditions or boundary conditions (ceteris paribus clause) may be known. Shackle's point seems to be that neither prediction nor explanation of human action can be deterministic because, even if all the conditions were known, the laws of action would still imply only a pattern of outcomes rather than a unique one.

25. This is because in a certainty model we can formally change our concept of action to remove any explicit contradiction. The logical problems emerges (1) when we suppose that it is possible to integrate the two models into a continuous and coherent series of approximations (that is, a single research program) and (2) when we try to derive conclusions from the certainty model that are applicable, without modification, to an uncertain world.

26. Lakatos, "Falsification," p. 142, italics suppressed.

27. Hempel, "Aspects of Scientific Explanation" in *Scientific Explanation,* p. 464.

28. Mises, *Human Action,* p. 20.

29. Compare the similarities and differences between our statement of the Austrian hard core and Latsis's statement of the neoclassical hard core: "(i) Decision-makers have correct knowledge of the relevant features of their economic situation. (ii) Decision-makers *prefer* the best available alternative given their knowledge of the situation and of the means at their disposal. (iii) Given (i) and (ii), situations generate their internal "logic" and decision-makers *act appropriately to the logic of their situation.* (iv) Economic units and structures display stable, coordinated behavior." See Spiro Latsis, "A Research Programme in Economics," in Latsis, *Method and Appraisal,* p. 22.

30. See, generally, Israel M. Kirzner, "Economics and Error," in Louis M. Spadaro, ed., *New Directions in Austrian Economics* (Kansas City: Sheed, Andrews and McMeel, 1978), pp. 57–76.

31. Abraham Kaplan, *The Conduct of Inquiry* (San Francisco: Chandler, 1964), pp. 97–98.

32. Compare Mises, *Human Action,* p. 250.

33. The explanandum statement or explananda statements are the sentences describing the phenomena that we are attempting to explain.

34. The changing of prices is costly to both producers and consumers.

35. Milton Friedman, "The Methodology of Positive Economics," in *Essays in Positive Economics* (Chicago: University of Chicago Press, 1953), pp. 3–43.

36. The explanans, or explanatory apparatus, consists of sentences describing the initial conditions and a general law.

37. Hempel and Oppenheim, "Logic of Explanation," p. 248.

38. Jack Melitz, "Friedman and Machlup on the Significance of Testing Economic Assumptions," *Journal of Political Economy* 73 (February 1965):42–44.

39. All these arguments apply to the independent testability of ceteris paribus clauses as well.

40. Hempel, "Scientific Explanation," pp. 475–476.

41. "Daily experience proves . . . that our fellow men are acting beings as we ourselves are." Mises, *Human Action,* p. 26; "It cannot be denied that [the assumption of purposefulness] works." Ibid., p. 24.

42. Hayek, "Degrees of Explanation," p. 10.

43. Hempel, "Scientific Explanation," p. 366. It is possible, of course, to subsume boundary conditions under the term *initial conditions,* since they are both logically antecedent conditions.

44. On the general criteria for revising theories, see later in chapter.

45. Ingvar Johansson "Ceteris paribus Clauses, Closure Clauses and

Falsifiability," *Zeitschrift für allgemeine Wissenschaftstheorie* 11 (1980): especially 18–19.

46. A closure clause can also specify the relevant initial conditions. In sum, it closes the system.

47. Hayek, *Counter-Revolution of Science,* p. 31.

48. In cases where the subjective element appears absent, as in discussions of the multiplier, velocity of circulation, and so on, it is usually implicit. See Alfred Schutz, "Common-Sense and Scientific Interpretation of Human Action," in Natarlson, *Philosophy of Social Science,* p. 334.

49. See the discussion in R.P. Dore, "Function and Cause," in *The Philosophy of Social Explanation,* ed. Alan Ryan (Oxford: Clarendon Press, 1973), p. 72.

50. The positive heuristic is in a sense part of the hard core, because the way in which a program is to be applied obviously must be consistent with the hard core.

51. Carl Menger, *Problems of Economics and Sociology,* 1883, reprint, trans. Francis J. Nock, ed. Louis Schneider (Urbana, Ill.: University of Illinois Press, 1963), p. 146.

52. Ibid., p. 139.

53. These have no direct relevance to the issue of general equilibrium, of course.

54. Hayek, *Counter-Revolution of Science,* p. 25.

55. See, generally, Alex Leijonhufvud, "Schools, 'Revolutions,' and Research Programmes in Economic Theory," in Latsis, *Method and Appraisal,* pp. 87–93.

56. Mises, *Human Action,* p. 32.

57. Ibid., pp. 64–69.

58. Leijonhufvud, "Schools, 'Revolutions,' " p. 80.

59. Lakatos, "Falsification," p. 134.

60. Ibid., p. 118.

61. Ibid.

62. Karl R. Popper, *The Logic of Scientific Discovery* (New York: Harper and Row, 1959), p. 60, n. 2; Lakatos, "Falsification," p. 116, n. 4. Prediction and postdiction are logically symmetrical. In the former case a statement describing an event is derived before it occurs, and in the latter it is derived after it occurs. In both cases, however, in contrast to explanation, the explanans is logically given and the explanandum must be derived. See note 24 of this chapter.

63. Elie Zahar defines a novel fact as follows: "A fact will be considered novel with respect to a given hypothesis if it did not belong to the problem situation which governed the construction of the hypothesis." Elie

Zahar, "Why Did Einstein's Programme Supersede Lorentz's?" *The British Journal for the Philosophy of Science* 1 (1973):103. This definition is proper only if the auxiliary hypotheses are not considered independently testable. Then the anomalous observation is automatically the evidence in favor of making a specific change in the protective belt.

    64. Israel M. Kirzner, *Economic Point of View,* pp. 171-172.

    65. Mises, *Human Action,* p. 18.

    66. Lakatos, "Falsification," p. 133.

    67. Ibid., p. 133, n. 4.

    68. Leijonhufvud, "Schools, 'Revolutions,' " p. 79.

Postscript

From the perspective of more than six months after this chapter was written, I would do a number of things differently. Most important, I would now locate the main differentiating characteristic of Austrian economics in the positive heuristic. In particular, the chapter's emphasis on the covering-law model of explanation (especially in the notes), stressing the logical deducibility of the explanandum statement from the explanans, seems inappropriate. An important distinction between Austrian economics and neoclassical economics is that the latter insists on deterministic explanations of the covering-law variety. Austrians, on the other hand, emphasize that explanations of human actions cannot be deterministic, and thus the most for which we can hope is a nondeterministic explanation of the principle. [For a detailed examination of this view, see my as-yet-untitled forthcoming book (with Gerald P. O'Driscoll, Jr.) to be published by Basil Blackwell in 1983.]

Fortunately, however, I do not believe that the applicability of Lakatos's general framework stands or falls with the covering-law model. One may believe, for example, that a theory in conjunction with initial conditions renders a phenomenon more intelligible (for example, more likely) and not determinate, while believing that Lakatosian distinctions among the hard core, positive and negative heuristics, and so on are useful. In fact, Lakatos's MSRP is on a higher level of generalization than the covering-law model and hence has no direct relationship to it.

7

Austrian Economics as Affirmative Science: Comment on Rizzo

Richard N. Langlois

Science does not give us absolute and final certainty. It only gives us assurance within the limits of our mental abilities and the prevailing state of scientific thought. A scientific system is but one station in an endlessly progressing search for knowledge. —Ludwig von Mises

One may, of course, show up the degeneration of a research programme, but it is only constructive criticism which, with the help of rival research programmes, can achieve real success. —Imre Lakatos

Rightly or wrongly, economists of the Austrian school generally concern themselves with questions of methodology to a far greater extent than do most of their compeers in the profession. To many of these Austrians, I suspect, Mario Rizzo's "rational reconstruction" of Austrian methodology on the framework of Lakatosian "research programs" will seem an untoward and dangerous revision.

Well, if this be revisionism, then count me a revisionist. In my view, Rizzo's analysis does Austrian economics a very great service—in at least two important ways.

Someone only cursorily familiar with the Austrian literature may be forgiven for seeing Austrians as excessively preoccupied with the negative—with what the economist should not do rather than with what he or she should do. Although this naive impression normally dissolves with greater exposure to Austrian thought, there nonetheless remains a certain negative cast to Austrian methodological discussions. The reason for this, one supposes, is that Austrian writers have long felt themselves under intellectual assault not merely from alternate views of economics but from what are fundamentally different philosophies of science—notably positivism and historicism.

Lance in hand, many present-day adherents to the Austrian viewpoint

---

Conversations with Gerald O'Driscoll (and Mario Rizzo) were helpful in writing this chapter. Material quoted in epigram comes from the following sources, respectively: Ludwig von Mises, *Human Action* (New Haven: Yale University, 1949), p. 7, and Imre Lakatos, "The Methodology of Scientific Research Programmes," in *Criticism and the Growth of Knowledge,* ed. Imre Lakatos and A. Musgrave (Cambridge: Cambridge University, 1970), p. 179.

continue valiantly to ride out against these same enemies. It is the first of Rizzo's contributions to point out that the methodological battlefield has changed considerably in the last two decades: the old enemies are still out there, but today it is they and not the Austrians who are the embattled minority. To put it another way, recent developments in the philosophy of science have vindicated much of what Mises and the others had been arguing.

His second contribution is closely related. If the issues between Austrian economics and mainstream economics (however construed) are no longer ones of fundamental philosophical principle, then they must be seen as issues of methodological detail or—more to the point—of "research program." This goes a long way toward transposing Austrian methodological discussions into an affirmative key, recommending that Austrians concern themselves less with arguing what is wrong with opposing viewpoints and more with specifying what is right about the Austrian approach. Rizzo takes an important step in this direction by asking wherein lies the hard core of Austrian economics and, especially, what constitutes its positive heuristic.

Mises and Lakatos

The principal timber in Rizzo's reconstruction is his explicit identification of Mises's "universally valid science of human action"[1] with the hard core of a Lakatosian research program.

There are some grounds for thinking that Mises might have disapproved of such an association. As Rizzo puts it, the "theoretical hard core of a research program consists of one or more statements that are *rendered irrefutable by the methodological decision of the scientists* working within the program."[2] To Mises, by contrast, the core of economics was scarcely a matter of methodological choice. "The starting point of praxeology," he asserts, "is not a choice of axioms and a decision about methods of procedure, but a reflection about the essence of action."[3] Mises saw his hard core as irrefutable—or, to use his own diction, "perfectly certain," "incontestible," and "apodictic"[4]—not out of (arbitrary) choice but because that hard core arose ineluctably from the categorical structure of the brain.

In short, Mises was what Lakatos would likely have described as a classical Kantian justificationist rationalist.[5] His position is Kantian in that he seeks to derive theory from the very logic of the brain's categorical structure; it is classically rationalist in that he sees truth as easily accessible to the rational mind once the delusive epiphenomena of empirical sense-data are swept away;[6] and it is justificationist in that he holds up his a priori methodology not merely as a good starting point for theory but actually as justifying theory—as proving its correctness.

This is a rather unusual—and indeed outdated—methodological position (which does not make it an incorrect position, of course—although I happen to think that it is).[7] If we view Mises in this light, then perhaps we can understand Mark Blaug's willingness to consign him to the dustbin of intellectual history as "cranky and idiosyncratic."[8]

But, if we choose, we can also tell the story in an entirely different way—a way far more favorable to Mises. For the history of the philosophy of science in this century may easily be read as the story of a retreat from empiricism; and, as the retreat progressed, modern methodological thought again and again found itself occupying positions long held by Mises.

At the time of Mises's early methodological writings, many thinkers—particularly in the natural sciences—upheld versions of empiricism we would now view as quaintly naive.[9] Many believed that empirical facts could prove theories in an unproblematical fashion, and others argued that empirical facts are somehow prior to theory and that the mind is a nondistortive receptor of nature's data. The first step in the retreat from strong empiricism was the doctrine of falsificationism, which crystallized in Karl Popper's 1936 *Logik der Forschung*.[10] This doctrine threw out the notion that empirical facts can prove or verify theories; instead, it held, facts can only disprove theories.[11]

Many modern Austrians are inclined to read Popper as a rabid empiricist noteworthy primarily for the bad influence he exerted on Hayek. But, in fact, Popper took the philosophy of science in very Misesian directions. He not only insisted that facts cannot prove theories, he also agreed, in rejecting the "Baconian myth" that theories are merely an inductive digest of experience, that theory is logically prior to experience.[12]

The crucial nail in the coffin of naive empiricism (if I may switch imagery abruptly) was forged by Michael Polanyi and driven in by Thomas Kuhn, whose *Structure of Scientific Revolutions* has achieved a level of influence approaching cult status.[13] Kuhn's work provided some additional victories for Mises. It underscored the active conception of mind favored by Mises (and Kant), arguing that the empirical facts are themselves a function of one's "paradigm." More importantly, Kuhn attacked the falsificationist doctrine that empirical facts are ultimately able to disprove theories, arguing on both historical and cognitive grounds that, even in the physical sciences, evidence from experience actually plays at best a minor role in validation or appraisal.[14]

"The iron law of wages," wrote Mises, "was not rejected because experience contradicted it, but because its fundamental absurdities were exposed."[15] A post-Kuhnian philosopher of science would be far more likely to assent to this statement than would his counterpart in 1933.

Lakatos's "methodology of scientific research programs," so well described by Rizzo, is in some ways an attempt to strike a compromise between Popper and Kuhn. As such Lakatos's ideas are arguably the mainstream of modern philosophy of science. And it is important to notice how much closer this mainstream is to the positions Mises defended than to those he attacked.

The Austrian Research Program

In Mises, the development of science comes across as a battle between a theory and logic. In Popper, it appears as a battle between a theory and empirical reality. But in Lakatos (as in Kuhn), the growth of knowledge progresses in the battle between (or among) rival theories (or research programs)—a battle fought with both logical and empirical weapons. As a consequence, the methodology of scientific research programs ultimately locates the primary criterion for scientific acceptance or rejection in the heuristic power of a body of theory rather than in the conformance of that theory with logic or fact.

To accept the Lakatosian approach is therefore to commit oneself to a very active program of theorizing: no theoretical program may rest on its laurels, however well deserved those may be. As I have already hinted, one side benefit to Austrians of accepting Lakatos's formulation might thus be a renewed emphasis on the positive heuristic of economics. If, as one increasingly hears suggested, the neoclassical program is "degenerating" or "in crisis," an activist Austrian economics would be in a better position to seize the day than one satisfied on methodological grounds with the truths of the past, content to gloss the ancient texts.

There is little doubt that the dominance of the neoclassical approach (or "marginalism") arises from the usefulness, simplicity, and ease-of-application of its positive heuristic. What may be less obvious—and more interesting—is that the Austrian complaint is precisely with the positive heuristic of neoclassical economics far more than with its hard core.

Indeed, as Kirzner has long maintained, the neoclassical formulation owes much to the philosophy of Mises.[16] Latsis, in discussing neoclassical economics as a research program, makes much the same point, arguing that Mises's basic approach "has . . . been tacitly adopted by most economists and methodologists of economics."[17]

Mises's "methodological dualism" and a priori approach, as Latsis correctly explains, is an attempt to steer between historicism and determinism—to preserve the possibility of theory while representing human agents as free beings. This is accomplished through the "rationality principle," according to which "human actions are adequate or appropriate to the situations in which they occur."[18] Neoclassicism applies the principle via a particular sort of situational determinism yielding the following hard-core propositions:

Decision makers have correct knowledge of the relevant features of their economic situation.

Decision makers prefer the best alternative given their knowledge and means.

Decision makers act appropriately to the logic of their situation.

Economic structures display stable, coordinated behavior.

What is significant about this hard core is that only one of the propositions—the first—should cause Austrians any trouble.[19]

And this immediately suggests wherein the Austrian point of view diverges from that of neoclassicism: Austrians do not wish to presuppose, in considering the logic of the decision maker's situation, that the framework for decision is automatically known by or a given to the agent. They prefer to see the agent not merely as possessing imperfect knowledge of a given decision situation (as in the modern mathematical economics of information and uncertainty) but as having the need (and sometimes the ability) first to perceive (or perhaps create) the decision situation—and only then to learn the relevant facts. In Kirzner's terms, Austrian economics adds the "entrepreneurial" element.[20] Furthermore, Austrians hold that the agent, who must live in an uncertain world, never has correct knowledge of his situation in an objective sense but always operates on the basis of expectations. (Latsis, incidentally, seems to object to the neoclassical formulation on much the same grounds. "The neoclassical approach," he says, "may perhaps fairly be termed as envisaging entrepreneurs without entrepreneurial functions or, to put it another way, decision-makers without decision procedures."[21] Phrasing it the first way gives you Kirzner; the second way gives you Herbert Simon.[22])

Consider now Rizzo's suggested "Austrian" hard core:

Individuals perceive a decision-making environment.

These perceptions take place in a world of uncertainty.

Individuals' perceptions are not always correct.

There is a tendency toward coordination of individual activities.

The fourth maxim—which we might call the "spontaneous order" postulate—is a reformulation of Latsis's fourth proposition. The other three are really reformulations of Latsis's first proposition along the "Austrian" lines I just described. But it is interesting that Rizzo leaves out Latsis's second and third propositions—what we might call the "situational determinism" postulates—for these are arguably the most Misesian of all the eight proposed maxims.

Kirzner has argued that neoclassical economics learned its Mises via Lord Robbins and that, in the process, it picked up only a narrow aspect of the human-action story.[23] Human action is more than Robbinsian "economizing." But what neoclassical economics did get right was situational determinism—not perhaps in the sense of what Latsis calls "single-exit" decision situations (Robbinsian economizing in another guise), but surely in the broader sense in which "human actions are adequate or appropriate to the situations in which they occur." This is what Popper described as analyzing the "logic of situations."[24]

With this in mind, let me try my own hand at articulating a hard core:

Agents perceive a decision-making situation (Rizzo's first proposition).

Agents act appropriately to the logic of their situations, and, specifically, prefer a best alternative given their knowledge and means (Latsis's second and third propositions).

Since agents operate in a world of complexity and uncertainty, their decisions, although correct in a subjective sense, are not necessarily correct in some objective sense (Rizzo's second and third propositions).

Nonetheless, there is a tendency toward coordination of activities (spontaneous-order postulate).

This differs from Rizzo's version only in retaining from Latsis what we might call a "situational-logic" axiom.

What about the positive heuristic? In a tacit sense, the neoclassical heuristic is well known to us all; in explicit terms, it goes roughly like this: formulate your problem as the (mathematical) maximization of an objective function subject to constraints; manipulate the assumptions until a determinate equilibrium obtains; now try more "realistic" assumptions.[25]

Rizzo's Austrian alternative has two parts. The first sets out the "fundamental problem," explaining "the unintended or undesigned results of the actions of many men."[26] This is the spontaneous-order postulate from another perspective and amounts to asking of economic phenomena what A. Leijonhufvud calls the "right question."[27] The second part of Rizzo's heuristic is a set of instructions for deflecting refutations from the hard core; these are: reconsider the expectational component of an explanation to see if a different set of expectations could explain inconsistent observations; and look for possible breakdowns in communication among economic agents. The only grounds one could possibly find for quibbling with this formulation are those of specificity.

I agree that economic analysis must involve "scientific creativity rather than mechanical surveying of a checklist"; indeed, as Polanyi and Kuhn have taught us, the heuristic of a science is actually learned largely in a tacit way through imitation.[28] Nevertheless, it might be useful—for purposes of discussion—to describe an Austrian heuristic that approaches more closely the cookbook specificity of the neoclassical version:

> Use the basic concepts of the classical-neoclassical tradition—"value, wealth, exchange, price, and cost," for example.[29]

> Consider the situational logic of the decision maker in an aggressively subjectivist way—including perceptions, expectations, and so on.

> Construct explicitly dynamic models—or "conjectural histories"—of how unintended results develop from individual actions.[30]

> Progressively enrich those aspects of the explanation that involve discovery and the growth and transmission of knowledge.

The procedures would be even more specific when applied to the various subfields of economics like macroeconomics or the theory of the firm.

Rizzo closed his chapter by considering the matter of appraising a research program. I shall close this chapter with a couple of observations on that point.

In the Lakatosian schema, one rejects a research program when it is "degenerating," that is, when it fails to yield "theoretically progressive problemshifts" involving some "excess empirical content over its predecessor."[31] It is certainly arguable that many aspects of Austrian theory qualify as progressive under this definition: the business-cycle theory explains elements of recession and predicts facts that rival theories do not. But, to ascertain whether a theory really does have "excess empirical content" over another, one needs a "background observational theory" like, say, econometrics.

For a number of quite good reasons, Austrians tend to reject the background observational theories of economics. Thus their attitude toward empirical economics is rather like that of the academic doctors who refused to look through Galileo's telescope because they believed the moons of Jupiter were an effect of his optics and not a phenomenon of nature. This does not mean that one should embrace econometrics. (Econometricians, along with their imitators in other disciplines, are the only Baconians left in the sciences.) But perhaps Austrians should give more attention to developing an "optics" of what Hayek calls "pattern prediction."[32]

There is a more general point. Mises, as we saw, believed that logic tests theories; and he turned his own logic on the theories of others, including the auxiliary theories like formalism in general and the use of mathematics in particular; statistical aggregation; certain kinds of simplifying assumptions;

and so on. The result is that the legacy of Mises is partly a large (and, of course, quite valuable) negative heuristic proscribing various techniques. My concern is that Austrians not let this protective belt become an iron maiden. It may turn out that one will have to resort to various off-limits sectors of the neoclassical toolbox to make a start on problems whose eventual solution can dispense with the proscribed tool. To put it another way, one may have to tolerate a little inconsistency in the beginning to get a truly progressive research program off the ground.

Notes

1. Ludwig von Mises, *Epistemological Problems of Economics,* Princeton, N.J.: D. Van Nostrand, 1960, p. 13.

2. Mario J. Rizzo, "Mises and Lakatos: A Reformulation of Austrian Methodology," chapter 6, p. 55, emphasis added.

3. Ludwig von Mises, *Human Action* (New Haven: Yale University, 1949), p. 39.

4. Ibid.

5. Imre Lakatos, "The Methodology of Scientific Research Programmes," in *Criticism and the Growth of Knowledge,* ed. Imre Lakatos and A. Musgrave (Cambridge: Cambridge University, 1970), p. 94.

6. "Our science, . . . disregarding the accidental, considers only the essential. Its goal is the comprehension of the universal, and its procedure is formal and axiomatic. It views action and the conditions under which action takes place not in their concrete form, as we encounter them in everyday life, nor in their actual setting, as we view them in each of the sciences of nature and of history, but as formal constructions that enable us to grasp the patterns of human action in their purity." (Mises, *Epistemological Problems,* p. 13.) On Mises's rationalism and neo-Kantianism, see also Lachmann's chapter 4 of this book.

7. This is not the place to detail my reasons for such a judgment. But perhaps I can outline the argument. The Kantian approach has been repeatedly discredited in the natural sciences—for example, by the invention of Riemannian geometry. In general, we have no reason to suppose that the categorical structure of the brain—if the brain even has a categorical structure—provides a path to unshakeable truth about natural phenomena. Mises's position is somewhat different, of course: he is asserting that logic is the path to truth about human action—the artificial rather than the natural—and here he is on far stronger ground than the Kantian natural scientist. (Being on strong ground is not the same as possessing apodictic certainty; the post-Humean mind rebels at the hubris of such a claim.) But even if we accept the validity of propositions about human action derived from logic, we must still ask how much this tells us about economic theory.

Logic may well tell us much about the basic economic concepts of human action—". . . value, wealth, price, and cost . . . valuing, scale of value and importance, scarcity and abundance, advantage and disadvantage, success, profit, and loss." (Mises, *Epistemological Problems,* p. 24.) But are we therefore entitled to think that "the quantity theory of money, the theory of the relation between the quantity of money and interest, the theory of fiduciary media, and the circulation-credit theory of the business cycle" also follow logically from the concept of action? (Mises, *Epistemological Problems,* p. 25.) In fact, the quantity theory and business-cycle theories are not strictly about human action: they are about the results of human action not of human design. Economic phenomena, as Hayek has stressed, are not artificial (that is, they do not operate according to the logic of action of an individual) any more than they are natural. A Kantian a priori economic theory would have to presuppose either (1) that the brain is wired with all the appropriate categories to understand directly the unintended results of human action (a notion no more plausible than it is with regard to natural phenomena) or (2) that one can logically deduce the laws of operation of such unintended results from the logic of individual action (which is a reductionist fallacy).

8. Mark Blaug, *The Methodology of Economics* (Cambridge: Cambridge University, 1980), p. 93.

9. The German edition of *Epistemological Problems,* called *Grundprobleme der Nationalökonomie,* was published in 1933.

10. The revised and updated translation of which is *The Logic of Scientific Discovery,* New York: Harper and Row, 1959.

11. In saying this I am intentionally glossing over Lakatos's distinction between naive (or "naturalistic" or "dogmatic") falsificationism and sophisticated (or "methodological") falsificationism. It is the latter, argues Lakatos, that Popper upheld.

12. Compare with Karl R. Popper, *Conjectures and Refutations; The Growth of Scientific Knowledge* (New York: Harper Colophon, 1965), p. 44.

13. Michael Polanyi, *Personal Knowledge: Towards a Post-Critical Philosophy* (Chicago: University of Chicago, 1958); Thomas Kuhn, *Structure of Scientific Revolutions* (Chicago: University of Chicago, 1962).

14. Whether this is a normative or merely a descriptive assertion is a major point of contention between Kuhn and his critics.

15. Mises, *Epistemological Problems,* p. 29.

16. See Israel Kirzner, *The Economic Point of View* (Princeton, N.J.: D. van Nostrand, 1960).

17. Spiro J. Latsis, "A Research Programme in Economics" in *Method and Appraisal in Economics,* ed. Spiro J. Latsis (Cambridge: Cambridge University, 1976), p. 5.

18. Ibid., p. 4, emphasis deleted.

19. The fourth proposition is a bit vague as worded, but it could be interpreted as the spontaneous-order principle of the Austrian hard core, on which see later in this chapter and also chapter 6.

20. Kirzner, *Competition and Entrepreneurship* (Chicago: University of Chicago, 1973).

21. Latsis, "Research Programme," p. 25.

22. See Herbert Simon, "From Substantive to Procedural Rationality," in Latsis, *Method and Appraisal,* p. 129. This is not the place to discuss the relationship of Austrian economics to Simon's "behavioralism" in any detail, of course.

23. Kirzner, *Economic Point of View,* chaps. 6, 7; see also, for example, Kirzner, *Competition and Entrepreneurship,* p. 33.

24. See Karl R. Popper, *The Poverty of Historicism* (New York: Harper Torchbooks, 1964), p. 149. I am indebted to Mario Rizzo for this reference.

25. Compare with Latsis, "Research Programme," p. 22.

26. F.A. Hayek, *The Counter-Revolution of Science* (Indianapolis: Liberty Press, 1979), p. 41.

27. A. Leijonhufvud, "Schools, 'Revolutions' and Research Programmes in Economics," in Latsis, *Method and Appraisal,* p. 89. Let me be clear that I do not mean a spontaneous-order postulate to imply a blind presumption that social phenomena are always orderly or that they represent some best-of-all-possible worlds. I mean only that social science should set itself the task of understanding the nature, determinants—and possible pathologies—of social order.

28. See chapter 6, p. 64.

29. Mises, *Epistemological Problems,* p. 24.

30. On which term see "Notes on the Evolution of Systems of Rules of Conduct," in F.A. Hayek, *Studies in Philosophy, Politics, and Economics,* (Chicago: University of Chicago, 1967), p. 75.

31. Lakatos, "Scientific Research Programmes," p. 118.

32. F.A. Hayek, "The Theory of Complex Phenomena," in Hayek, *Studies,* p. 24.

8 Equilibrium and the Market Process

S.C. Littlechild

Introduction

For many years, the concept of the market process made little headway against the prevailing concept of equilibrium. However, during the last decade or so, there has been increasing dissatisfaction with the straightjacket of equilibrium and an increasing willingness to explore ideas of process. Uncertainty, expectations, learning, and revision of plans are phrases nowadays in common use.

Ironically, the leaders in this movement include mathematical economists, those whom Ludwig von Mises derided for "vain playing with mathematical symbols, a pastime not suited to convey any knowledge" (Mises 1966, p. 250). It seems appropriate therefore, to explore how far the latest ideas and models of mathematical economists are consistent with Austrian concepts of equilibrium and the market process and, specifically, with the views of the two major figures in the modern Austrian school: Ludwig von Mises and F.A. Hayek.

For this purpose, we shall examine the stimulating and provocative inaugural lecture given by F.H. Hahn (1973b) at the University of Cambridge, entitled "On the notion of equilibrium in economics."[1] This lecture is of interest and importance for several reasons. It contains a nontechnical guide to the rapidly growing mathematical literature going beyond the Arrow-Debreu model of general equilibrium, written by one who has been actively involved in those developments. It represents a major position statement on methodology by a sometime president of the Econometric Society. Finally, it constitutes a call for economists to take into consideration the sequential process by which actual economies evolve, a topic that until then had largely been neglected by mainstream economic theories.

We begin with an outline and comparison of the views of Mises and Hayek and then attempt to relate Hahn's ideas to this context. In the final sections we appraise Hahn's suggestion for the direction of future research in this area.

I should like to acknowledge helpful comments by F.H. Hahn, L.M. Lachmann, and G.J. Stigler on some early notes for this chapter and valuable discussion with I.M. Kirzner and L.H. White at the New York conference. Hahn and Lachmann have also commented on the revised version (see postscript).

It is perhaps unnecessary to emphasize that a great number of economists, of very diverse backgrounds, have made useful and often potentially important contributions to the understanding of the market process.[2] Limitations of time and space prevent a comprehensive survey, valuable though that could be. In the confines of this chapter it seems most fruitful to concentrate on a detailed comparison of the ideas of three leading figures.

Mises's Views on Equilibrium and Market Process

For Mises, the market is a process. The state of the market is continually changing. The market process is characterized by profits and losses as the judgments made by entrepreneurs turn out to be correct or incorrect. A system in which there is no uncertainty about the future, and hence no profits and losses, is not a possible state of affairs. However, an important role in Mises's scheme of thought is played by the equilibrium concept of an "evenly rotating economy," which is characterized by the elimination of change and stability of prices. How can this be?

Mises certainly acknowledges—indeed emphasizes—that the perfect foresight implied by such an economy is not characteristic of the real world, but to analyse the problems of change one has to confront them with a fictitious state in which change is absent.

> Such a rigid system is not peopled with living men making choices and liable to error, it is a world of soulless unthinking automatons; it is not a human society it is an ant-hill.

> These insoluble contradictions, however, do not affect the service which this imaginary construction renders for the only problems for whose treatment it is both appropriate and indispensable: the problem of the relation between the prices of products and those of the factors required for their production, and the implied problems of entrepreneurship and of profit and loss (Mises 1966, p. 248).

The concept of evenly rotating economy is useful, in Mises's view, precisely because of "the tendency, prevailing in every action, toward the establishment of an evenly rotating economy" (1966, p. 250). He explains that the logical (nonmathematical) economist shows how

> the activities of enterprising men, the promoters and speculators, eager to profit from discrepancies in the price structure, tend toward eradicating such discrepancies and thereby also toward blotting out the sources of entrepreneurial profit and loss. He shows how this process would finally result in the establishment of the evenly rotating economy (1966, pp. 355-356).

The use of the concept of the evenly rotating economy reflects Mises's view that "the method of economics is the method of imaginary constructions" (Mises 1966, p. 236). This involves "abstract[ing] from the operation of some conditions present in actual action. Then we are in a position to grasp the hypothetical consequences of the absence of these conditions and to conceive the effects of their existence" (p. 237). Parenthetically, we may question whether "the method of imaginary constructions is justified by its success" (p. 236). Do we really need the concept of the evenly rotating economy "to grasp the function of enterpreneurship and the meaning of profit and loss" (p. 248), or to obtain "the insight that dealing with the uncertain conditions of the unknown future—that is, speculation—is inherent in every action, and that profit and loss are necessary features of acting which cannot be conjured away by any wishful thinking" (p. 250)?

Finally, we may emphasize once again that Mises does not claim that equilibrium is—at least in certain places, at certain times, and for certain purposes—a reasonably close approximation to the real world. Unlike (most) neoclassical economists, Mises explicitly rejects such a claim:

> It is furthermore absurd to believe that the services rendered by the construction of an evenly rotating economy are the more valuable the more the object of our studies, the realm of real action, corresponds to this construction in respect to absence of change. The static method, the employment of the imaginary construction of an evenly rotating economy, is the only adequate method of analyzing the changes concerned without regard to whether they are great or small, sudden or slow (1966, p. 248).

Similarly, part of Mises's criticism of mathematical economists is that "they deal with equilibrium as if it were a real entity and not a limiting notion, a mere mental tool" (p. 250).

Hayek on Economics and Knowledge

Hayek has championed the cause of process versus equilibrium just as vigorously as Mises. "The Meaning of Competition" is devoted to the thesis that "competition is by its nature a dynamic process whose essential characteristics are assumed away by the assumptions underlying static analysis" (Hayek 1946, p. 94). This general coincidence of views is not surprising, given that Hayek was a pupil of Mises and educated in the same Austrian school of thought. Nevertheless, the direction and extent of influence are by no means clear. Hayek's seminal paper on "Economics and Knowledge" was delivered in London in 1936, and he refers to a related idea inherent in an article published in German in 1928. In contrast, the first edition of *Human Action* was not published until 1949, although it is based to some extent on a treatise written in German in 1940, and it has been suggested that Mises probably conceived the idea of the market process around 1910 (Lachmann 1971, p. 193).

"Economics and Knowledge" contains the most explicit statement of Hayek's views on equilibrium. He defines the actions of a person as in equilibrium insofar as they can be understood as part of a single plan. Since equilibrium is a relationship between actions, which must necessarily take place successively in time, "it is obvious that the passage of time is essential to give the concept of equilibrium any meaning" (Hayek 1937, p. 37). Following this line of approach, a society can be said to be in equilibrium at a point in time, but only in the sense that the different plans of the individuals comprising it are mutually compatible. Such an equilibrium, once it exists, will continue only so long as the external data correspond to the common expectations of the members of the society.

Equilibrium is thus defined, not in terms of prices and quantities, but in terms of expectations and plans. As a result, the concept of equilibrium is clearly separated from the concept of a stationary state. Hayek's role in the origination of this idea has recently been affirmed (Milgate 1979). [Surprisingly he makes no reference to Hayek's own view that "this is no more than the necessary outcome of a process which has been going on for a fairly long time" (Hayek 1937, p. 41, n. 6); this was the idea already inherent in the paper written in 1928.]

In the present context, it is appropriate to point out that, although the concept of the evenly rotating economy assumes no change in the underlying data, nonetheless Mises emphasized that it was misleading to call it a static equilibrium and a bad mistake to confuse it with a stationary economy. Mises's approach is less advanced than Hayek's in this respect, but in retrospect we can see that it is in the same spirit, and arguably the Hayekian equilibrium concept can be used for the same purposes as Mises used the evenly rotating economy.

Hayek then enquires into "the reasons for our concern with the admittedly fictitious state of equilibrium:

> the only justification for this is the supposed existence of a tendency toward equilibrium. It is only by the assertion that such a tendency exists that economics ceases to be an exercise in pure logic and becomes an empirical science. . . . [This] assertion can hardly mean anything but that, under certain conditions, the knowledge and intentions of the different members of society are supposed to come more and more into agreement. . . . [This] is clearly an empirical proposition (1946, pp. 44–45).

Commentators in the Austrian literature have emphasized and discussed the contrast between Hayek's view that the tendency to equilibrium is an empirical matter and Mises's view that it follows logically from the "activities of enterprising men."[3] This is not our present concern. We emphasize instead the agreement between Mises and Hayek that (1) equilibrium is a "fictitious," not a realistic, state of the economy; (2) an equilibrium concept is important only because of the *tendency* to equilibrium; and (3) this tendency relies on an aspect of human nature—call it entrepreneurial alertness or learning—which (as Israel Kirzner has repeatedly emphasized) is not encompassed by Robbinsian economising or choice in the face of given data.

Hayek goes on to confess that "we are still pretty much in the dark about (a) the conditions under which this tendency is supposed to exist and (b) the nature of the process by which individual knowledge is changed" (1937, p. 45). The first question involves the investigation of whether particular hypotheses about learning are necessary and sufficient to explain a movement to equilibrium in particular circumstances; the second involves the investigation of how people actually do learn. In effect, Hayek is sketching out a program of research that might involve the use of formal mathematical models to tackle the first question and applied psychology to tackle the second.

Such a program of research would not, of course, commend itself to Mises, chiefly because from his point of view it would be unnecessary and outside the scope of economics. Somewhat more surprisingly, Hayek does not pursue this line of research either; nor does he encourage others to do so. Admittedly he is not a mathematician, but in his Nobel lecture he was at pains "to avoid giving the impression that I generally reject the mathematical method in economics," and emphasized the qualitative insights that mathematics could provide: "We could scarcely have achieved that comprehensive picture of the mutual interdependencies of the different events in a market without this algebraic technique" (Hayek 1974, p. 252). Nor is Hayek a psychologist, but he is one of the very few economists to have published a book embodying original research in psychology.

The reason Hayek gives for abandoning this line of enquiry is that "there seems to me to be another and more fruitful way of approach to the central problem," namely, to pose the further question "how much knowledge and what sort of knowledge the different individuals must possess in order that we may be able to speak of equilibrium" (1937, p. 50). For Hayek, this "problem of the division of knowledge" is "the really central problem of economics as a social science." He points out that the (minimum) relevant knowledge that each person must possess for equilibrium to exist is certainly not all the knowledge that might be useful to him. Consequently, an equilibrium is not necessarily "a sort of optimum position" (1937, p. 53). This raises the further question of what conditions are necessary and sufficient "in order that the results of the combination of individual bits of knowledge should be comparable to the results of directions by an omniscient dictator.'' In effect, Hayek is enquiring into the conditions for the existence and (as we would now say) Pareto efficiency of equilibrium.

To summarize, in the first part of his paper, Hayek introduces the concept of equilibrium as mutual compatibility of plans over time, which is in principle distinct from the concept of stationarity. This aspect of his work is beginning to receive general notice. In the middle part of the paper he argues (contra Mises) that the existence of a tendency to equilibrium is an empirical matter. This is the part that most Austrian commentators have emphasized. In the last part of the paper he in effect sketches out two alternative programs of research that follow from the earlier insights. The first program focuses on the nature of the market process and the conditions for it to converge to equilibrium; the second focuses on the conditions for the existence and efficiency of equilibrium. For our present purposes, it is this last part of the paper that is of most interest. And what is of greatest significance is that Hayek opts for the second research program rather than the first—that is, for the study of equilibrium rather than process.

Hahn on Equilibrium in Economics

The central argument of Hahn's lecture may be summarized quite briefly. Equilibrium is a central organizing idea in economics. The various different concepts of equilibrium have in common the notion of mutual consistency of plans. The Arrow-Debreu model of equilibrium has the advantage of clarity and is of great use for many purposes, but it also presents three specific difficulties: (1) it is possible to define equilibrium states (the core) that in general are not equal to the Arrow-Debreu equilibrium; (2) when there are increasing returns there may be no equilibrium; and (3) the Arrow-Debreu model is inadequate to handle uncertainty (since it might necessitate contingent futures markets that might not exist). What is required is an equilibrium notion that reflects ''the sequential character of actual economies'' in an ''essential'' way. It will need explicitly to incorporate concepts of information, expectations, and uncertainty. Hahn proposes a formal model that can be used to analyze these problems and then discusses the nature, existence, and efficiency of equilibrium in this model. The last part of his lecture is devoted to refuting certain objections to his approach and exploring some of its implications.

For Hahn, the Arrow-Debreu model has the advantage of being ''precise, complete and unambiguous'' (1973b, p. 3). With the aid of it, ''it is often possible to say something about the direction in which some variables will move next,''—for example, when the economy is in a state of disequilibrium (1973b, p. 9).[4] It is not claimed that the Arrow-Debreu model is a realistic description of the actual world: Hahn elsewhere explicitly rejects that claim.[5] In fact, the model makes "a significant contribution to the understanding of Keynesian economics just by describing so precisely what would have to be the case if there were to be no Keynesian problems" (1973b, p. 34).[6] "This negative role of Arrow-Debreu equilibrium I consider almost to be sufficient justification for it" (1973b, p. 14).

To summarize, the Arrow-Debreu general equilibrium model has the advantage of clarity, may be used to indicate directions of change, is not claimed to be a realistic description, and may (arguably) be used in the method of "imaginary constructions." But as shown, these are precisely the same claims that Mises makes for his model of the evenly rotating economy. Thus the first point to make is that Hahn and Mises share a similar view of the role of general equilibrium (in its timeless sense).

Despite its usefulness, Hahn does not believe that the Arrow-Debreu concept of equilibrium is the most useful one. What is required is an equilibrium notion that reflects "the sequential character of actual economies" in an essential way, that is, it should not be possible to reformulate the model in a nonsequential way (1973b, p. 16). "This in turn requires that information processes and costs, transactions and tranactions costs and also expectations and uncertainty be explicitly and essentially included in the equilibrium notion. This is what the Arrow-Debreu construction does not do" (1973b, p. 16).

These concepts that Hahn emphasizes, such as ignorance and uncertainty, theories and perception, information and expectations, learning and plan revision, all lie at the heart of the subjectivist approach. The term "sequential character" of actual economies surely refers to the market process, and indeed Hahn remarks that "we should like to be able to describe and predict the course of economic processes in great detail" (1973b, p. 10). His concluding remarks not merely acknowledge the importance of perceptions and expectations but urge further work in this direction as a matter of first priority.

> . . . the main progress to be made now is to recognize quite explicitly the sequential structure of the economies which we study and to wrestle with some of the very serious conceptual problems which this raises. In particular *the distinction between the perceived environment and the environment* and the consequential importance of the theories which are held by agents seems to be bound to become increasingly important in analysis (Hahn 1973b, p. 40). (Emphasis added.)

Thus, the second point to make about Hahn's lecture is that, compared to most previous work in mathematical economics, it represents an important step forward in the direction of subjectivism.

To analyze these problems, Hahn proposes the following model (1973b, pp. 18-20, 25-26). At any time, an economic agent holds a *theory* that comprises, roughly speaking, his conditional predictions about the way in which the economy will develop and about the consequences of his own actions. He is said to be learning if his theory changes over time. (Here, learning does not refer to the mere updating of a conditional forecast in the light of more recent information, nor does the absence of learning mean that the forecast must be constant. Rather, learning means a change in the *method* of making forecasts.) The agent is assumed to abandon his theory when it is sufficiently and systematically falsified. The agent also has a *policy,* which specifies his actions conditional on any pattern of development in the economy.

The agent is said to be in equilibrium if his policy does not change over time. This in turn requires (1) that he is not learning and (2) that his objectives do not change. The economy is said to be in equilibrium when it develops in such a way that it does not cause agents to change the theories that they hold or the policies that they pursue. This requires, roughly speaking, that the actions of agents not be systematically and persistently inconsistent and that the agents hold subjective probability distributions that converge to observed frequencies.

We are now in a position to make a third point of comparison. The concepts of individual and general equilibrium that Hahn defines are in principle the same as those proposed by Hayek. To be sure, they are defined more rigorously, using more sophisticated mathematical and statistical techniques. But for both authors (1) an individual is in equilibrium as long as his actions form part of a single plan, uninterrupted by learning; (2) an economy is in equilibrium when the plans of its members are mutually compatible; and (3) the concept of equilibrium is quite distinct from that of the stationary state. In effect, Hahn's equilibrium is a stochastic version of Hayekian equilibrium.

Once Hahn has set up his model and defined his concept of equilibrium, his instinct is to look immediately for an existence theorem. "But I must note an important and interesting open question of a technical kind before I justify the approach. In order that any kind of equilibrium, even in simple cases, can be shown to exist, I must show that there are theories which, if agents held them, would in that economy not be falsified" (1973b, p. 27). He recognizes that this will be a difficult task in the complex model he has constructed, but it is not merely a technical mathematical question that is at issue: there is a real problem that lies behind it. "For what one is asking in the last resort is whether it is possible to have a decentralized economy in which agents have adapted themselves to their economic environment and where their expectations in the widest sense are in the proper meaning not falsified" (1973b, p. 28). Almost immediately thereafter, on discussing the problems raised by increasing returns, Hahn takes up the question of whether one can any longer speak of the efficient allocation of resources, and he notes the kind of global problems that decentralization may pose.

Once again, this is reminiscent of Hayek who, recall, identified two directions for further research: analysis of the market process leading to equilibrium and analysis of the conditions for the existence and efficiency of equilibrium. Hayek recommended the second approach to explain how a decentralized economy is not only possible but efficient, and this is precisely the line that Hahn has taken.

To summarize, in examining Hahn's lecture we have been led to four conclusions. First, the Arrow-Debreu equilibrium concept plays substantially the same role for Hahn as the evenly rotating economy does for Mises. Second, Hahn's paper represents a significant step for mathematical economics in the direction of subjectivism. Third, the revised concept of equilibrium that Hahn proposes as a means of analyzing the sequential character of actual economies is essentially a stochastic version of Hayekian equilibrium, both being couched in terms of compatibility of plans over time and both quite distinct from the concept of a stationary state. Finally, as a means of understanding the properties of a decentralized economy, both Hayek and Hahn consider it fruitful to concentrate on studying the conditions for the existence and efficiency of equilibrium.

We are thus led to a very striking overall conclusion. Recent developments in mathematical economics, as expounded and encouraged by Hahn, have returned economic theory precisely to the path that Hayek sketched out in 1937. The techniques of analysis are of course more sophisticated, and in that sense a useful advance has been made, but the underlying philosophies are the same.[7] With respect to this branch of economic theory, as Lachmann has observed in a private communication, Austrians can hardly complain that their ideas have been overlooked: the mathematical economists, albeit unwittingly, have done precisely what Hayek asked of them!

Equilibrium versus Market Process?

In recommending the study of equilibrium, it is fairly clear that Hayek is not counseling that the study of market processes should be abandoned. He notes that "this question of the empirical probability that people will learn" is not "lacking in unsolved and highly interesting questions" (1937, pp. 49–50). But these questions "have at least received some attention in past discussions," whereas the problem of the knowledge required for equilibrium is "at least equally important but one which appears to have received no attention at all." We may safely take it, from Hayek's other writings if not from this paper, that the study of equilibrium is advocated to obtain additional insights and not to preclude the futher formal study of the market process. Only a few years later, for example, he is arguing strongly that competition is properly to be viewed as a process of discovery, and not as an equilibrium state (Hayek 1946).

This is not the view that Hahn takes. Remarks scattered throughout his lecture give the impression that he favors the study of equilibrium to the *exclusion* of the study of process. He gives three quite different reasons: first, that equilibrium (in his modified sense) is a realistic description of the world; second, that it would be impossible to construct a theory of process anyway, so that equilibrium represents the limit of what economists have to say; and third, that it is the particular duty of economists to study equilibrium. We shall examine these arguments in turn and contrast them with the Austrian position.

Hahn's first argument is that equilibrium (in the extended Hayek-Hahn sense) is useful in practice because it is a realistic description of the world. ". . . it is precisely the empirical claim for the usefulness of the equilibrium notion that the theories and motives of agents are sufficiently stable and we are not allowed to invoke changing theories or motives to help us out of falsified predictions" (Hahn 1973b, p. 23). Now it is not entirely clear that this argument is valid. To make and test predictions it is necessary that the observer be able to specify the theories and motives of the agents, and these may or may not be stable. For example, one might test the hypothesis that during times of inflation people have changing theories of price expectations against the null hypothesis that they have stable theories. Hahn also seems to be in error in claiming that if a "higher-level" theory of the learning process were available the concept of equilibrium would be otiose. "If a definite behaviour pattern can be established for all situations then nothing would be gained by labelling any particular behaviour as equilibrium behaviour" (Hahn 1973b, p. 11). It would certainly be true that the omniscient observer could explain or predict an agent's behaviour over any period of time, regardless of whether the agent was in equilibrium over the whole of that period. *But the agent himself would not know this "higher-level" theory.* (If he did, this knowledge would become part of his own theory, and he would no longer be learning.) As Hayek himself emphasized, the point is not whether any particular behavior is equilibrium behaviour but whether particular actions are in an equilibrium relationship with other actions (1948, p. 36). It is useful to be able to describe certain actions as part of one plan, and other (subsequent) actions as part of a different plan adopted as a result of learning.

However, the main point to make here is that the view that the economy is or can be in a state of equilibrium (for any significant period of time) is diametrically opposed to the Austrian position. We have already noted the views of Mises and Hayek on the "fictitious" nature of equilibrium; Lachmann has made the point quite explicitly. ". . . we must assume that Professor Hahn envisages some time sequences in which nothing is learned by a participant and others in which something is learned. Needless to say, the former variety cannot exist. Time and knowledge belong together. As soon as we permit time to elapse, we must permit knowledge to change. The pattern of knowledge never stands still" (1976, p. 36).

For the Austrians, the concept of equilibrium is used to characterize not the *state* of the economy but the direction of *changes* in the state. To use Kenneth Boulding's analogy of the dog chasing the cat, equilibrium for the dog is where the cat is—but the dog might never catch the cat! The concept is nevertheless useful because it explains the direction in which the dog is running. To assume the existence of equilibrium in empirical work can thus provide so-called insights that are positively misleading, and quite inappropriate suggestions for policy may be derived (Littlechild 1981).

Hahn's second argument is that a model involving learning would necessitate a "higher-level" theory of the learning process. "Such a theory is not available at present. . . . In our present state of knowledge however it is routine behaviour and not behaviour which we can hope to describe. Indeed one of the reasons why an equilibrium notion is useful is that it serves to make precise the limits of economic analysis" (1973b, p. 21). That we do not have a theory of the learning process is not disputed. Some would argue with L.M. Lachmann that we *cannot* have one: "Expectations, it is true, are largely a response to events experienced in the past, but the modus operandi of the response is not the same in all cases even of the same experience. This experience, before being transformed into expectations, has, so to speak, to pass through a 'filter' in the human mind, and the undefinable character of this process makes the outcome of it unpredictable" (Lachmann 1943).

We should realize, nevertheless, that all applications of economic theory—even the application of insights from the Arrow-Debreu model—involve implicit assumptions about learning. For example, in the illustration given by Hahn, an excess of intended investment over intended savings will begin to take effect only when, and as fast as, frustrated borrowers and alert lenders recognize the true nature of the situation and react accordingly.

The most appropriate avenue for research, as Lachmann suggests, is probably to explore the effects of different assumptions about learning:[8]

Under these circumstances, what can the economist do but construct various hypothetical types of expectations conceived as responses to various hypothetical situations, and then leave the process of selection to empirical verification in the light of economic history? Several such "ideal types" either of expectations, like Lord Keynes' "long-term" and "short-term" expectations, or of the holders of expectations, like Professor Schumpeter's "static producer" and "dynamic entrepreneur" or Professor

Hicks' "sensitive" and "insensitive" traders, have already been evolved
and served to elucidate important dynamic problems (Lachmann 1943).

This approach would seem to worry Hahn, who earlier remarked "Of
course, one of the reasons why so much of our effort is devoted to the study
of equilibria is that they are singularly well suited to study. We all know the
endless variety of adjustment models, not uncongenial to commonsense,
one is capable of constructing. No unifying principle, such as maximization, seems available" (Hahn 1970, p. 1). (The discussant questioned
whether *any* of the adjustment models so far developed are congenial to
commonsense!) Lachmann's argument is that variety is not a defect: "we
need not deplore unduly the indeterminateness of expectations, for it is
intelligibility and not determinateness that social science should strive to
achieve" (1943).

At this point we may acknowledge a related objection raised by Mises,
namely, that market processes are incapable of being modelled mathemati-
cally:

> The problems of process analysis, i.e., the only economic problems that
> matter, defy any mathematical approach. The introduction of time para-
> meters into the equations is no solution. It does not even indicate the essen-
> tial short-comings of the mathematical method. The statements that every
> change involves time and that change is always in the temporal sequence are
> merely a way of expressing the fact that as far as there is rigidity and
> unchangeability there is not time. The main deficiency of mathematical
> economics is not the fact that it ignores the temporal sequence, but that it
> ignores the operation of the market process.

> The mathematical method is at a loss to show how from a state of nonequil-
> ibrium those actions spring up which tend toward the establishment of
> equilibrium. It is, of course, possible to indicate the mathematical opera-
> tions required for the transformation of the mathematical description of a
> definite state of nonequilibrium into the mathematical description of the
> state of equilibrium. But these mathematical operations by no means
> describe the market process actuated by the discrepancies in the price struc-
> ture (Mises 1966, p. 356).

The objection has validity, but is it perhaps overstated? Consider the case of
arbitrage. One possibility is to model entrepreneurial alertness by a positive
probability of discovering hitherto-unknown arbitrage opportunities. (Littlechild 1979; Littlechild and Owen 1980) Perhaps, in a similar way, one
could model the "creation" of longer-term investment opportunities, or the
adoption by an agent of a new theory (in the sense of Hahn).

Discussion of these problems would take us too far afield, however. I
simply wish to establish here that the lack of an accepted theory of learning
does not preclude the development of formal economic models of market

processes and that the concept of equilibrium certainly does not represent "the limit of economic analysis."

Hahn's final argument is that economists are better engaged studying equilibrium than the laws of motion of a capitalist society: "I am certain that in such an ambitious intellectual programme the expertise of the economist will only be a very small part of what is required. In the meantime there are many important problems in all societies which if they are not understood by economists will not be understood by anyone and it is here that our main obligation must lie" (1973b, pp. 39–40).

An opposite view may also be advanced. The study of economic processes can be done usefully on a scale less grand than the aforesaid "laws of motion." Particularly important, for example, is the study of how markets generate, disseminate, and respond to information. Insofar as only very general propositions about learning are involved, and ideal types are used for illustration, the study of economic processes does not require significant inputs from disciplines other than economics. (More precisely, the economic theory of such processes requires no more noneconomic inputs than the economic theory of equilibrium. Applied studies may require further inputs in either case.) It follows that the study of economic processes is just as much the proper domain of the economist as is the study of equilibrium; indeed for Mises, as for all Austrian economists, the "imaginary constructions such as equilibrium . . . are only tools of reasoning. The sole task of economics is analysis of the actions of men, is the analysis of processes" (1966, p. 357). Moreover, no one else will study economic processes if the economist does not.

This is not the place to appraise the relative merits of process and equilibrium per se. However, since the study of economic processes has been almost entirely neglected during the past half-century (in contrast to the half-century preceding Hayek's paper), it seems more likely that, in the immediate future, a higher return is to be obtained from studying processes rather than from further refining the equilibrium concept.[9]

Conclusions

We set out to discover how far the recent developments in mathematical economics, as exemplified by Hahn's inaugural lecture, are consistent with the ideas of Austrian economists, notably Mises and Hayek. We found that (1) Hahn's view of the nature and role of Arrow-Debreu equilibrium is substantially the same as Mises's view of the evenly rotating economy; (2) Hahn's emphasis on "the distinction between the perceived environment and the environment" reflects a central tenet of the subjectivist approach; (3) Hahn's redefinition of equilibrium as mutual compatibility of plans over time is a stochastic version of Hayekian equilibrium; and (4) Hahn's focus on the existence and properties of equilibrium, rather than on the nature of the market process, parallels the earlier argument of Hayek. However, we argued that Hayek, unlike Hahn, did not mean to exclude the study of process; that Hahn's view that the (modified) equilibrium is a useful concept precisely because it realistically describes the world is not shared by Austrians; that Austrians would agree with Hahn that there cannot be a definitive higher-level theory of the learning process but that, nevertheless, models can be built to analyze plausible types of learning process; and that, contra Hahn, there is likely to be a higher payoff in the immediate future from studying processes rather than equilibrium.

Hahn has provided us with a clear and colorful map of largely unfamiliar territory. He has described the country we know and the reports currently coming in from the advance scouts and has sketched out his own view of the terrain ahead. Furthermore, in advising on our route, he has drawn attention to the beauty of some familiar features and warned against the impenetrable forests elsewhere. We must be grateful to him for the map, but perhaps the forests are not so impenetrable as they seem, and the glimpses we have already had through them suggest that the less familiar routes will provide better access to more exciting vistas beyond.

Notes

1. Hahn's lecture has elsewhere been appraised by Coddington (1975), Loasby (1976), and Hutchison (1977, chap. 4).

2. Notably L.M. Lachmann, I.M. Kirzner, and G.L.S. Shackle from the Austrian/subjectivist camp, and R. Radner and J.M. Grandmont among mathematical economists.

3. Compare Lachmann (1943; 1971; 1974; 1976), Kirzner (1974; 1979; chaps. 2, 9), White (1976).

4. "In an economy with unemployed resources an excess of intended investment over intended savings is used to predict that incomes will not persist at their present level and indeed are very likely to rise." (p. 9) Compare Hayek (1974, p. 251) "We have indeed good reason to believe that unemployment indicates that the structure of relative prices and wages has been distorted . . . and that to restore equality between the demand and supply of labour in all sectors changes of relative prices and some transfer of labour will be necessary." Both Hayek and Hahn immediately make the point that one may not be able to specify in quantitative, as opposed to qualitative, terms what the final point of equilibrium will be.

5. "It was, I believe, always understood that the equilibrium of Arrow-Debreu is not a description of an actual economy" (Hahn 1973a, p. 329). See also p. 323.

6. This last argument is by no means convincing. Even if the Arrow-Debreu model is conceded to demonstrate that under certain assumptions there will be no Keynesian problems, this does not imply that the converse is true. A similar difficulty arises with Hahn's assertion that the Arrow-Debreu model may be used to dispose of a false claim about natural resources. See Coddington (1975, pp. 552–556), Loasby (1976, p. 47), Hutchison (1977, pp. 86–87), and Lachmann (1976, pp. 36–37) for vigorous criticism.

7. A fuller account of these developments would of course need to consider the important contributions of Hicks, who in turn remarks in his preface to *Value and Capital* that "they were not by any means entirely my own ideas; they came into being as a sort of social process which went on among the people who were working there [at LSE], at that time, under the leadership of Professor Robbins" (1939).

8. L.M. Lachmann, "The Role of Expectations in Economics as a Social Science," *Economica* 10 (February 1943). All quotes reprinted with permission.

9. As Hutchison points out, Hahn himself once questioned the marginal utility of further elaboration of general equilibrium analysis (1977, pp. 82–83). "It cannot be denied that there is something scandalous in the spectacle of so many people refining the analysis of economic states which they give no reason to suppose will ever, or have ever, come about" (Hahn 1970, p. 1). Presumably this reservation referred only to the Arrow-Debreu equilibrium concept.

References

Coddington, A. December 1975. The rationale of general equilibrium theory. *Economic Inquiry* 13:539–558.

Dolan, E.G., ed. 1976. *The foundations of modern Austrian economics.* Kansas City: Sheed & Ward.

Hahn, F.H. 1970. Some adjustment problems. *Econometrica* 38:1–17.

———. 1973a. The winter of our discontent. *Economica* 40:322–330.

———. 1973b. On the notion of equilibrium in economics. Inaugural lecture. Cambridge: Cambridge University Press.

Hayek, F.A. 1937. Economics and knowledge. *Economica* 4:33–54. Page references to reprint in Hayek (1948).

———. 1946. The meaning of competition. Stafford Little Lecture, Princeton University, May 1946. Page references to reprint in Hayek (1948).

———. 1948. *Individualism and economic order.* Chicago: University of Chicago.

———. 1974. The pretence of knowledge. Nobel Memorial Lecture.

Hicks, J.R. 1939. *Value and Capital.* London: Oxford University Press.

Hutchison, T.W. 1977. *Knowledge and ignorance in economics.* Oxford: Basil Blackwell.

Kirzner, I.M. 1974. On the method of Austrian economics. Lecture given at Austrian Economics Conference, South Royalton, Vermont, June 1974. Reprinted in Dolan (1976, pp. 40-51).

———. 1979. *Perception, opportunity and profit.* Chicago: University of Chicago.

Lachmann, L.M. 1943. The role of expectations in economics as a social science. *Economica* 10:12-23. Reprinted in Lachmann (1977, pp. 65-80).

———. 1971. Ludwig von Mises and the market process. In *Toward Liberty: Essays in Honor of Ludwig von Mises,* ed. F.A. Hayek. 2 vols. Menlo Park, Calif: Institute of Humane Studies, 2:38-52. Reprinted in Lachmann (1977, pp. 181-193).

———. 1974. On the central concept of Austrian economics: market process. Lecture given at Austrian Economics Conference, South Royalton, Vermont, June 1974. Reprinted in Dolan (1976, pp. 126-132).

———. 1976. From Mises to Shackle: an essay. *Journal of Economic Literature* 14:54-62.

———. 1977. *Capital, expectations and the market process.* Kansas City: Sheed, Andrews & McMeel.

Littlechild, S.C. 1979. An entrepreneurial theory of games. *Metroeconomica* 31:145-165.

———. 1981. Misleading calculations of the social costs of monopoly power. *The Economic Journal* 91:348-363.

Littlechild, S.C., and Owen, G. 1980. An Austrian model of the entrepreneurial market process. *Journal of Economic Theory* 23:361-379.

Loasby, B.J. 1976. *Choice, complexity and ignorance.* Cambridge: Cambridge University.

Milgate, M. 1979. On the origin of the notion of "intertemporal equilibrium. *Economica* 46:1-10.

Mises, Ludwig von. 1966. *Human Action.* 3d ed. Chicago: Henry Regnery.

White, L.H. 1976. Entrepreneurship, imagination and the question of equilibrium. Unpublished paper.

Postscript

F.H. Hahn and Ludwig Lachmann have indicated their general sympathy with this chapter, but their comments on two aspects should be noted.

As to "the limit of economic analysis," Hahn writes the following (private communication dated 21 October 1981):

> I spent the flower of my youth on "processes" e.g. tâtonnement and non-tâtonnement, heterogeneous capital goods, etc. The conclusion I reached was that the kind of theory which was attainable differed in kind from that which equilibrium provides. In the latter, one can proceed from first principles; in the former, this seems impossible. To take just one simple point: there is no "primitive" account of the lag structure of all the error-correcting mechanisms which we postulate; that structure is completely ad hoc. But the behaviour of the system is very sensitive to that structure. So there is really an epistemological point involved. Equilibrium theory, even in its sequential and expectational form, is as robust as its sparse axioms; process theory seems totally unrobust and therefore strictly contingent. That is, while for equilibrium analysis functional form is almost inessential, it is almost everything for process analysis.
>
> It is in *this* sense that I used "the limit of economic analysis." I did not wish to imply that, given "plausible" or even "empirical" adjustment rules, economists could not or should not study their implications. What I doubted was the possibility of going "behind such rules" to ground them in basic theory. But, as I am about to say again in a lecture at Warwick, equilibrium *is* only half of the story. It is relevant to processes in the weak sense I gave, and processes are relevant to it in the sense that they define critical points.

Lachmann (private communication, 25 October 1981) is concerned at Hahn's definition of learning as merely a *change* in the agent's theory of the world:

> TO LEARN means to acquire knowledge. When we say that we have learned a language or calculus or how to drive a car, or call somebody "a learned man," we mean that such knowledge, once acquired, will last a lifetime as a rule. Business knowledge in a competitive world (i.e., knowledge of markets) is of course altogether different since IT CANNOT LAST. Such knowledge is, on the contrary, continuously jeopardised by obsolescence, and therefore its continuing validity has to be MONITORED. In fact, a good deal of what is wrongly called "learning" becomes necessary precisely because the knowledge acquired in such processes will not last! How is a "higher level theory of the learning process," whatever thay may mean, to help us, or the businessmen whose conduct we attempt to

"model," with this central problem? To the businessman the "list of our customers" is knowledge, but how far can he rely on it in planning next year's sales campaign? Are you suggesting that there may one day be a "higher level theory" which tells us how firms manage to keep customers instead of losing them?

I take it there is no difference of substance between Lachmann and Hahn on this point. Lachmann emphasizes that in a changing world we cannot learn the kind of knowledge (about the future) that would be necessary to achieve equilibrium. Hahn's definition and use of the term *learning* is not inconsistent with this view, and his later writing acknowledges that "Put at its mildest, the sequence economy has presented problems of market expectations which are not yet resolved" (Frank Hahn, "General Equilibrium Theory," *The Public Interest,* Special Issue (1980):133.

9

Mises, Hayek, Hahn, and the Market Process: Comment on Littlechild

Lawrence H. White

S.C. Littlechild's chapter is a careful piece whose major points are well argued. This chapter, therefore, will be limited largely to minor amplifications here and minor revisions there. I shall consider, following the order of his chapter, what Littlechild has to say about Mises's, Hayek's, and Hahn's views on equilibrium and the market process. Lastly I shall comment briefly on the alternative methods available for theorizing about market processes.

Littlechild on Mises

Littlechild correctly emphasizes Mises's recognition that the conditions necessary for general equilibrium cannot be met in the real world (Mises 1966, pp. 247–248). It is not so much that the future is unrealistically certain in the general equilibrium construct of the evenly rotating economy but rather that in a real sense that economy has no future. It has no future in the sense that all originative choices have already been made: "Today does not differ from yesterday and tomorrow will not differ from today." There is only the carrying out of chosen plans. Mises makes it clear in this passage, part of which Littlechild quotes, that the impossibility of equilibrium in the real world in no way constitutes a valid objection to the proper use of the equilibrium construct.

Littlechild seems a bit confused as to what Mises means by "the method of imaginary constructions" in which the construction of the evenly rotating economy plays a role. Part of the difficulty lies with Mises's use of an unusual phrase. Although the phrase has not been widely used, the method certainly has. The best-known use of the method of imaginary constructions is the comparative-statics exercise, the device of the ceteris paribus clause with which every economist is well acquainted. Certainly the success of this method cannot be questioned. That this is his meaning is clear in Mises's discussion of another imaginary construction, that of the unhampered market economy (1966, pp. 237–238).[1] The economist studies the hypothetical construct of a market free of minimum-wage laws or tariffs to elucidate by contrast the difference that these government policies make, ceteris paribus.

In a similar way the economist studies a hypothetical construct of a market free of entrepreneurs to elucidate by contrast the difference that entrepreneurs make. Mises uses the construct of the evenly rotating economy—a general equilibrium through time characterized by absence of change in the external data—in this way. I argue later in this chapter that the Hayekian concept of general equilibrium could be used in the same way. This exercise is not of course a comparative-statics exercise in the usual sense, but something broader.

The questions that Littlechild poses regarding the usefulness of the construct for this purpose should be answered in the affirmative. We do learn something about the entrepreneurial role by comprehending that there is no room for it in a general equilibrium. It is certainly true that the method of imaginary constructions has not been widely used in the analysis of entrepreneurship. But that merely reflects the unfortunate fact that economists have generally paid too little attention to the subject of entrepreneurship.

Littlechild's final paragraph on Mises quotes, but does not comment on, his criticism of mathematical economists for "deal(ing) with equilibrium as if it were a real entity and not a limiting notion, a mere mental tool." Today we would want to distinguish more carefully than did Mises between the broader camp of economists who use mathematical tools (virtually the entire profession, including many Austrian economists) and the narrower group who apply such tools (typically high-powered ones) to the tasks of general equilibrium analysis. The use of mathematics in developing equilibrium concepts is not the object of Mises's criticism here. The object is rather the fallacy of misplaced concreteness with regard to equilibrium concepts. Surely the virtual neglect of the problems of entrepreneurship by the economics profession, and the Ricardian zeal with which equilibrium concepts are applied to real-world policy questions, testify sadly to the continuing applicability of Mises's critique (1966, p. 250).[2]

Littlechild on Hayek

Littlechild claims that the Hayekian concept of equilibrium "marks an advance on Mises's thought" because it is more general than the concept of the evenly rotating economy. This claim, I have discovered in the course of making it myself, is controversial within Austrian circles. Some elaboration and defense of it may therefore be in order.

There is first a small terminological matter to be cleared up. For F.A. Hayek the concept of general equilibrium is indeed "separate from the concept of a stationary state" as Littlechild notes, and this does mark his departure from Mises. Littlechild points out that Mises also insists that "it is a bad mistake to confuse (the concept of the evenly rotating economy) with the imaginary construction of a stationary economy'' (1966, p. 247). Mises makes this statement because he reserves the term ''stationary economy'' to denote an economy of constant per-capita wealth and income, which need not be an evenly rotating economy. The Misesian evenly rotating economy does exhibit stationarity. Even rotation is sufficient but not necessary for stationarity in Mises's sense.

The Hayekian general equilibrium (HGE) and the Misesian evenly rotating economy (ERE) have in common that they are concepts of equilibrium through time. This distinguishes them from the Arrow-Debreu or neo-Walrasian general equilibrium, which is an entirely ex ante concept.[3] In the HGE or ERE the market clears every day. In Arrow-Debreu it clears once-and-for-all, and what happens ''next'' is outside its logic. What makes the HGE more general and more subjectivist than the ERE is that it drops the stipulation that the external data (tastes, technology, resources) be unchanging in an objective or absolute sense. What is stipulated instead is only that the data not change relative to the (unanimously held) expectations regarding the data embodied in agents' plans. One might argue that unanimity of expectations is implausible outside an ERE. But that is irrelevant to the logical point.

The two areas where Mises claims that use of the ERE ''is both appropriate and indispensable'' are (1) imputation, or the pricing of factors of production, and (2) entrepreneurship, or profit and loss (1966, p. 248). In both these areas, however, the HGE will serve just as well or better. It is certainly the case that anticipation of changes in the data, and not only actual changes, are important for the pricing of capital goods, for instance. And it is not changes in the data, as such, but otherwise unforeseen changes that make room for an ongoing entrepreneurial role. That is, we need not abstract from all change in the data (or from all nonseasonal change) to eliminate the scope for entrepreneurship. We need only to eliminate unforeseen change. Consider, for example, an otherwise evenly rotating economy in which a meteorite is seen to be approaching a forest. Suppose the meteorite's impact on the timber crop is unanimously and correctly foreseen. Then the actual arrival of the meteorite, although it will change the datum of resource-availability flows, need not upset equilibrium in the Hayekian sense of continuous plan fulfillment and no surprise. The scope for entrepreneurship has disappeared, although the even flow will be upset.

Ludwig Lachmann has criticized Cassellian and neoclassical equilibrium-growth models for the ''lack of realism'' inherent in their assumption that entrepreneurs perfectly foresee changes in tastes (Lachmann 1977, pp. 186–187). For the concrete descriptive uses to which these models have typically been put, Lachmann's criticism is pertinent and telling. But the presence of the same assumption (or rather, condition) in the Hayekian general equilibrium, although it undoubtedly means that the concept is ''unrealistic," does not make the concept useless. It may still be validly used for the same illuminatory purposes to which Mises turned the ERE concept.[4] Mises would himself be the first to argue, paraphrasing a passage quoted by Littlechild, that it is "absurd to believe that the services rendered by (a) construction . . . are the more valuable the more the object of our studies, the realm of real action, corresponds to (that) construction" in respect to its characteristic features (1966, p. 248).

Littlechild performs a great service in drawing our attention to the abandoned Hayekian research program on the question of the equilibrating process. As I have argued before, this is a question that merits further investigation (White 1976, p. 15). A similar call to action has been issued by a leading neo-Walrasian mathematical economist who in a valuable survey of their work candidly recognizes that he and his coworkers have by no means answered the question in a satisfactory manner (Fisher 1976). Littlechild's suggestion that an answer might require a conjunction of "formal mathematical models" and "applied psychology" is questionable and in any case need not be taken as an injunction against approaches more in the Misesian tradition. But I certainly agree with Littlechild that junking the question of equilibrium in favor of existence proofs leaves important issues unresolved.

Littlechild on Hahn

Hahn's 1973 lecture hardly represents, at this date, a guide to the latest in the mathematical-economic thought going beyond Arrow-Debreu. The formal model it proposes has not, to my knowledge, actually been constructed. That research program seems to have been abandoned. What interest the lecture retains lies in its methodological position statements and its suggestions for the route future research should take.

The "significant step in the direction of subjectivism" that Littlechild observes in Hahn (1973b), may also be observed elsewhere. Fisher (1976) and Rothschild (1973) have expressed a sincere concern over the lack of subjectivist intelligibility of available mathematical treatments of the equilibrating process. All the same, the neo-Walrasian general-equilibrium theorists have not yet discovered the need to incorporate the entrepreneur or speculator into their analysis. Although the first sentence of the following remark by Mises has become outdated with the recent proliferation of mathematical price-adjustment models, the second sentence remains timely[5]:

> The mathematical economists disregard dealing with the actions which, under the imaginary and unrealized assumption that no further new data

will emerge, are supposed to bring about the evenly rotating economy. They do not notice the individual speculator who aims not at the establishment of the evenly rotating economy but at profiting from an action which adjusts the conduct of affairs better to the attainment of the ends sought by acting, the best possible removal of uneasiness (1966, p. 250).

There is however one exception to the absence of entrepreneurial action from the models of mathematical economics, a paper of which Littlechild is coauthor (Littlechild and Owen 1980). The existence of this paper is no doubt related to the fact that he takes a rather more charitable attitude toward mathematical economics than does Mises. To evaluate the degree of success this paper achieves in modeling entrepreneurship would be to transgress the limits of my duties. But I certainly wish Littlechild all success in stimulating the readers of the *Journal of Economic Theory* to turn their analytical minds toward Austrian ideas.

Littlechild wants to argue that "Hahn and Mises share a similar view of the role of general equilibrium (in its timeless sense)." It is true that both recognize its lack of correspondence to the real-world market economy. But while Mises (1966, p. 247) sees this as part and parcel of the equilibrium construct—it deliberately abstracts from change in order to aid in analyzing the problems of change—Hahn (1973b, p. 3) views it as a defect to be remedied. His stated aim in the lecture Littlechild discusses is "to examine the theoretical and conceptual difficulties which arise with the Arrow-Debreu paradigm when it is modified to serve descriptive purposes" and to deal with such difficulties.[6] Littlechild is on firmer ground when he notes the similarity between Hahn's and Hayek's conceptualizations of an equilibrium through time. Hahn's concept might indeed be thought of roughly as a stochastic version of Hayekian general equilibrium.

The question remains: to what use does Hahn intend to put his notion of general equilibrium? Littlechild effectively refutes the policy arguments Hahn bases on the Arrow-Debreu paradigm, showing that Hahn commits what logicians term the fallacy of the denial of the antecedent. Brian Loasby has also neatly disposed of Hahn's use of the Arrow-Debreu paradigm as the basis for policy pronouncements (1966, pp. 46–48). But it seems from recent evidence that Hahn has taken little heed of his critics on this score (1980, pp. 123, 126). This time it is the argument for free trade proclaiming its "optimality" that Hahn finds uninformed of the subtleties of the Arrow-Debreu model, on which Hahn evidently believes that the argument must be based. Of course it is true that a free-trade policy is not sufficient to zip the economy straightaway to a Paretian optimum whose existence requires zero error and zero contracting costs. Free trade may nonetheless, because it strikes down artificial barriers to mutually beneficial trade, be the policy most consistent with optimality.

Equilibrium and Market Process

Littlechild quotes Hahn's expression of frustration at "the *endless variety* of adjustment models, not uncongenial to commonsense." Littlechild's parenthetical remark that some would question "whether any of the adjustment models so far developed are congenial to common sense" refers to a statement of mine that was based on an earlier survey of the literature of price-adjustment models.[7] The models making up that literature have been unintelligible in three principal ways. Some have failed to locate price adjustment in the actions of individual market participants, postulating instead a central price-adjusting auctioneer. Others, although providing for atomistic price adjustment, have failed to motivate the postulated behavior of the price-adjusting agents, specifying instead senseless behavioral rules that have no basis in self-interest. Still other models are informationally incoherent, requiring decision-making agents either to know more than they could possibly have learned or to ignore what they should have learned within the logic of the model.[8]

If Mises's categorical statement that the "problems of process analysis . . . defy any mathematical approach" is regarded as unwarranted (1966, p. 356), the fact remains that they have almost entirely defied mathematical approaches thus far, Littlechild's model possibly excepted (1980). The reason is that process analysis raises in conjunction the problems of Knightian uncertainty, rivalrous competition, and non-predetermined discovery, none of which has so far proven amenable to mathematical treatment. This is not said to discourage mathematical treatment of the problems of market process—quite the contrary. It is said to emphasize that there have been and remain gains to be made from nonmathematical treatment as well. Littlechild would no doubt agree, his enthusiasm for "the development of formal economic models of market processes" notwithstanding.

Notes

1. One must resist the translation of "imaginary construction" as "model." That translation garbles more of Mises's message than it transmits.

2. Every practicing economist's toolbox comes equipped with a large Ricardian vise. It is a tool considered indispensable for clamping down the real world.

3. For this reason Littlechild's remark that the ERE "may be thought of as a special case of Arrow-Debreu" is unhelpful (see chapter 8).

4. Lachmann (1977, p. 36) levels a similar criticism of unrealism (or unrealizability) against Hahn's conception of equilibrium through time, a

criticism that would again apply equally to Hayekian general equilibrium. Again the same defense may be made: its unrealism does not mean that a concept cannot help illuminate the real world, although obviously we must use it carefully.

5. One may question, however, whether the architects of price-adjustment models have dealt with *actions* in the sense in which Mises uses that term, that is, non-predetermined choices. For a critical survey from an Austrian perspective see White (1978). That paper was written in ignorance of the survey by Fisher (1976), which makes many of the same criticisms.

6. See Coddington for an attack on this enterprise based on a defense of abstraction (1975, pp. 540–542).

7. The remainder of this paragraph draws on White (1978, pp. 4–5).

8. Informational incoherence is also a problem with rational-expectations macromodels. There has not yet been a reasonable story told of how agents outside the rational-expectations equilibrium could learn what is required for them to arrive at the rational-expectations equilibrium. A volume of conference papers on this problem is forthcoming under the editorship of Roman Frydman.

References

Coddington, Alan. 1975. The rationale of general equilibrium theory. *Economic Inquiry* 13:539–558.

Fisher, Franklin M. 1976. The stability of general equilibrium: results and problems. In *Essays in economic analysis,* ed. M.J. Artis and A.R. Nobay. Cambridge: Cambridge University.

Hahn, F.H. 1973a. The winter of our discontent. *Economica* 40:322–330.

———. 1973b. *On the notion of equilibrium in economics.* Cambridge: Cambridge University.

———. 1980. General equilibrium theory. *The Public Interest.* Special issue: 123–138.

Hayek, F.A. 1948. Economics and knowledge. In *Individualism and economic order.* Chicago: University of Chicago.

Lachmann, Ludwig. 1977. Ludwig von Mises and the market process. In *Capital, expectations, and the market process,* ed. Walter E. Grinder. Kansas City: Sheed Andrews and McMeel.

Littlechild, S.C., and Owen, G. 1980. An Austrian model of the entrepreneurial market process. *Journal of Economic Theory* 23:361–379.

Loasby, Brian J. 1976. *Choice, complexity and ignorance.* Cambridge: Cambridge University.

Mises, Ludwig von. 1966. *Human Action,* 3d ed. Chicago: Henry Regnery.

Rothschild, Michael. 1973. ''Models of market organization with imperfect information: a survey. *Journal of Political Economy* 81:1283–1308.

White, L.H. 1976. ''Entrepreneurship, imagination, and the question of equilibration.'' (Unpublished ms.)

————. 1978. Entrepreneurial price adjustment. Paper delivered at Southern Economic Association Meetings, November 1978.

Economics of Dispersed and Incomplete Information

Brian J. Loasby

Self-Interest and Knowledge

Many people are familiar with Adam Smith's observation: "It is not from the benevolence of the butcher, the brewer, or the baker, that we expect our dinner, but from their regard to their own interest" (1976a, 1:26–27). It would, however, be quite wrong to regard this sentence as testimony to the virtue of self-interest. For consider what precedes it. "In civilized society [man] stands at all times in need of the co-operation and assistance of great multitudes, while his whole life is scarce sufficient to gain the friendship of a few persons." That is a tragic utterance at the personal level and might yet prove so for the human race. "Sympathy," which figures so largely in Smith's *Theory of Moral Sentiments* (1976b), can, and indeed must, serve as a partial substitute for friendship; but it is not enough. Some other stimulus to cooperation must be found, and it is found in self-interest.

But we cannot simply assume that self-interest will produce harmony, or even stability. Probably no less well-known than the sentence first quoted is Smith's comment that "People of the same trade seldom meet together, even for merriment and diversion, but the conversation ends in a conspiracy against the publick, or in some contrivance to raise prices" (1976a, 1:145). Self-interest is not, after all, benevolence. Thus if self-interest is to be employed to economise on what has been appropriately called the scarce resource of love, it needs to be employed in an appropriate setting. The question of in what circumstances and within what framework self-interest is likely to produce the best attainable results has been in one form or another the central issue of political economy for the last two hundred years.

The role of moral sentiments in directing and constraining self-interest is not often given the consideration it deserves, although there is a standard assumption (except in some quarters of Chicago) that economic agents are naturally law abiding. In mainstream economics, attention has been concentrated on two issues: the effect of market structure on the allocation of resources and the overall level of resource utilization. These two issues are conventionally allotted to micro and macroeconomics respectively. Austrian economists have declined to accept this division of their subject, and economists of other persuasions seem to be gradually coming round to their view. That both successful coordination and coordination failure need to be explained in terms of individual human decisions is a basic premise of this chapter.

There is a second basic premise that should be stated now, although it will not enter the argument for some pages to come. It is that any explanation of the working of an economy will be incomplete (although not necessarily useless) unless it is capable of handling the evolution of knowledge as part of the economic process itself. Adam Smith placed economic evolution at the forefront of the *Wealth of Nations,* in his discussion of the progressive extension of the division of labor. Now the division of labor creates a need for coordination, and this seems to call for an analysis of exchange in terms of equilibrium. But the scope for division of labor is increased by the greater incomes generated by earlier applications of the same principle, and its forms include innovation in product, technology, and organizational arrangements: such processes do not fall naturally within the scope of equilibrium models.

This second aspect of Smith's work has been emphasized by G.B. Richardson, who also points out that Alfred Marshall resisted the obvious attractions of static equilibrium in order to preserve a theory of development (1975). A fairly casual reading of Book IV of A. Marshall's *Principles* is sufficient to indicate that Marshall had an entrepreneurial theory of the firm and an entrepreneurial theory of competition (1920). (Austrians will not be surprised to find entrepreneurship and competition so closely linked.) Marshall's own treatment of entrepreneurship and economic progress deserves consideration on another occasion; at present, we need simply to observe that in Marshall's work the conflicting theoretical requirements of equilibrium and of evolution, which Smith's loosely integrated structure can accommodate without too much strain, generate a tension that calls for some resolution. This resolution was achieved, as we all know, by the dominance of equilibrium analysis. It is not, of course, impossible to construct equilibrium models of economic growth; but these are not models of evolution, as Smith and Marshall sought to provide, since they cannot, by the very principles of their construction, accommodate novelty. It is, I believe, fundamentally because we need some means of analyzing the generation of novelty—and not merely the response to exogenous novelty—that we need to think, as Austrians habitually do, in terms of processes.

Equilibrium and Its Attainment

To this use of a theory of processes we shall come in due course. But we will begin our consideration of economic processes by examining the difficulties that have to be fudged by equilibrium theorists, even when claiming to analyze the problems that they have set for themselves.

General equilibrium theorists seek to discover what conditions are sufficient to sustain an equilibrium. The best known of such theories is the Arrow-Debreu system, in which a perfectly competitive economy of price takers, if provided with an appropriate price vector, will generate a set of compatible actions. Although the need to provide these prices is well recognized as an awkward theoretical problem, there is a further difficulty that is rarely mentioned—the readiness of all economic agents to act on those prices. Richardson deserves much more credit than he has yet received for pointing out that actions, which necessarily relate to the future, depend on beliefs and that a theory of equilibrium actions requires a theory of equilibrium beliefs (1960). The need for such a theory is hidden in the Arrow-Debreu system, first by simply defining each agent as a price taker, so that he is compelled to accept as correct whatever price he sees, and second by extending the model to include markets for all future contingent commodities, thus effectively abolishing the distinction between present and future. Modern theories of "rational expectations" require agents to believe what the analyst knows to be true.

Once in equilibrium, economic agents take no action that is not fully prescribed by the parameters of the system; since this is the focus of study, scarcely any attention is paid to the question of what might happen out of equilibrium. Analysis of change normally proceeds by the comparison of equilibria appropriate to the data before and after the change, and it is then simply assumed that somehow the economy will move from the first equilibrium to the second, with no consideration of what is involved in this movement.

Such an analytical program produces misleading prescriptions for policy. Those prescriptions are derived from the study of a system that is fully adjusted to existing data and in which there is no expectation that these data could ever change: thus any elements that might be necessary to recognize and respond to change are strictly superfluous. Once everthing is agreed—and within the analytical convention, finally agreed—there is no further need for any of the apparatus of enquiry, communication, and control which might have been required to secure agreement. It is all to be condemned as (according to taste) organizational slack, x-inefficiency, wastes of competition, or monopolistic misallocation. There is not even any reason for the existence of firms. It is not my purpose here to enlarge on the policy errors that flow from treating competition as an equilibrium state instead of a discovery process. Some comments will be made when considering the requirements of an effective process, which, it will be argued, are not quite as simple as they appear in the Austrian literature.

One important point, however, should be made here. General-equilibrium theorists do not take too seriously their fables of the auctioneer or of recontracting. They seem to assume that an economy in practice moves toward equilibrium by (unanalyzed) trial and error. But as soon as we permit any contracts at nonequilibrium prices, we introduce the possibility of income effects that may invalidate the equilibrium toward which the economy is supposed to move. Marshall, so concerned with the applicability of formal models, observed that if exchange is by barter, an initial deal that is favorable to one party may affect the terms on which both are willing to make further exchanges. Since, in Marshall's view, such a course of events was rather probable, he concluded that a bartering sequence would be likely to end in an accidental equilibrium and not in the "true equilibrium" that might be deduced by an analyst from the initial data. The chances of approximating the latter are, however, much improved (he argued) if commodities are exchanged for money; the initial deal is not likely to be so favorable as to significantly affect either party's marginal valuation of general purchasing power (Marshall 1920, app. F). This argument leads to the paradox that microeconomic equilibrium cannot safely be analyzed in real terms (as is the standard practice) except in a monetary economy. Now if it is only a monetary economy that can justifiably be analyzed in real terms, it can hardly be argued that monetary issues are somehow distinct from the problems of the "real economy." Mises, of course, placed a good deal of emphasis on the fact that goods are exchanged, not directly for other goods, but for money. However, as he also emphasized, money is not neutral, and so the very circumstances that are necessary to justify the use of equilibrium analysis also require some modification of it (1949, p. 203). The processes we have to study are monetary processes, and, as we shall see, monetary processes are not necessarily stable.

The Price System and Entrepreneurship

A central theme of Austrian analysis is the central role of prices in permitting the effective mobilization of local knowledge. Whereas a centrally planned economy needs to concentrate within the planning organization knowledge of available resources, of production techniques, and (assuming that the plan is intended to reflect these) consumers' preferences, a decentralized economy needs only to establish a set of prices. Each economic agent can then apply his own specific knowledge of resources and of technology and his own particular pattern of preferences to those prices: there is no need for information about these matters to be communicated. What is more, as F.A. Hayek, for example, has emphasized, no one needs to know why the price of some particular commodity is whatever it is. A particular material may rise in price because its supply is becoming exhausted, because new uses have been found for it, or because existing uses are becoming more popular. The cause does not matter: whatever that may be, the consequence is that more effort should now be devoted to ways of increasing the supply, using it more effectively, or replacing it by some alternative. But in a pure market economy no one needs to be instructed to do any of these things. The increased price provides the only signal needed, and anyone who has the knowledge, or the particular pattern of preferences, to contribute in any of these ways will do so. Thus local knowledge will be effectively put to use.

However, Hayek's explanation of the economy of knowledge through the use of the price mechanism still leaves us with one problem of general-equilibrium theory: how are these prices to be arrived at? In his simple story, agents are price takers, just as in general-equilibrium models. Something more is needed—a theory of price setting.

Such a theory has been provided by Israel Kirzner, building on the work of Mises. In Kirzner's system, the price setter is the entrepreneur. Thus, although entrepreneurial competition is atomistic competition, it is not perfect competition. But neither is it the kind of imperfect competition associated with Joan Robinson, for whereas the theory of imperfect competition is an equilibrium theory, entrepreneurial competition can exist only in disequilibrium.

Kirzner offers a theory of an equilibrating process, which is directed to the question that general-equilibrium theorists evade. It is therefore appropriate that it is designed to be readily comparable with a general-equilibrium model. In both, all economic agents are presumed to act as individuals, under the motivation of self-interest, and in both the endowment of original resources, preferences and the set of technologies are exogenous. The critical differences are that (1) in Kirzner's system economic agents do not merely respond to prices that are somehow provided but actively determine prices, and (2) endowments, preferences, and technology are not assumed to be generally known. Instead, each individual has his own particular subset of knowledge. In conventional terms, such limitations produce local-knowledge monopolies, and allow for some pricing discretion; but the very act of using that discretion must tend to break down the monopoly by diffusing the knowledge on which it is based. As knowledge is more widely spread, so the scope for monopoly profits diminishes and the allocation of resources approaches more closely to equilibrium; when there is no longer any special knowledge to be exploited, equilibrium has been reached.

Since equilibrium seems to be so closely associated with the idea of perfect knowledge (a viewpoint shared by Austrians and general-equilibrium theorists) it is peculiarly appropriate that the process detailed by Kirzner should embody knowledge acquisition as virtually the dual of equilibration. It is then easy to demonstrate, within a context general-equilibrium theorists should find familiar, that some of the welfare propositions derived from equilibrium theory need to be reversed for the equilibrating process.

Differences in price for an apparently homogeneous product and supernormal profit, for example, are necessary features of that process.

Entrepreneurship and Equilibration

Kirzner's theory is designed to maximize the chances of a satisfactory outcome. He explicitly contrasts his analysis with that of Schumpeter. Whereas Schumpeterian entrepreneurs are innovators, for Kirzner "entrepreneurship . . . is not so much the introduction of new products or of new techniques of production as the ability to *see* where new products have become unsuspectedly valuable to consumers and where new methods of production have, unknown to others, become feasible. For me the function of the entrepreneur consists not of *shifting* the curves of cost or of revenues which face him, but *of noticing that they have in fact shifted"* (Kirzner, 1973, p. 81). This specification ensures (given the usual assumptions) that there is an equilibrium toward which the economy can move. It does not, however, ensure that the economy will necessarily move toward it.

Two problems may be briefly dealt with. The first is that entrepreneurs' perceptions may be false. In the passage just quoted this possibility is implicitly denied; alternatively it may be argued that the "testing of plans in the market" is an effective mechanism for correcting errors. Neither of these arguments is conclusive; but the issues become more critical at a later stage in this chapter. So does the second problem, which is the effect on the final equilibrium of initial out-of-equilibrium exchange. That such exchanges should actually occur is essential to the model, since entrepreneurs will not long be motivated by the expectation of profits that are never realized. The market process redistributes income, and a redistribution of income entails a redefinition of equilibrium. Even if entrepreneurial perceptions are not originally false, it is therefore possible that they may be falsified by the entrepreneurs' own actions. It is perhaps unlikely that entrepreneurial action will be found, according to the new equilibrium, to have led in the wrong direction, especially if we invoke Marshall's argument about the stabilizing effect of monetary exchanges. When we go beyond Kirzner's model, as we shall do shortly, we become much less certain.

Within Kirzner's system, more attention needs to be given to a difficulty that he recognizes: "each market participant, in laying his buying or selling plans, must pay careful heed not only to the prospective decisions of those to whom he hopes to sell or from whom he hopes to buy, but—as an implication of the latter—also to the prospective decisions of others whose decisions to sell or to buy may compete with his own" (1973, p. 11). But how is he to form reasonable expectations about the actions of possible rivals? As Richardson has observed, "a general profit opportunity, which is both known to everyone and equally capable of being exploited by everyone, is, in an important sense, a profit opportunity for no-one in particular'' (1960, p. 57). Richardson's criticism was directed at the inadequacy of perfect competition as an adjustment mechanism, but it applies to any rivalrous process in which the outcome of one person's decision depends on the actions of others. This, as we have seen, is a fundamental objection to the Arrow-Debreu system, concealed by the myth of the auctioneer. Joseph Schumpeter avoids it by focusing on innovation, which is naturally associated with monopoly. How does Kirzner's theory compare?

Kirzner clearly regards entrepreneurship as relatively rare in relation to any particular opportunity. The great majority of economic agents can be relied on to conform in most respects to their regular, and therefore predictable, patterns of behaviour and to act as entrepreneurs in only a few of the multitude of markets that comprise a competitive economy. Thus an entrepreneur may be justified in believing that an opportunity that he has perceived will remain generally unnoticed long enough for him to exploit it. (Kirzner implicitly assumes that he will believe this.) Richardson makes the point explicitly: "ignorance, by checking the response of some, may be a necessary condition for any response by others" (1960, p. 57). In this way, limitations of knowledge help to resolve the problems that they create.

Why different people should perceive different changes in technology or preferences is a question that Kirzner does not discuss; he seems satisfied that it is so. But although every theory must take for granted the truth of many important facts, differential knowledge is so fundamental to Austrian theories of the market process—to Mises and Hayek as well as to Kirzner—that there seems a major theoretical issue here. It is a standard assumption in almost all theories of the firm that all firms are alike in the sense that each is potentially capable of doing whatever others are doing, at the same long-run costs; and in many contexts it is a misleading assumption. The most obvious exception to this class of theories is E.T. Penrose's *Theory of the Growth of the Firm,* in which the capabilities and the perceptions of each firm are molded by its historical experience and constrained by the particular patterns of effective behavior that have evolved among its managers as a result of that experience (1959). Penrose's theory may be regarded as a natural development of Adam Smith's account of economic evolution through the exploitation of the division of labor: new opportunities are created through the increased income that is generated by the innovative exploitation of previous opportunities. Further development of this idea may require the introduction of a theory of knowledge into the theory of the firm, and some tentative proposals have been put forward elsewhere (Loasby 1982).

It seems a natural corollary of Penrose's theory that prospective entrepreneurs should be able to identify their most likely rivals. This proposition may also be derived from Marshall, whose firms operate within a network of regular suppliers, regular customers, and regular competitors. Richardson has expanded this theme to explain how a firm's market connections, traditionally dismissed as an objectionable source of monopoly profit, may provide some protection for prudent expansion (1960, pp. 64–65). He goes beyond this, however, and argues that in some—certainly not all—circumstances tacit collusion between firms, or even specific agreements, may actually assist the process of adjustment to new data. In conditions of limited knowledge, unrestricted competition may not permit adequate information.

One form of agreement, which is not much discussed in the orthodox literature, is an agreement to make complementary investments. It sometimes happens that a particular course of action by one entrepreneur appears profitable if, but only if, some other entrepreneur, or possibly several other entrepreneurs, take appropriate and timely decisions. This is particularly likely when the requirements for success are very specific: for example, the effective administration of the inhalant-anaesthetic halothane demanded much closer control by the anaesthetist than was possible with the equipment then available, which was designed to suit the existing range of inhalant anaesthetics. Without the development of new apparatus by an equipment firm, a decision to produce halothane would not be profitable; but without a decision to produce halothane, why should anyone design equipment that would otherwise be unnecessarily precise and unnecessarily expensive (Bradbury, McCarthy, and Suckling 1972)?

This kind of coordination can hardly be left to a market process that relies entirely on price signals, although it will not be achieved without the prospect of entrepreneurial profit for all who cooperate. In a later article, Richardson has illustrated the range of imperfectly specified contracts between firms in Britain to assist the coordination of entrepreneurial activity (1972). Such agreements do not banish competition, for firms can, and do, change partners, and there is a great gulf between a freely formed network of such arrangements and centralized planning; they do, however, point to the limitations of any model of atomistic competition either as a guide to the working of an economy or as a basis for policy. It is one of the merits of Mises's approach that such entrepreneurial cooperation to exploit productive opportunities can be comfortably accommodated in a theory of competition.

Uncertainty and Imagination

Kirzner's theory of the market process is well designed to serve as a critique of general equilibrium models; but for that very reason it offers only a partial analysis of the problems of an economy in which knowledge is dispersed and incomplete. We have noted some qualifications within its own terms of reference; more fundamental are the limitations prescribed by the theory itself. Kirzner's entrepreneurs perceive a change that has already taken place. But decisions relate to the future: therefore what these entrepreneurs perceive is already too late for action—except as it guides their expectations.

It is here that we see the critical distinction between the conceptions of Kirzner and of G.L.S. Shackle, two authors whose vision of the economy is in many respects very similar. In Kirzner's scheme a profit opportunity arises from the difference between the current market valuation of an asset, or group of assets, and a new valuation derived from a change in underlying conditions that is as yet perceived only by the entrepreneur (but which is expected to persist). For Shackle, the future is unknowable, and this new valuation is the product of the entrepreneur's imagination. Kirzner's entrepreneurs are alert, Shackle's are creative.

Shackle has extended the principle of subjective valuation to a point where its connection with objective knowledge becomes problematic. In his contribution to this book, Kirzner takes explicit account of uncertainty and recognizes, as does Mises (1949, p. 58), that entrepreneurs must create the future. He argues, however, that they are motivated to overcome uncertainty and will tend to be successful. I believe that this should not be assumed. In the remainder of this chapter, I shall review briefly some of the issues raised by the recognition that entrepreneurs do not merely discover but can—and must—invent the future that they seek to exploit and that their inventions may turn out to be misconceived.

Consumer Welfare

The conventional association of market imperfections with welfare losses has been effectively challenged by Kirzner: the challenge is strengthened by a recognition of the prevalence of innovation. Rather than commenting further on market-structure arguments, it is worth considering the familiar criticism of capitalism that wants are "manufactured" by producers and that in a better-ordered system production would be directed toward people's needs. Kirzner avoids such an accusation by specifying that his entrepreneurs perceive what already exists. But once we allow for entrepreneurial imagination this path is no longer open. However, the criticism must be considered in the proper context, which is a context of incomplete and dispersed knowledge. In that context it is reasonable to argue that the increase of consumers' knowledge, and with it the extension of consumers' sovereignty, will normally be fostered by the market process.

This is not simply an Austrian idea. Marshall's vision of the world was one in which both wants and production methods changed over time and in which these changes occurred in large part through the agency of competing businessmen, who "must have the power of forecasting the broad movements of production and consumption, of seeing where there is an opportunity of supplying a new commodity that will meet a real want or improving the plan of producing an old commodity" (Marshall 1920, p. 297). Competition is important, not only in providing a stimulus to seek such opportunities but also in encouraging creative ideas and the diversity of experimentation, which is necessary to progress. Moreover, Marshall makes it clear that some wants may not be perceived by consumers until they are offered a means of satisfying them: he describes as "a characteristic task of the modern manufacturer . . . that of creating new wants by showing people something which they had never thought of having before; but which they want to have as soon as the notion is suggested to them" (1920, pp. 280–281).

It will be recalled that E.H. Chamberlin was very careful not to draw any simple conclusions from his model of monopolistic competition about exploitation of the consumer (1933). Indeed, his reluctance to do so was a source of great annoyance to Robinson, who wished to link his model to her own deceptively similar analysis to demonstrate the inherent and unacceptable failings of free enterprise. In the preface to the second edition of her *Economics of Imperfect Competition,* she comments as follows: "I said very little about non-price competition, such as artificial product differentiation, advertising and sales promotion, which in fact accounts for the greatest part of the wastefulness of imperfect markets. (The twin to my book, Chamberlin's *Monopolistic Competition,* opened up these subjects, but in the subsequent controversies Chamberlin appeared to be more concerned to defend the market system than to expose its drawbacks)" (1969, p. ix). But Chamberlin's analysis, although cast in the mold of static equilibrium, is, as Romney Robinson argues, intended to deal with competitive search in unorganized markets (1971, p. 34). In such markets, producers have to discover what consumers want, and the process of discovery involves product differentiation and product creation, advertising, and the promotion of sales. (Indeed, as has been argued, there is no clear distinction between production costs and selling costs, all being incurred to secure a market.) Romney Robinson leaves his readers to infer that Chamberlin is denying the relevance of perfect competition to a world of incomplete knowledge; if that is accepted, then it is possible to argue that, despite the sharpest contrast in form, the spirit of Chamberlin's analysis is remarkably similar to that of Kirzner.

Imperfect-competition theory, as portrayed by Joan Robinson, also depends on incomplete knowledge; for if consumers were as well informed as our models of perfect competition assume, how could they possibly be bamboozled to the extent that she assumes? To call for state regulation of production to meet consumers' "real preferences" seems to assume that the consumers' lack of knowledge is not shared by the regulators. This, of course, is a view that is held on the paternalist right as well as on the authoritarian left; it is a view that perhaps reflects more strongly the preferences of those who hold it for particular kinds of behavior by other people than any reasonably corroborated theory of systematic distortion.

This is not to say that there is no distortion. Incomplete knowledge entails the possibility of mistakes, and consumers may—perhaps often do—misjudge the effectiveness of products in satisfying their wants. Since, moreover, enterpreneurship is based on superior knowledge in some particular, it is open to an entrepreneur to seek profit through misleading those with whom he proposes to trade. We must not forget that we are relying on self-interest to perform what is beyond the scope of benevolence; and although we should not assume that "sympathy," in Adam Smith's sense, plays no part in entrepreneurial decisions, neither should we assume that it is always sufficient to preclude attempts at exploiting ignorance. There are obvious remedies within the system: consumers can learn from bad experiences, and other entrepreneurs may see profitable opportunities in offering protection against deception and exposing fraud. But it is absurd to assume that these remedies will avoid any significant loss. For example, although no great harm may be done by purchasing an unappetizing brand of cornflakes, the purchase of a car that is difficult to control may be fatal, and within a large corporation it is not always easy to ensure that blame is properly attributed for misdemeanor or neglect. Those who wish to defend the market system should not confuse the claim that it is, on the whole, better than the available alternatives with the claim that it is faultless.

Thanks, in substantial measure, to the work of James Buchanan, it is no longer easy simply to invoke market failure as a sufficient justification for governmental action. By applying the same principles traditionally used to predict misallocation through markets to the choices of politicians and bureaucrats, it has been demonstrated that governmental decisions are likely to violate the welfare ideal, even on the assumption that knowledge is equally available in either system. The virtues of the market in using dispersed knowledge, and in encouraging the discovery and creation of new knowledge, must also be taken into account as soon as that assumption is discarded. But we can go one step further. In a regulated economy, entrepreneurship, which, we must remember, is based on self-interest, may be turned in a new direction. The more attractive—certainly the more assured—profit opportunities are now to be found not in satisfying customers but in securing governmental favor, either by direct contracts or through a favorable regulatory structure. If government seeks to control business, we should not be surprised if business seeks to control government. Evidence in

Britain and the United States suggests that it is likely to be fairly successful, often in collusion, tacit or open, with trade unions. Governmental control of industry for the public benefit demands both more knowledge and more benevolence than we have any right to expect.

Speculative Markets

Let us now turn to some of the problems of coordination. Economists have been very wary of allowing decisions to depend in any way on the imagination of economic agents—for good cause, as we shall see. For a start, it must be recognized that uncertainty about the future reacts back on to the present. The current demand for and supply of any nonperishable commodity depends on estimates of its future value; thus the markets for all such commodities are speculative. This influence from the future extends, through the usual relations of substitution and complementarity, to perishable commodities; it extends in particular to those perishable commodities that can be converted to nonperishables through the productive process—most notably to the value of labor services. Thus the current values, which provide the basis of comparison against which future potential must be measured to identify a profit opportunity, are themselves determined not simply by what is already known but also in part by imagination.

It is immediately obvious that this extension of our inquiry aggravates all the problems raised by Kirzner's scheme. What assurance can we have that entrepreneurial perceptions will not be so seriously in error as to lead them in quite the wrong direction, or indeed that there can be any assurance of action at all?

If many—perhaps most—markets are speculative, in the sense that current actions, and current prices, are based on expectations not only about the immediate future but about situations months, or even a few years, hence, then the testing of plans in the market cannot be conclusive. Each market test applies to only a part, often a small part, of the set of expectations, and its relevance to the remainder of the set is not certain. The apparent failure of an entrepreneurial plan may, for example, indicate that a shift of preferences is proceeding more slowly than had been anticipated or that a substantial demand will occur only when incomes have risen further. (Both causes of entrepreneurial failure seem to have been operative in the British market for dishwashers, in which a number of entrepreneurs have lost money.) Alternatively, initial success may not provide the justification for sustained high-volume output that it is believed to offer, particularly where customers simply wish to acquire a stock that will thereafter be turned over very slowly. Thus error correction may be both faltering and incomplete.

J.M. Keynes emphasized how insecure are the foundations of many of our long-term expectations: "If we speak frankly, we have to admit that our basis of knowledge for estimating the yield ten years hence of a railway, a copper mine, a textile factory, the goodwill of a patent medicine, an Atlantic liner, a building in the City of London amounts to little and sometimes to nothing; or even five years hence. In fact, those who seriously attempt to make any such estimate are often so much in the minority that their behavior does not govern the market" (1936, pp. 149–150). Conventional equilibrium theorists appear to believe that such estimates are easily made; but anyone who gives due weight to the limitations of knowledge can hardly agree. Nor is this a difficulty that time will resolve. When the five years, or the ten, have passed we can calculate what the yield has been, but that will not resolve our problems of determining the best course of action at that time, unless we have some method of inferring new estimates from our experience. Of course people do learn from their mistakes, but they do not learn enough, and they may not even learn correctly. Just consider what various economists claim to have learned from the attempts to apply incomes policies.

Investment Decisions and Coordination Failure

Errors in investment decisions may have serious consequences, not only for output but also for employment. We shall approach this issue by considering the familiar Austrian explanation of monetary disorder, as set out comprehensively in Hayek's *Prices and Production* (1931). We begin by recalling that, to justify the analysis of an economy in real terms, it is necessary to assume that exchanges are made against money. But money brings new dangers, one of which is its propensity to disturb relative prices. Hayek's concern is with the effect of monetary expansion on intertemporal prices, an effect that arises directly from the economy of information which characterizes a price mechanism working effectively.

It will be convenient for our later discussion to begin by assuming that there is a shift of preferences from present to future consumption. Some alert entrepreneurs will perceive that the resources hitherto employed in the production of goods for immediate use are no longer all required for that purpose, and they will also notice that consumers are diverting a greater part of their income to loans, which might therefore be obtained at lower rates. This combination of underemployed real resources and cheaper and easier credit would then be seen by some people as an opportunity for a profitable shift toward longer production processes with higher productivity. (Whether those processes are already known or are invented in order to make better use of the newly available resources is of secondary importance, denoting merely the difference between Kirznerian and Marshallian entrepreneurship.) At least some of these longer processes would require a substantially different outfit of capital goods, the provision of which entails a lengthy period of adjustment to build up, stage by stage, an interrelated series of investments. (The problem of achieving these complementary investments has been noted earlier.) A very large scale example of such a longer process is a system of electricity generation using fast-breeder reactors; a smaller-scale example is the development of postschool education.

Let us now suppose that while these elaborate schemes of investment are in mid-course the pattern of consumer preferences reverts to its original state. We would then be left with a partly finished capital outfit that was unusable in its existing state but no longer worth finishing. Some parts might be adaptable to other uses, but much of it would need to be abandoned. Industries that had expanded to meet the new demand would be faced with large-scale cancellation of orders. A good deal of unemployment would be created, much of it impossible to alleviate until the economy had readjusted.

What Hayek argued is that monetary expansion can create the illusion of just such a shift of preferences, but it is an illusion that cannot persist. The creation of credit increases the supply of loans, which entrepreneurs can thus obtain at lower rates, in much the same way as an increase in personal savings at the expense of consumption. It is no part of the potential borrowers' business to enquire into the reasons for this reduction in interest rates: A market system economizes on information by making response independent of cause. Thus entrepreneurs in this situation would respond in similar fashion to those in the case previously discussed. There would be one immediate difference, which would presumably have some influence on the set of entrepreneurial plans: since consumption is not being reduced, resources would not be automatically released—instead of becoming available at lower prices they would have to be attracted by higher offers. Although one would expect the movement to be less, nevertheless resources would be diverted from present consumption.

But in this instance there has been no shift in preferences. The demand for consumption goods has been maintained; and so, as their supply is reduced, entrepreneurs begin to see opportunities for charging higher prices for them and thus for bidding resources away from investment. This increase in the prices of present goods counteracts the effects of the reduced interest rates in favoring future goods and lengthy production methods. The true opportunity costs of roundabout methods reassert themselves; the assumptions on which the investment programs were launched are shown to be false. The programs are abandoned, much capital is wasted, and unemployment results.

The only method of avoiding this result (short of engineering a shift in preferences to accommodate the new structure of production) is to continue the expansion of credit at a pace that will allow the rate of discount applied to future income to fall fast enough to offset the rise in current prices, thus perpetuating the misallocation of resources. The temptation to continue credit expansion may be strong, for the restoration of a pattern of production that conforms with people's unforced desires to save implies the liquidation of misguided investment and a period of considerable unemployment. Both of these unwelcome consequences appear to result from a tightening of credit, and therefore apparently could be relieved very simply and painlessly by a policy of easy money.

Hayek has sought to explain how monetary mismanagement can cause serious damage. (His explanation is microeconomic rather than macroeconomic in that it works through shifts in relative prices rather than through aggregate demand: microeconomics deals mostly with price effects and substitution, macroeconomics with income effects and complementarity.) But his belief that without such mismanagement, or other political interventions that result in false price signals, such large-scale errors will not occur seems too optimistic. Mises, by contrast, seems ready to accept that irremediable lack of knowledge may lead even the most efficient market economy into substantial malinvestment (1949, p. 391). Since our knowledge is incomplete, may we not guess wrong; and since our knowledge about the medium-term future is particularly inadequate and cannot be adequately corrected through the market process until that medium-term future arrives, may we not go particularly wrong in our investment decisions? To return to our example, entrepreneurs may anticipate a future pattern of demand that seems to justify the diversion of resources from current consumption, for example to develop new energy sources with very long lead times, and they may discover after some years that this demand shows no sign of appearing.

If, as Keynes says, we have very little basis for estimating the yield of a textile factory even five years hence, is there not a substantial chance that textile factories will be built and then found not worth operating, while we find ourselves short, say, of capacity for microprocessors? It may be the distribution, rather than the total, of investment that goes awry, but the results will be fairly similar. The present states of the world shipbuilding and synthetic fibre industries are examples. To what extent the entrepreneurial misjudgements that have contributed to these disasters were influenced by credit policy or other kinds of government intervention I do not propose to enquire. Although those influences were hardly negligible, it seems reasonably clear that many firms both overestimated the growth of demand, by extrapolating too easily from experience, and were too sanguine about their own market share. The difficulty of estimating attainable market share with inadequate knowledge of the intentions of other firms is one of the critical information problems of investment in atomistic competition (to which Richardson has drawn attention); and firms commonly seem to assume that their own marketing skills are peculiarly fitted to give them a competitive edge.

The consequences of these major investment errors have been idle plants and large-scale redundancies; and suggestions to mitigate these consequences by credit creation or by some kind of special treatment have not been lacking. Both are more likely to aggravate than to cure the problem. Credit creation, of course, leads straight to the situation analyzed by Hayek; and proposals designed to encourage premature scrapping and replacement of existing ships simply transfer orders from the future to the present and exacerbate the problem of overcapacity when such a scheme is completed.

No firm can make investment errors as big as those of governments, and none has done; but some of them have been big enough. Even though the direct financial losses fall on those who invested in the company, there are plenty of others who suffer: employees, suppliers, shopkeepers who lose trade because their customers have lost income, and so on. Neither the possibility nor the consequences of major errors should be dismissed. It is important to look for ways of improving performance, for example by seeking to explore future possibilities rather than producing a "best forecast"— in other words by acknowledging more candidly the extent of our ignorance. While our ignorance exists, mistakes cannot be avoided, even by the most efficient market process, and this too needs to be admitted.

Money, Information, and Confidence

The difficulties are increased by another of the dangers that accompanies the indispensable means of exchange—money. When someone offers a commodity for barter he must decide what commodity he is willing to accept in exchange: thus the supply of one good is necessarily a demand for a specific other good. But if he sells for money, there is, at the time of exchange, no demand for any other specified commodity. Now this deficiency is usually remedied quickly, as the seller uses the proceeds of his sale to make purchases elsewhere; and such minor time-differences between purchase and sale do not invalidate an analysis in terms of direct multiple exchange. But the proceeds of a sale do not have to reappear quickly as a specific demand; and if those proceeds are intended to be used for future consumption, they rarely will. In a pure barter economy, the only ways of providing for future consumption are by storing present purchases or by exchanging goods against a contract for future delivery. In the former case, there is no need to consider future demand; in the latter, the purchaser knows at once what he has to make available and at what date. But in a monetary economy, provision for the future is primarily sought through the accumulation of financial assets.

This method avoids the need for storage or for future contracts and alleviates the consumer's problems that arise from inadequate knowledge by allowing him to defer decisions to a time when he may expect to be better informed, as Shackle has observed (1972, p. 160). The means of exchange also serves as a store of value. In the former role, as in the latter, money is extremely convenient. But this convenience has an opportunity cost. In comparison with a barter economy the consumer's escape from premature commitment has the effect of destroying the producer's information. He does not know how consumers will choose to spend their savings; indeed consumers probably have no more than a very rough idea themselves. Thus, in making decisions that are directed toward supplying goods and services some years ahead, entrepreneurs cannot rely on the perception of changes that have already taken place but must use their imagination in an attempt to anticipate changes in the future. We should not be surprised if they make mistakes.

Like everyone else, entrepreneurs may seek to conceal the extent of their ignorance, by assuming a degree of continuity between past and future that cannot possibly be assured and that may well be greater than the continuity achieved in the past; alternatively they may place exaggerated reliance on the apparent plans of other entrepreneurs, who are credited with superior foresight. Entrepreneurial competition encourages a variety of opinions and of plans; but faced with the total inadequacy of any basis for rational expectation, we may sometimes find excessive conformity, both in undertaking particular kinds of business strategy and in abandoning such strategies. To rely on one's own imagination, and to await the eventual market test, requires greater resolution, perhaps greater arrogance, than most of us possess.

The importance of business confidence was noted by Marshall and emphasized by Keynes. Where there is no adequate basis for confident predictions a few years ahead, entrepreneurs may lack the confidence to act on any prediction. They may envisage a wide range of possibilities, each calling for a different course of action, and for any single project the chance of profit may seem to be outweighed by the risk of loss. Therefore no project is undertaken; instead profit is sought from current operations or is not sought at all.

One possibility is that entrepreneurs will devote their attention not to anticipating real changes in the economy but to forestalling shifts of opinion about the prospects of such changes. Since speculative markets are so common, there is no lack of scope for such activities, and the structure of taxation—especially the differential treatment of income and capital gains—may encourage the search for profit through the purchase of assets in order to sell them a little later at a higher price to someone who hopes to resell at a higher price still. Such concentrations of entrepreneurial effort, fuelled by credit creation, have been observed in commodity markets, property markets, and even the market for corporations.

Entrepreneurs, motivated by self-interest, must be expected to seek profit where they believe they can find it; and it is not difficult to so arrange our affairs that some of them can find it in ways that contribute nothing to the public weal. One of the dangers of inflation is that entrepreneurs will learn the lesson, which Hayek teaches, that the apparent prospects of profit generated by current interest rates are illusory, and go on to infer that any prospect of profit is likely to be deceptive. A further danger is that people may find it impossible to distinguish at all clearly between price movements that reflect changes in relative scarcity—and therefore suggest opportunities for entrepreneurship—and movements that are simply part of the continuing but uncoordinated upward drift of prices. Our knowledge is so slight, and in such need of supplementation by imagination and faith, that we can ill-afford anything that attenuates that scanty knowledge, paralyses imagination, and destroys faith.

Conclusion

The performance of an economy in which decisions are taken by individuals pursuing their own interest has provided the principal subject matter of our discipline for two hundred years. Throughout that time it has been generally recognized that this performance depends on the conditions within which self-interest is pursued. (That it depends also on the tempering of self-interest, in the narrow sense, by "moral sentiments" has sometimes been forgotten.) Probably the most distinctive Austrian contribution to this analysis has been the insistence that one of the conditions is an environment of limited and dispersed knowledge. Many of the conventional questions of economics are wrongly posed because they take no account of ignorance, and the answers are therefore incomplete and often misleading. In particular, the questions require individuals to respond, but not to initiate, with the unsurprising consequence that initiative appears disruptive of good order.

Mises's treatise is entitled *Human Action,* not *Programmed Response* (1949). Action, as Shackle has consistently argued, is originative and must derive from the actor's own estimate of its consequences. The gaps in his knowledge must be filled from his own imagination, and if he is unable or unwilling to so fill them, then he cannot act. It follows that we cannot assume that entrepreneurship will always be in adequate supply; we should therefore be chary of discouraging it. It also follows that entrepreneurs sometimes make mistakes, and although many of these mistakes will be quickly discovered and corrected, it is idle to believe that this will always happen. Entrepreneurs may be able to cope with ignorance; they cannot abolish it.

Indeed, if the future cannot be known, there is logically no means by which we can choose in advance the best way to deal with it. Not only is it impossible to be certain, now, what is the most effective method of providing for (or reducing) our energy needs in twenty-five years or the forms of business organization that will be most appropriate; we cannot be certain what form of economic system will be best. Those who believe in the market system because of its superior ability to generate and use knowledge cannot legitimately assume the perfection of knowledge (implying some variety of economic determinism), which advocates of other systems use to bolster their case. An advocate of human freedom—which is necessarily a freedom to choose wrongly, even foolishly—can never be certain that he is right on the grounds of efficiency, which provide the conventional terms of debate. It is one of the strengths of his position that he can freely admit that he may be wrong.

References

Bradbury, F.R., McCarthy, M.C., and Suckling, C.W. 1972. Patterns of innovation: Part II—the anaesthetic halothane. *Chemistry and Industry:* 109.

Chamberlin, E.H. 1933. *The theory of monopolistic competition.* Cambridge, Mass.: Harvard University.

Hayek, F.A. 1931. *Prices and production.* London: Routledge.

Keynes, J.M. 1936. *The general theory of employment interest and money.* London: Macmillan.

Kirzner, I.M. 1973. *Competition and entrepreneurship.* Chicago: University of Chicago.

Loasby, B.J. 1982. Knowledge, learning and enterprise. In *Beyond positive economics?* ed. J. Wiseman. London: Macmillan.

Marshall, A. 1920. *Principles of economics.* 8th ed. London: Macmillan.

Mises, L. von 1949. *Human action.* London: William Hodge.

Penrose, E.T. 1959. *The theory of the growth of the firm.* Oxford: Basil Blackwell.

Richardson, G.B. 1960. *Information and investment.* Oxford: Oxford University.

———. 1972. The Organisation of industry. *Economic Journal* 82:883–896.

———. 1975. Adam Smith on competition and increasing returns. In *Essays on Adam Smith;* ed. A.S. Skinner and T. Wilson, pp. 350–360. Oxford: Oxford University.

Robinson, J.V. 1969. *The economics of imperfect competition.* 2d ed. London: Macmillan.

Robinson, R. 1971. *Edward H. Chamberlin.* New York: Columbia University.

Shackle, G.L.S. 1972. *Epistemics and economics.* Cambridge: Cambridge University.

Smith, A. 1976a. *An Inquiry into the nature and causes of the wealth of nations,* ed. R.H. Campbell, A.S. Skinner, and W.B. Todd. Two Volumes. Oxford: Oxford University.

————. 1976b. *The theory of moral sentiments,* ed. D.D. Raphael and A.L. Macfie. Oxford: Oxford University Press.

11

Austrian Economics as the Middle Ground: Comment on Loasby

Roger W. Garrison

Introduction

In chapter 10, which deals with the economics of dispersed and incomplete knowledge, Brian Loasby discusses a broad range of topics that have traditionally been of interest to the Austrian school. In fact, the headings of the chapter's ten sections could well serve as a syllabus for a survey course dealing with the Austrian contribution. It will be instructive to identify the implicit organizing theme that underlies much of Loasby's discussion. Critical passages can then be evaluated in the light of this theme.

The underlying theme is exemplified by the phrase *incomplete knowledge,* which appears in the title of the chapter. This phrase delineates a middle ground between omniscience and total ignorance. In the Austrian view it is only with respect to this middle ground that economists have anything of consequence to say. At either extreme of the "knowledge spectrum" economic theory loses most, if not all, of its relevance. This aspect of the economics of extrema—or what might better be called the "noneconomic" nature of extrema—has more manifestations in economic theory than are conventionally recognized. Identifying a number of spectrums to be labeled with such terms as "knowledge," "uncertainty," "stability of expectations," and so forth, and considering the nature of the extrema for each spectrum, will take us a long way toward understanding the nature of economics. It will also help to locate the Austrian position on many of the issues raised by Loasby and to compare the Austrian school with the more conventional approach to economic issues.

In might be helpful to begin with an idea that spans all, or nearly all schools of thought. The concept of scarcity or scarce goods and services has rightly been accorded a prominent place in every introduction to economic theory. We can imagine a "scarcity spectrum" with one extreme representing the complete absence of goods and services and the other representing a complete satiation with respect to all goods and services. Theories of resource allocation, whether Robbinsian or Kirznerian, are simply inapplicable to these polar positions. The economic void and the economic bliss point serve only to bracket the wide band of the scarcity spectrum to which economic theory is applicable. And the virtual inconceivability of the two polar positions serves to dramatize just how wide that band is.

The Knowledge Spectrum

Although nearly all schools of thought stay between the poles of the scarcity spectrum, the modern mainstream has gravitated to one of the poles of the knowledge spectrum. This marks a sharp break between the Austrian theorists and the mainstream. Perfect knowledge—or perfect knowledge camouflaged beneath an assortment of frequency distributions—has been the primary domain of standard theory for several decades now. But this pole on the knowledge spectrum has no more relevance to the "economic problem" than does the bliss pole on the scarcity spectrum. This was the message in F.A. Hayek's now-famous article on "The Use of Knowledge in Society." The determination of the optimal allocation of resources given all the relevant information "is emphatically *not* the economic problem which society faces."[1] Hayek was urging that we move away—a long way away—from the polar position on the knowledge spectrum. But he was not urging that we rush to the opposite pole. This, unfortunately, has been the interpretation of many readers both inside and outside the Austrian camp. Loasby, it appears, has embraced this particular misinterpretation. Excerpts from chapter 10 can be offered as evidence: "[T]here is *no* need for information about [resources, technology, and preferences] to be communicated. [A]s F.A. Hayek . . . has emphasized, *no one* needs to know why the price of some particular commodity is whatever it is. . . . The increased price provides the *only* signal needed." (Emphasis added.) Loasby prefaced his discussion of Hayek with the assessment that things "are not quite as simple as they appear in the Austrian literature." He went on to conclude that "Hayek's explanation of the economy of knowledge through the use of the price mechanism still leaves us with one problem of general-equilibrium theory: how are . . . prices to be arrived at?" If only we recognize that Hayek stopped just short of the perfect-ignorance pole on the knowledge spectrum, we see that this problem does not in fact arise, I quote Hayek's celebrated example of the use of knowledge in society in which the price of tin has risen:

> There is no need for the *great majority* of [tin users] even to know where the more urgent need [for tin] has arisen, or in favor of what other needs they ought to husband the supply. If only *some of them* know directly of the new demand, and switch resources over to it, and if *people who are aware* of the new gap thus created in turn fill it from still other sources, the effect will rapidly spread throughout the whole economic system . . . and all this without the *great majority* of those instrumental in bringing about

these substitutions knowing anything at all about the original cause of these changes.[2] (Emphasis added.)

We see then that Hayek allows for, and depends on, the existence of some individuals whose knowledge bridges the gap between strictly local knowledge and knowledge derived strictly from prices. These are the people—we call them entrepreneurs—who set the prices and thus solve the problem posed by Loasby. Hayek's studied choice of the word *marvel* to describe the market process has new meaning in the context of the present discussion. He "deliberately used the word 'marvel' to shock the reader out of the complacency with which we often take the working of the market for granted."[3] Now that we have come to take Hayek for granted it is necessary to point out that the word is marvel and not miracle. Hayek called our attention to the marvel of the market economy functioning as it does on the basis of such little knowledge; he did not insist on a miracle in which the economy functions in the total absence of knowledge.

The Existence of Equilibrating Tendencies

Yet another spectrum can shed some light on one of the most fundamental issues in economics. At several points in Loasby's chapter he touches on the question of whether there is a tendency toward equilibrium. This is a question that all schools of thought have had to answer either explicitly or implicitly and a question on which the Austrian writers have poured much ink. The issue can be put into perspective by imagining a spectrum on which we gauge the volatility of economic data (or alternatively, on which we gauge the conformity of expected changes in the economic data to actual changes). At one end of the spectrum the underlying data, that is, preferences, resource availabilities, and technology, do not change at all. Here, apart from the path-dependency issue, the equilibrating tendency is not in doubt. This pole of the spectrum has been the popular stomping ground for neoclassical theorists who prefer to skirt the more fundamental issue and to get on with the description of alternative equilibrium states. At the opposite pole the economic data are more volatile than we care to imagine. In these circumstances we can predict not only that the question of an equilibrating tendency would be answered in the negative but also that economic science, in which such a question could be raised, would itself be nonexistent. Hayek has reminded us that it is only insofar as individual actions result in unintended order that economic science has a subject matter.[4] We must take Ludwig von Mises literally when he suggests that the only way we can conceive of markets is to conceive of a tendency toward equilibrium.[5] Once again, the poles represent the extreme circumstances under which economic theory is either trivial or impossible. It is on that expansive band between the two poles that Mises's concept of human action, the ultimate source of the equilibrating tendency, has applicability.

As an aside let me suggest that the modern discussions of the existence of equilibrating tendencies should induce a feeling of déjà vu. They parallel both in form and in substance the debate between Malthus and Ricardo on the issue of gluts. Gluts, after all, are just a particular form of disequilibrium. The similarity of the issues, then, should not be surprising. Their resolutions, it can be argued, are also similar. Although we can conceive of a temporary glut in a particular market or even a short-run economywide glut caused, say, by the collapse of the currency, the thought of a sustained economywide glut of goods and services is totally alien to the economic way of thinking. Similarly, we can conceive of the equilibrating tendencies being blocked for a particular market, and we can understand how, say, perverse monetary policy can disrupt the equilibrating tendencies on an economywide basis, but the idea of a general lack or ineffectiveness of equilibrating tendencies in a market economy is alien to our way of thinking. To deny the existence of equilibrating tendencies or even to plead agnosticism on the issue is to deny or doubt the possibility of an economic science.

Other Spectrums

Framing these issues in terms of polar positions and the spectrum between the poles helps to put other related issues into perspective. For instance, general-equilibrium theory, whose applicability is confined to one of the polar positions, is sometimes described as institutionless. Economic institutions would be superfluous in a world where perfect order already exists. At the opposite pole, where no order is attainable, institutions could not emerge. It is only in that broad middle ground, where individual actions give rise to a spontaneous order, that economic institutions have a role to play. This accounts for the Austrians' continual attention to the role of institutions in their economic theory and for the inattention on the part of general-equilibrium theorists.

Finally, let me suggest a spectrum that has relevance to sections of Loasby's chapter dealing with intertemporal coordination and monetary disturbances. In an illuminating discussion of these issues Hayek referred to money as the "loose joint" in the system.[6] This view clearly marks off a middle position between two polar views. Theorists whose attention is confined strictly to the real factors are implicitly viewing money as a tight joint; theorists who reason in terms of fixed price levels and liquidity traps see money as a broken joint. Clearly, Hayek's view is the most insightful. The fact that money joins nominal supply and nominal demand is what validates

Say's law correctly understood. The fact that the joint is a loose one is what keeps Say's law from being true in the vulgar sense.

Loasby sees Mises as recognizing that the looseness of the monetary joint can give rise to malinvestment in an unhampered market and takes Hayek to believe that only a misguided monetary authority can induce malinvestment. But unless we take *Prices and Production* as Hayek's final word, this contrast is unfounded. Both theorists took a middle-ground position. Whereas Hayek used the imagery of the loose joint, Mises viewed money as a tool, but not a foolproof tool, of economic calculation. In each case it was understood that individual investors can and do make investments that turn out to be unsound. This is unavoidable so long as we reject the polar position of tight-jointed money. (It is true that Mises and Hayek were more concerned with the attempts of government to take political advantage of the loose joint, in the process inducing systematic economy-wide distortions in the structure of production. Loasby recognizes the difference between individual investment errors and government-induced malinvestment when he remarks that "no firm can make investment errors as big as those of government.")

On many key economic issues, such as economic knowledge, equilibrating tendencies, economic institutions, and the nature of money, the Austrian theorists take what might be described as a middle-of-the-road position when compared to the mainstream counterpart. This is the theme that underlies much of Loasby's discussion. There may be some Austrians who are uncomfortable with this characterization. After all, are not the Austrians supposed to be radicals? Indeed they are. And rejecting a contrary-to-fact polar position in today's academic environment can be a radical thing to do. Let me conclude this portion of my comments with a casual observation about the Austrian school and the modern mainstream. On the analytical issues the mainstream adopts a polar position, but the corresponding policy prescriptions, for example, those concerned with monopoly, externalities, and public goods, can be characterized as middle of the road. That is, perfect-knowledge models yield interventionist policies. Conversely, the Austrians, who take a middle-of-the-road position in analyzing the market process, tend to adopt a polar position on policy issues. The economics of dispersed and incomplete knowledge tend to imply a policy of laissez faire.

Loasby on the Business Cycle

Loasby's chapter contains a fairly standard exposition of the Austrian theory of the business cycle. Rather than to comment specifically on this exposition, it may be more worthwhile to ask why this theory is so poorly received by the more conventional macroeconomic theorists. There are clues to an answer in Loasby's chapter. In raising the business-cycle issue Loasby off-handedly describes Hayek's *Prices and Production* as a comprehensive Austrian explanation of monetary disorder. The view that this small book is, or is intended to be, a comprehensive statement and that modern theorists working in the Austrian tradition so regard it may be more common than we realize. In truth the book is, and is intended to be, a skeletal outline of the Austrian theory of business cycles. This is made perfectly clear in the preface to the second edition. Hayek explains that the book is based on a series of lectures he was invited to deliver at the University of London during the session of 1930-1931. He further explains that the invitation "came at a time when I had arrived at a clear view of the outlines of a theory of industrial fluctuations but before I had elaborated it in full detail or even realized all the difficulties which such elaboration presented."[7] In recent years Hayek has remarked that if he had been invited a year earlier, he could not have given those lectures, and if he had been invited a year later, he would not have given them. However thankful we may be that the invitation came in 1930, we should not take the lectures as the last word in business-cycle theory. To so regard *Prices and Production* is to misrepresent Hayek and to do a disservice to the Austrian school.

The extent of the difficulties in elaborating the theory is evidenced by the sheer volume of Hayek's *Pure Theory of Capital* published ten years after the London lectures. This volume, as its preface indicates, was intended to serve as a foundation for a more adequate analysis of the problem of industrial fluctuations.[8] The follow-on volume, which was to have analyzed monetary disturbances in the light of this capital theory, was never written primarily because of the shift in Hayek's interest from theoretical economics to political science. Modern theorists working in the Austrian tradition, notably, Murray Rothbard, Gerald O'Driscoll, and Richard Wagner, have partly filled the void left by Hayek. These more modern contributions are evidence that the theory of monetary disturbances is a living issue in the Austrian tradition. Unfortunately, economists outside the Austrian school persist in the belief that Austrian business-cycle theory consists of some pat story fabricated in final form in 1930. If the modern Austrians can overcome this misunderstanding, they will have gone a long way toward greater acceptance.

A second source of misunderstanding is manifest in Loasby's discussion of knowledge and expectations. This issue was treated separately from the theory of the business cycle but has direct relevance for the particular course of events that constitute any given monetary disturbance. In effect Loasby criticizes the Austrians for not explaining why different people know different things and have different expectations. The issue of differential knowledge is symptomatic of a larger problem faced by any school of thought that does not follow every trend in the way of thinking of the mainstream. The repeated use of contrary-to-fact assumptions, such as perfect knowledge or homogeneous products, can blunt our ability to deal with reality as it actually exists. The standardization of such assumptions can eventually lead us to require that the recognition of facts-as-they-are be accompanied with special justification. A hypothetical example can serve to illustrate this problem.

Suppose that in the near future an economist devises a model in which it becomes convenient to assume that all goods are made out of rubber. (This otherwise outrageous assumption may initially be justified on the basis of the empirical soundness of the model's predictions.) If this rubber-goods model were to sweep the profession, it would eventually become unnecessary to restate the underlying assumption each time the model is employed. Eventually, it would be necessary to reject explicitly the all-rubber assumption if the fact that different goods are made from different materials is instrumental for a particular line of reasoning. The first theorist to make this explicit rejection would be regarded as having a brilliant insight by some, while others would demand an explanation for the multimaterial view of the world. Soon enough, historians of thought would begin combing through the early literature looking for clear evidence that Smith, Ricardo, and Menger realized that some things are not made out of rubber. Such is "life among the Econ"—to use a phrase coined by a modern Econ-watcher.

In the Austrian tradition the fact of differential knowledge literally goes without saying. The "assumption" that different people know different things is on a par with the "assumption" that not all goods are made out of rubber. In fact, to a methodological individualist the idea that different people know different things is inherent in the very concept of an individual. Differential knowledge remains a puzzle only to those economists whose understanding has been numbed by the continual contrary-to-fact assumptions of identical individuals and identical firms as represented by the corresponding homothetic indifference curves and production functions. Yet, Loasby considers the fact of differential knowledge a "major theoretical issue" and calls on the Austrians to justify their assumption. Surely this demand should be seen as a commentary on the current mind set of the modern mainstream and not as an imperative for modern Austrian scholars.

These remarks, inspired by Loasby's discussion of Austrian business-cycle theory, are intended to suggest that those who are convinced of the basic soundness of the Mises-Hayek theory should proceed on two fronts. They should strive, of course, to elaborate and refine the analysis offered by these earlier Austrian theorists. But they should also attempt to advance on the strategic front. Identifying and overcoming misunderstandings can be as important—and as difficult—as arriving at the understanding in the first place.

Conclusion

Loasby has touched on many more issues that I have been able to consider. But the general approach I have taken to put a few of the issues into perspective could well be extended beyond Loasby's discussion. If nothing else, the approach has served to keep one important distinction in sharp focus. It has made us realize which issues are truly controversial and which ones are only controversial in the light of some contrary-to-fact mainstream view. This is a distinction that modern Austrian theorists should keep in mind.

Notes

1. F.A. Hayek, "The Use of Knowledge in Society," *Individualism and the Economic Order* (Chicago: University of Chicago, 1948), p. 77.
2. Ibid., p. 85f.
3. Ibid., p. 87.
4. "It is only in so far as some sort of order arises as a result of individual action but without being designed by any individual that a problem is raised which demands a theoretical explanation." F.A. Hayek, *The Counter-Revolution of Science* (New York: Free Press of Glencoe, 1955), p. 39.
5. "The only method of dealing with the problem of action is to conceive that action ultimately aims at bringing about a state of affairs in which there is no longer any action . . ." Ludwig von Mises, *Human Action,* 3d rev. ed. (Chicago: Henry Regnery, 1966), p. 244.
6. F.A. Hayek, *The Pure Theory of Capital* (Chicago: University of Chicago, 1941), p. 408ff.
7. F.A. Hayek, *Prices and Production,* 2d ed. (New York: Augustus M. Kelley, 1967), p. vii.
8. Hayek, *Pure Theory of Capital,* p. v.

12 Uncertainty, Discovery, and Human Action: A Study of the Entrepreneurial Profile in the Misesian System

Israel M. Kirzner

A central element in the economics of Ludwig von Mises is the role played by the entrepreneur and the function fulfilled by entrepreneurship in the market process. The character of that process for Mises is decisively shaped by the leadership, the initiative, and the driving activity displayed and exercised by the entrepreneur. Moreover, in an intellectual edifice built systematically on the notion of individual *human action*—on the manner in which reasoning human beings interact while seeking to achieve their individual purposes—it is highly significant that Mises found it of relevance to emphasize that each human actor is always, in significant respects, an entrepreneur.[1] The present paper seeks to explore the character of Misesian entrepreneurship, with special reference to the influence exercised by the inescapable uncertainty that pervades economic life. Both at the level of isolated individual human action and at the level of entrepreneurial activity in market context, we shall be concerned to determine the extent to which the Misesian entrepreneur owes his very existence and his function to the unpredictability of his environment and to the ceaseless tides of change that undergird that unpredictability.

On the face of it, this question may not seem worthy of new research. Mises, it may be pointed out, expressed himself quite clearly on numerous occasions to the effect that the entrepreneurial function is inseparable from speculation with respect to an uncertain future. For example he wrote that "the entrepreneur is always a speculator."[2] Or, again, he wrote that "entrepreneur means acting man in regard to the changes occurring in the data of the market."[3] Moreover when Mises points out that every individual acting man is an entrepreneur, this is because "every action is embedded in the flux of time and thus involves a speculation."[4] In other words the entrepreneurial element cannot be abstracted from the notion of individual human action, because the "uncertainty of the future is already implied in the very notion of action. That man acts and that the future is uncertain are by no means two independent matters, they are only two different modes of establishing one thing."[5]

Thus it might seem that the essentiality of uncertainty for the Misesian entrepreneur hardly needs to be established anew. Certainly any thought of questioning that essentiality must, it might appear, be quickly dismissed.

What I shall argue in this chapter is not that the role of uncertainty in the function of the Misesian entrepreneur may be any less definitive than these clear-cut statements imply but that this role is a more subtle one than may on the surface appear to be the case. It is this subtlety in the role played by uncertainty in the Misesian system, I believe, that sets that system apart in significant respects from the views of other economists (such as Knight or Shackle) who have emphasized the phenomenon of uncertainty in the context of the market.

The Background of the Present Exploration

In earlier forays into the field of the Misesian entrepreneur, I developed an interpretation of the entrepreneurial function in which the role of uncertainty, while recognized and certainly not denied, was not emphasized. This failure to emphasize uncertainty was quite deliberate and was indeed explicitly acknowledged.[6] Instead of emphasizing the uncertainty in which entrepreneurial activity is embedded, these earlier treatments stressed the element of *alertness to hitherto unperceived opportunities* that is, I argued, crucial for the Misesian concept of entrepreneurship.[7] Since my position explicitly recognized the element of change and uncertainty, while it claimed to be able to explicate the elusive quality of entrepreneurship without need to emphasize the uncertainty element, it is perhaps not surprising that my treatment has drawn fire from two different perspectives. A number of critics have felt rather strongly that failure to emphasize the role of uncertainty renders my understanding of entrepreneurship fundamentally defective. At least one critic, on the other hand, has been persuaded by my exposition of entrepreneurship to the point that even my frugal references to uncertainty as an inescapable characteristic of the entrepreneurial scene appear altogether unnecessary and are seen as productive of confusion. Since all these critics are basically in agreement with me, I believe, on the broad accuracy of the general entrepreneurial character of the market process that I ascribe to Mises, it has for some time been my hope to delve into these questions more thoroughly. Some further brief recapitulation of these earlier discussions seems in order as an introduction to our present exploration.

My emphasis on alertness to hitherto unperceived opportunities as the decisive element in the entrepreneurial function stemmed from my pursuit of a didactic purpose. This purpose was to distinguish the analysis of the market *process* (a process in which the entrepreneur plays the crucial role) as sharply as possible from the analysis of equilibrium states (in which all scope for entrepreneurial activity has been assumed away). In equilibrium, it turns out, all market decisions have somehow come already into complete mutual coordination. Market participants have been assumed to be making their respective decisions with perfectly correct information concerning the decisions that all other participants are making at the same time.[8] So long as the underlying present consumer attitudes and production possibilities prevail, it is clear that we can rely on the very same set of decisions being made in each of an indefinite number of future periods. On the other hand, in the absence of such complete equilibrium coordination of decisions, a market process is set in motion in which market participants are motivated to learn more accurately to anticipate the decisions of others; in this process the entrepreneurial, profit-motivated discovery of the gaps in mutual coordination of decisions is a crucial element. Entrepreneurial activity drives this market process of mutual discovery by a continually displayed alertness to profit opportunities (into which the market automatically translates the existing gaps in coordination). Whereas entrepreneurial activity is indeed speculative, the pursuit of profit opportunities is a purposeful and deliberate one, the "emphasis on the element of alertness in action [was] intended to point out that, far from being numbed by the inescapable uncertainty of our world, men *act upon their judgments of* what opportunities have been left unexploited by others."[9]

In developing this aspect of entrepreneurship I was led to emphasize the capture of pure entrepreneurial profit as reducible essentially to the exploitation of arbitrage opportunities. Imperfect mutual awareness on the part of other market participants had generated the emergence of more than one price for the same bundle of economic goods; the entrepreneur's alertness to the profit opportunity presented by this price discrepancy permits him to win these profits (and, in so doing, tends to nudge the prices into closer adjustment with each other). In so emphasizing the arbitrage character of pure profit, emphasis was deliberately withdrawn from the speculative character of entrepreneurial activity that wins pure profit by correctly anticipating *future* price movements.[10]

A number of (otherwise friendly) critics expressed serious reservations concerning my deliberate lack of stress on the speculative character of entrepreneurial activity. Henry Hazlitt pointed out that my repeated references to the entrepreneur's perceiving of opportunities fail to make clear that at best the entrepreneur *thinks* that he perceives opportunities; that what an entrepreneur "acts on may not be a perception but a *guess*."[11] Murray Rothbard has endorsed a discussion by Robert Hébert in which my definition of the entrepreneur is sharply distinguished from that of Mises: "Mises conceives of the entrepreneur as the uncertainty bearer. . . . To Kirzner, on the other hand, entrepreneurship becomes reduced to the quality of *alert-*

ness; and uncertainty seems to have little to do with the matter."[12] Although conceding that my treatment of the entrepreneur has "a certain amount of textual justification in Mises," Rothbard sees this not as providing genuine support for my reading of the Misesian entrepreneur but as being the result of a "certain uncharacteristic lack of clarity in Mises' discussion of entrepreneurship."[13]

In a most thoughtful paper by Lawrence H. White several years ago, he too deplored my deliberate failure to emphasize uncertainty in the analysis of entrepreneurship. This treatment White argues, fosters neglect of important features of entrepreneurial activity that arise precisely from the passage of time and from the uncertainty generated by the prospect of unanticipated changes bound to occur during the journey to the future. To compress entrepreneurial activity into an arbitrage box is, in particular, to fail to recognize the highly important part played by entrepreneurial *imagination.* [14]

On the other hand my treatment of entrepreneurship has been criticized by J. High from a diametrically opposite point of view. High accepts the definition of entrepreneurship in terms of alertness to opportunities for pure profit. He proceeds to point out that "[n]othing in this definition requires uncertainty. The definition requires ignorance, because the opportunity has not been discovered earlier; it requires error, because the opportunity could have been discovered earlier, but the definition does not require uncertainty."[15] High is therefore critical of passages in which uncertainty is linked specifically with entrepreneurship.[16]

Clearly the role of uncertainty in the entrepreneurial environment, and in particular its relationship to the entrepreneur's alertness to error, demands further explication. What follows may not satisfy my critics (from both wings). I trust, however, that my discussion of some of the perhaps less obvious links between uncertainty and alertness will, if it does not quite absolve me of the charge of intransigence, at least bear witness to my grateful acknowledgement of the very deep importance of the problems raised by my critics.

Our inquiry will be facilitated by a careful examination of the sense in which each individual engaging in human action is, as already cited from Mises, exercising entrepreneurship.[17] Or, to put the issue somewhat differently, it will be helpful to explore more precisely what it is that distinguishes human action from purely calculative, allocative, economizing activity.

I have argued in earlier work that the concept of human action emphasized by Mises includes an ineradicable entrepreneurial element that is absent from the notion of economizing, of the allocation of scarce resources among competing ends, that was articulated by Lord Robbins.[18] On the face of it there appear to be two distinct aspects of Misesian human action that might be considered to set it apart from Robbinsian economizing activity. We shall have to ask whether these are indeed two distinct aspects of human action and how they relate to the entrepreneurial element that human action contains (but which Robbinsian allocative activity does not). These two aspects of human action (not present in economizing activity) may be identified as (1) the element in action that is beyond the scope of "rationality" as an explanatory tool, and (2) the element in action that constitutes discovery of error. Let us consider these in turn.

The Limits of Rationality

Perhaps the central feature of purely economizing activity is that it enables us to explain behavior by reference to the postulate of rationality. With a given framework of ranked goals sought, and of scarce resources available to be deployed, rationality (in the narrow sense of consistency of behavior with the relevant given ranking of ends) assures a unique pattern of resource allocation; decision making can be fully understood in the light of the given ends-means framework. There is no part of the decision that cannot be accounted for; given the framework, the decision taken is fully determined (and therefore completely explained); any other decision would have been simply unthinkable.

On the other hand the notion of Misesian human action embraces the very adoption of the ends-means framework to be considered relevant. The adoption of any particular ends-means framework is a step which is logically (although not necessarily chronologically) prior to that of allocating means consistently with the given ranking of ends. If the human decision is to be perceived as including the selection of the ends-means framework, then we have an element in that decision that cannot, of course, be explained by reference to rationality. Consistency in action is not sufficient to account for that ranking of ends in terms of which consistency itself is to be defined. So that the totality of human action cannot, even in principle, be explained on the basis of rationality. A science of human action cannot fail to acknowledge—even after full recognition of the formidable explanatory power of the postulate of rationality—that human history, depending as it does on unexplained adoption of goals and awareness of means, contains a strong element of the unexplained and even the spontaneous. These are themes that have, of course, been extensively developed by G.L.S. Shackle. "Choice and reason are things different in nature and function, reason *serves* the chosen purposes, not performs the selection of them."[19] "A man can be supposed to act always in rational response to his 'circumstances': but those 'circumstances' can, *and must,* be in part the creation of his own mind. . . . In this loose-textured history, men's choices of action being choices among thoughts which spring indeterminately in their minds, we can deem them to *initiate* trains of events in some real sense."[20]

In an earlier era, much criticism of the role of the rationality postulate in economic theory focused on the place of apparently nonrational behavior, behavior arising out of impetuous impulse or out of unthinking habit.[21] It is simply unrealistic, these criticisms ran, to assume that economic activity represents the exclusive result of deliberation. Man acts all too often without careful deliberation; he does not weigh the costs and benefits of his actions. This is not the place to evaluate these criticisms or deal with the debates that they engendered three-quarters of a century ago and more. But it is perhaps important to point out that limits of rationality discussed in this section have little to do with the arguments based on impulsiveness and on habit bondage. It is not at all being argued here that human action involves the *thoughtless* selection of goals. Human decision making may of course involve the most agonizingly careful appraisal of alternative courses of action to choose that which seems likely to offer the most estimable of outcomes. In emphasizing that the rationality postulate is unable to explain the selection of the relevant ends-means framework, we are not suggesting that that selection occurs without deliberation, but merely that the results of that deliberation cannot be predicted on the basis of the postulate of consistency; that deliberation is essentially creative. One may predict the answer that a competent mathematician will arrive at when he tackles a given problem in computation (in the same way that one may know in advance the answer to that problem that will be yielded by an electronic computer); but one cannot, in the same way, predict which computational problem the mathematician will deliberately choose to tackle (as one may not be able to predict which problems will be selected to be fed into the electronic computer).

The matter may be presented in an alternative version. One may always distinguish, within each human decision an element into which thought enters in self-aware fashion from an element into which thought enters without self-awareness. A man desires a specific goal with great eagerness; but deliberation persuades him, let us imagine, that it is in his interest not to reveal that eagerness to others (say, because others might then spitefully wish to deny that goal to him). The studied nonchalance with which he masks his pursuit of the goal exhibits scope for both elements: (1) his apparent nonchalance is indeed deliberate and studied, he knows precisely the reason why it is important that he pretend disinterest; but (2) he may not be at all self-aware as to how he arrived at this judgment to act on the assumption that others may spitefully seek to frustrate his achievement. He simply decides so to act. His decision is to refrain from naively pursuing with evident eagerness that which he eagerly desires; but his decision is yet naive in the sense that he has not, for example, sought (as reasons having to do with long-term strategy might well suggest) to ostentatiously pretend unawareness of the spitefulness of the others. No matter how calculative a man's behavior may be, it seems impossible to avoid having accepted, without calculation, some framework within which to self-consciously engage in cost-benefit comparisons. A man decides to display behavior *a*. We may call the mental activity of making that decision, activity *b*. Now the man *may* have decided (in the course of decision-making activity *c*) to engage in decision-making activity *b*, (or he may have simply and impulsively engaged in decision-making activity *b*). But even if engaging in decision-making activity *b* (as a result of which behavior *a* was chosen) was itself the outcome of "higher" decisions, at some level our decision maker's highest decision was made quite unselfconsciously.

This extra-Robbinsian aspect of human action, the aspect which involves the creative, unpredictable selection of the ends-means framework, can also be usefully stated in terms of *knowledge*. Given his knowledge of the relevant ends-means framework, man's decision can be predicted without doubt; it is simply a matter of computation. To the extent, however, that man must "decide" what it is, so to speak, that he knows, and that this determination is not, in general, based ineluctably on other knowledge unambiguously possessed, man's behavior is not at all predictable. What a man believes himself to know is not itself the result of a calculative decision.[22] This expression of the notion of the existence of limits to rationality will facilitate our insight into the important linkage that exists between these limits and the phenomenon of uncertainty.

In the absence of uncertainty it would be difficult to avoid the assumption that each individual does in fact already know the circumstances surrounding his decision. Without uncertainty, therefore, decision making would no longer call for any imaginative, creative determination of what the circumstances really are. Decision making would call merely for competent calculation. Its results could, in general, be predicted without doubt. Human judgment would have no scope. "With uncertainty absent, man's energies are devoted altogether to doing things; . . . in a world so built . . . it seems likely that . . . all organisms [would be] automata. . . ."[23] "If man knew the future, he would not have to choose and would not act. He would be like an automaton, reacting to stimuli without any will of its own."[24] Thus the extra-Robbinsian aspect of human action, the aspect responsible for rendering human action unpredictable and incompletely explainable in terms of rationality, arises from the inherent uncertainty of human predicament. If, then, one chooses to identify entrepreneurship with the function of making decisions in the face of an uncertain present or future environment, it certainly appears that Misesian human action does (while Robbinsian economizing does not) include an entrepreneurial element.

But before making up our minds on this point, we must consider that second element, mentioned at the end of the preceding section, that distinguishes Misesian human action from Robbinsian allocative decision making.

The Discovery of Error

To draw attention to this element in human action I shall draw on an earlier paper in which I attempted to identify that which might represent "entrepreneurial profit" in successful individual action in a Crusoe context.[25] Entrepreneurial profit in the Crusoe context, it turned out, can be identified only where Crusoe discovers that he has up until now attached an erroneously low valuation to resources over which he has command. Until today Crusoe has been spending his time catching fish with his bare hands. Today he has realized that he can use his time far more valuably by building a boat or making a net. "He has discovered that he had placed an incorrectly low value on his time. His reallocation of his labor time from fishing to boatbuilding is an entrepreneurial decision and, assuming his decision to be a correct one, yields pure profit in the form of additional value discovered to be forthcoming from the labor time applied."[26] This (Crusonian) pure profit arises from the circumstance that at the instant of entrepreneurial discovery Menger's law is violated. Menger's law teaches that men value goods according to the value of the satisfactions that depend on possession of those goods. This law arises from man's propensity to attach the value of ends to the means needed for their achievement. At the moment of entrepreneurial discovery Crusoe realizes that the ends achievable with his labor time have higher value than the ends he had previously sought to achieve:

> The value Crusoe has until now attached to his time is *less* than the value of the ends he now seeks. This discrepancy is, at the level of the individual, pure profit. . . . Once the old ends-means framework has been completely and unquestionably replaced by the new one, of course, it is the value of the new ends that Crusoe comes to attach to his means. . . . But, during the instant of an entrepreneurial leap of faith . . . there is scope for the discovery that, indeed, the ends achieved are more valuable than had hitherto been suspected. *This,* is the discovery of pure (Crusonian) entrepreneurial profit.[27]

Scope for entrepreneurship thus appears to be grounded in the possibility of discovering error. In the market context, the state of general equilibrium, providing as it does absolutely no scope for the discovery of profitable discrepancies between prices and costs, affords no opportunity for entrepreneurial discovery and turns out to be populated entirely by Robbinsian maximizers. In the same way, it now appears, the situation in which Crusoe is errorlessly allocating his resources—with the value of ends being fully and faultlessly attached to the relevant means in strict accordance with Menger's law—affords no scope for the entrepreneurial element in human action. Human action, without scope for the discovery of error, collapses into Robbinsian allocative activity.

Clearly this way of identifying the entrepreneurial element that is present in Misesian human action but absent in Robbinsian economizing activity fits in well with the approach that defines enterpreneurship as alertness to hitherto unperceived opportunities.[28] In the market context entrepreneurship is evoked by the presence of as yet unexploited opportunities for pure profit. These opportunities are evidence of the failure of market participants, up until now, to correctly assess the realities of the market situation. At the level of the individual too, it is then attractive to argue, an entrepreneurial element in action is evoked by the existence of as-yet-unexploited private opportunities. To act entrepreneurially is to identify situations overlooked until now because of error.

Uncertainty and/or Discovery

Our discussion has led us to identify two apparently distinct elements in human action, each of which possesses plausible claims as constituting that entrepreneurial element in action that sets it apart from purely calculative economizing activity: (1) On the one hand we saw that it appears plausible to associate entrepreneurship with the department within human action in which the very framework for calculative economizing activity is, in an open-ended, uncertain world, selected as being relevant. It is here that we would find scope for the unpredictable, the creative, the imaginative expressions of the human mind—expressions that cannot themselves be explained in terms of the postulate of consistency. Thus entrepreneurship, at the Crusoe level, arises uniquely and peculiarly from the circumstance that, as a result of the inescapable uncertainty of the human predicament, acting man cannot be assumed to be sure of the framework relevant for calculative activity. He must, using whatever entrepreneurial gifts he can display, *choose* a framework. (2) On the other hand, as we have seen, it appears perhaps equally plausible to associate entrepreneurship with that aspect of human action in which the alert individual realizes the existence of opportunities that he has up until now somehow failed to notice. Scope for entrepreneurship, at the Crusoe level, arises then not from the present uncertainty that must now be grappled with in decision making but from earlier error from which entrepreneurial discovery must now provide protection.

We must emphasize that these alternative identifications of the entrepreneurial element in action do appear, at least on a first scrutiny, to be genuinely different from one another. It is of course true that past error (from which, on the one view, we look to entrepreneurial discovery to provide a rescue) may be attributed to the pervasive uncertainty that characterizes our world (and to the inevitably kaleidic changes responsible for that uncertainty.) But to discover hitherto unnoticed opportunities (unnoticed because of past failure to pierce correctly the fog of uncertainty) does not at all seem to be the same task as that of selecting between alternative present scenarios for the future within which calculative activity is to be undertaken. Moreover, whatever the possible reasons for past error, error itself implies merely ignorance, not necessarily uncertainty.[29] To escape ignorance is one thing; to deal with uncertainty is another.

This tension that we have discovered at the level of human action in the Crusoe context, between present uncertainty and earlier error as sources of entrepreneurship, is clearly to be linked immediately with our more general exploration in this chapter. This chapter is concerned with determining the extent to which the Misesian entrepreneur is to be perceived as the creature of uncertainty. The tension we have now discovered between present uncertainty and earlier error corresponds exactly to the disagreement that we encountered between those who see the Misesian entrepreneur as essentially the bearer of market uncertainty and those who see him as the discoverer of earlier market errors. It is my contention that our awareness of this apparent tension can in fact shed light on certain subtleties in the concept of entrepreneurship likely otherwise to be overlooked. Our procedure to develop this claim will be as follows: We will seek to show that, on a deeper understanding of the meaning of uncertainty and of the discovery of error at the level of individual action, the tension between them dissolves in a way that will reveal the full significance of entrepreneurial alertness at the level of the individual. Thereafter we will pursue the analogy between the scope of entrepreneurship at the individual level and that of the entrepreneurship at the level of the market, drawing on this analogy to identify precisely the relative roles, in market entrepreneurship, of uncertainty and of alertness.

Action and Alertness

Man acts, in the light of the future as he envisages it, to enhance his position in that future. The realized consequences of man's actions, however, flow from the impact of those actions on the actual (as contrasted with the envisaged) course of future events. The extent to which man's plans for the enhancement of his future prospects are fulfilled depends on the extent to which the future as he has envisaged it corresponds to the future as it in fact occurs. There is no natural set of forces or constraints assuring correspondence between the envisaged future and the realized future. The two may, it seems at first glance, diverge from one another with complete freedom. The future course of events is in general certainly not constrained by past forecasts; nor, unfortunately, are forecasts constrained by the actual future events these forecasts seek to foretell. On the face of it, then, with nothing to guarantee correspondence between the actual future and the future as it is envisaged, it might seem as if successful action were entirely a matter of good fortune. Indeed, if man is aware of this apparent lack of ability to envisage the future correctly except as a matter of sheer good fortune, it is not clear why (apart from the joys of gambling itself) man bothers to act at all. But of course the overwhelming fact of human history is that man does act, and his choices are made in terms of an envisaged future that, although by no means a photographic image of the future as it will actually unfold, is yet not entirely without moorings in regard to that realized future. "To be genuine, choice must be neither random nor predetermined. There must be some grounds for choosing, but they must be inadequate; there must be some possibility of predicting the consequences of choice, but none of perfect prediction."[30] "The essence of the situation is action according to *opinion*, . . . neither entire ignorance nor complete and perfect information, but partial knowledge."[31] The genuine choices that do, we are convinced, make up human history express man's conviction that the future as he envisages it does hold correspondence, in some degree, to the future as it will in fact unfold. The uncertainty of the future reflects man's awareness that this correspondence is far from complete; the fact that he acts and chooses at all reflects his conviction that this correspondence is far from negligible. Whence does this correspondence, incomplete though it may be, arise? If there are no constraints assuring correspondence, how is successful action anything but the sheerest good fortune?

The answer to this dilemma surely lies in the circumstance that man is *motivated* to formulate the future as he envisages it, as accurately as possible. It is not a matter of two unfolding tapestries, one the realized future, the second a fantasized series of pictures of what the first might look like. Rather, acting man really does try to construct his picture of the future to correspond to the truth as it will be realized. He really does try to glimpse the future, to peer through the fog. He is thus motivated *to bring about* correspondence between the envisaged and the realized futures. Man's purposeful efforts to better his condition are responsible not only for his choices as constructed against a given envisaged future; that purposefulness is, perhaps even more importantly, responsible for the remarkable circumstance that that envisaged future does overlap significantly with the future as it actually unfolds. (Of course, these forecasts need not be made, explicitly, prior to action; they are embedded, possibly without self-awareness, in action itself.) We call this motivated propensity of man to formulate an image of the future man's *alertness*. Were man totally lacking in alertness, he could not act at all: his blindness to the future would rob him of any framework for action. (In fact, were man totally lacking in potential for alertness, it would be difficult to identify a notion of error altogether: were unalert man to act, it would not be on the basis of an erroneously forecast future. It would be on the basis of no relevant forecast at all. Not recognizing that he might—had he been more alert—have avoided the incorrect picture of the future, he could not in any meaningful sense blame himself for having erred.)

It will surely be acknowledged that this alertness—which provides the only pressure to constrain man's envisaged future toward some correspondence with the future to be realized—is what we are searching for under the phrase "the entrepreneurial element in human action." Robbinsian allocation activity contains no such element, because within the assigned scope of such defined activity no possible divergence between a future as envisaged and a future to be realized is considered. What is incomplete in the notion of purely allocative activity is surely to be found precisely in this abstraction from the desperately important element of entrepreneurship in human action.

It should be observed that the entrepreneurial alertness we have identified does not consist merely in "seeing" the unfolding of the tapestry of the future in the sense of seeing a preordained flow of events. Alertness must, importantly, embrace the awareness of the ways in which the human agent can, by imaginative, bold leaps of faith, and determination, in fact *create* the future for which his present acts are designed. As we shall argue in a subsequent section, this latter expression of entrepreneurial alertness does not affect its essential formal character—which remains that of assuring a tendency for the future context envisaged as following present action to bear some realistic resemblance to the future as it will be realized.

We must notice, in understanding this entrepreneurial element in human action, two aspects of it: (1) We note what provides the scope for entrepreneurship. This scope is provided by the complete freedom with which the future as envisaged might, without entrepreneurial alertness, diverge from the future as it will in fact be. Entrepreneurial alertness has a function to perform. (2) We note what provides the incentive that switches on entrepreneurial alertness. This incentive is provided by the lure of pure entrepreneurial profit to be grasped in stepping from a less accurately envisaged future to a more accurately envisaged one. Each step taken in moving toward a vision of the future that overlaps more significantly with the truth is not merely a step toward truth (that is, a positive entrepreneurial success); it is also a profitable step (that is, a step that enhances the value of the resources with which action is available to be taken).

Viewed from this perspective, the tension between the uncertainty-environment in which action occurs, on the one hand, and the discovery-of-error aspect of action, on the other, can be seen to dissolve at a glance. These two aspects of action can be seen immediately as merely two sides of the same entrepreneurial coin. If uncertainty were merely an unpleasant condition of life to which man must passively adjust, then it would be reasonable to distinguish between the quite separate activities of bearing uncertainty on the one hand and of discovering error on the other. Escaping from current errors is one thing; grappling with the uncertainty of the future is another. But, as we have noticed, to choose means to *endeavor,* under the incentive to grasp pure profit, to identify a more truthful picture of the future. Dealing with uncertainty is motivated by the profit to be won by avoiding error. In this way of viewing the matter the distinction between escaping current error and avoiding potential future error is unimportant. The discovery of error is an interesting feature of action because it offers incentive. It is this incentive that inspires the effort to pierce the fog of uncertainty that shrouds the future. To deal with uncertainty means to seek to overcome it by more accurate prescience; to discover error is merely that aspect of this endeavor that endows it with incentive attraction. The imagination and creativity with which man limns his envisaged future are inspired by the pure gains to be won in ensuring that that envisaged future is in fact no less bright than that which can be made the truth.

We shall find in the next section that these insights surrounding entrepreneurship at the level of individual action have their exact counterparts in entrepreneurship in the market context. It will be useful to summarize briefly the key points we have learned about individual entrepreneurship:

1. Entrepreneurship in individual action consists in the endeavor to secure greater correspondence between the individual's future as he envisages it and his future as it will in fact unfold. This endeavor consists in the individual's alertness to whatever can provide clues to the future. This alertness, broadly conceived, embraces those aspects of imagination and creativity through which the individual may himself *ensure* that his envisaged future will be realized.

2. Scope for entrepreneurship is provided by the uncertainty of the future. For our purposes uncertainty means that, in the absence of entrepreneurial alertness, an individual's view of the future may diverge with total freedom from the realized future. In the absence of entrepreneurial alertness it is only sheer chance that can be responsible for successful action.

3. Incentive for the "switching on" of entrepreneurial alertness is provided by the pure gain (or avoidance of loss) to be derived from replacing action based on less accurate prescience by action based on the more realistically envisaged future. The avoidance of entrepreneurial error is not merely a matter of being more truthful, it happens also to be profitable.

Entrepreneurship in the Market

Our examination of the entrepreneurial element in individual action permits us to see the role of entrepreneurship in the market in a fresh light. We shall discover, in the market context, elements that correspond precisely to their analogues in the individual context. Let us consider what happens in markets.

In a market exchanges occur between market participants.[32] In the absence of perfect mutual knowledge, many of the exchanges are inconsistent with one another. Some sales are made at low prices when some buyers are buying at high prices. Some market participants are not buying at all because they are unaware of the possibility of buying at prices low enough to be attractive; some are refraining from selling because they are unaware of the possibility of selling at prices high enough to be attractive. Clearly the actions of these buyers and sellers are, from the perspective of omniscience, uncoordinated and inconsistent. We notice that, although the assumption of perfect knowledge that is necessary for market equilibrium would constrain different transactions in the market to complete mutual consistency, the actuality of imperfect knowledge permits these different transactions in different parts of the market to diverge with apparently complete freedom. What alone tends to introduce a modicum of consistency and coordination into this picture, preventing a situation in which even the slightest degree of coordination could exist only as a matter of sheerest chance, is market entrepreneurship, inspired by the lure of pure market profit. We are now in a position to identify, in the market context, elements that correspond to key features already identified in the context of individual entrepreneurship.

Corresponding to uncertainty as it impinges on individual action we have market discoordination. The freedom with which an individual's envisaged future may diverge from the future to be realized, corresponds precisely to the freedom with which transactions made in one part of the market may diverge from transactions made elsewhere. In the absence of entrepreneurship it is only out of the purest chance that market transactions by different pairs of buyers and sellers are made on anything but the most wildly inconsistent terms. There is nothing that constrains the mutually satisfactory price bargain reached between one pair of traders to bear any specific relation to corresponding bargains reached between other pairs of traders.

Corresponding to error at the level of the individual, we have price divergence at the level of the market. Perfect knowledge (such as in Robbinsian individual allocative activity) precludes error. Market equilibrium (implied by universal perfect knowledge) precludes price divergences.

The individual entrepreneurial element permits the individual to escape from the distressing freedom with which divergences between envisaged futures and realized futures may occur; the entrepreneur fulfills the same function for the market. The function of the entrepreneur is to bring different parts of the market into coordination with each other. The market entrepreneur bridges the gaps in mutual knowledge, gaps that would otherwise permit prices to diverge with complete freedom.

Corresponding to the incentive for individual entrepreneurship provided by more realistic views of the future, we have, at the market level, the incentive provided by opportunities for pure entrepreneurial profit. Market profit consists in the gap between prices generated by error and market inconsistency—just as the source for private gain is to be discovered in a present divergence between the imagined and the actual future.

The following are propositions, in the context of the market, that concern entrepreneurship; they correspond precisely to those stated at the conclusion of the preceding section:[33]

1.° Entrepreneurship in the market consists in the function of securing greater consistency between different parts of the market. It expresses itself in entrepreneurial alertness to what transactions are in fact available in different parts of the market. It is only such alertness that is responsible for any tendency toward keeping these transactions in some kind of mutual consistency.

2.° Scope for market entrepreneurship is provided by the imperfect knowledge that permits market transactions to diverge from what would be a mutually inconsistent pattern.

3.° Incentive for market entrepreneurial activity is provided by the pure gain to be won by noticing existing divergences between the prices at which market transactions are available in different parts of the market. It is the lure of market profits that inspires entrepreneurial alertness.

Time, Uncertainty, and Entrepreneurship

Our analogy between entrepreneurship at the level of the individual and entrepreneurship in the market emphasized only the most salient respects of the analogy. Certain additional features of the entrepreneurial function in the market need to be dealt with more extensively. In the individual context the divergence (which it is the function of entrepreneurship to limit) was a divergence between anticipated and realized future. Its source in uncertainty was immediately apparent. In the market context the divergence (which it is the function of entrepreneurship to limit) was a divergence between the transactions in different parts of the market. Its source was stated in terms of imperfect mutual knowledge among market participants. Its relationship to uncertainty was not asserted. This requires both amplification and modification.

Our statements concerning market entrepreneurship were couched in terms of the market for a single commodity within a single period. It should be clear that nothing essential is lost when our picture of the market is expanded to include many commodities and, in particular, the passage of time. This should of course not be understood to mean that the introduction of the passage of time does not open up scope for additional insights. We merely argue that the insights we have gained in the single-period context for entrepreneurship are not to be lost sight of in the far more complex multiperiod case.

When we introduce the passage of time, the dimensions along which mutual ignorance may develop are multiplied. Market participants in one part of today's market not only may be imperfectly aware of the transactions available in another part of that market; they also may be imperfectly aware of the transactions that will be available in next year's market. Absence of consistency between different parts of today's market is seen as a special case of a more general notion of inconsistency that includes also inconsistency between today's transactions and those to be transacted next year. A low price today may be in this sense inconsistent with the high prices that will prevail next year. Scope for market entrepreneurship, in the context of the passage of time, arises then from the need to coordinate markets also across time. Incentive for market entrepreneurship along the intertemporal dimension is provided not by arbitrage profits generated by imperfectly coordinated present markets but, more generally, by the speculative profits generated by the as yet imperfectly coordinated market situations in the sequence of time. And, of course, the introduction of entrepreneurial activity to coordinate markets through time introduces, for individual entrepreneurs engaged in market entrepreneurship, precisely the considerations concerning the uncertain future that we have, until now, considered only in the context of the isolated individual.

It is because of this last circumstance that we must acknowledge that the introduction of the passage of time, although leaving the overall formal function of market entrepreneurship unchanged, will of course introduce substantial modification into the way we must imagine entrepreneurship to be exercised concretely. It is still the case, as noted, that the entrepreneurial function is that of bringing about a tendency for transactions in different parts of the market (conceived broadly now as including transactions entered into at different times) to be made in greater mutual consistency. But whereas in the case of entrepreneurship in the single-period market (that is, the case of the entrepreneur as arbitrageur) entrepreneurial alertness meant alertness to present facts, in the case of multiperiod entrepreneurship alertness must mean alertness to the future. It follows that market entrepreneurship in the multiperiod case introduces uncertainty as facing the entrepreneur not only as in the analogy offered in the preceding section—where the market analogue for uncertainty turned out to be the freedom with which transactions in different parts of today's market may unconstrainedly diverge from being mutually consistent—but also as in the simple sense of the entrepreneur's awareness of the freedom with which his own envisaged future (concerning future market transactions) may diverge from the realized future. In particular the futurity that entrepreneurship must confront introduces the possibility that the entrepreneur may, by his own creative actions, in fact *construct* the future as *he* wishes it to be. In the single-period case alertness can at best discover hitherto overlooked current facts. In the multiperiod case entrepreneurial alertness must include the entrepreneur's perception of the way in which creative and imaginative action may vitally shape the kind of transactions that will be entered into in future market periods.

Thus the exercise of entrepreneurial alertness in the multiperiod market context will indeed call for personal and psychological qualifications that were unneeded in the single-period case. To be a successful entrepreneur one must now possess those qualities of vision, boldness, determination, and creativity that we associated earlier with the entrepreneurial element in isolated individual action with respect to an uncertain future. There can be no doubt that in the concrete fulfillment of the entrepreneurial function these psychological and personal qualities are of paramount importance. It is in this sense that so many writers are undoubtedly correct in linking entrepreneurship with the courage and vision necessary to *create* the future in an uncertain world (rather than with merely seeing that which stares one in the face).

However, the function of market entrepreneurship in the multiperiod context is nonetheless still that spelled out in the preceding section. What market entrepreneurship accomplishes is a tendency for transactions in different parts of the market (including the market at different dates) to become coordinated. The incentive that inspires this entrepreneurial coordinaton is the lure of pure profit—the difference in market values resulting from hitherto less complete coordination. These insights remain true for the multiperiod case no less than for the arbitrage case. For some purposes it is no doubt important to draw attention to the concrete psychological requirements on which successful entrepreneurial decision making depends. But for other purposes such emphasis is not required; in fact such emphasis may divert attention from what is, from the perspective of the overall functioning of the market system, surely the essential feature of entrepreneurship: its market-coordinative properties.

Let us recall that at the level of the individual, entrepreneurship involved not merely the bearing of uncertainty but also the overcoming of uncertainty. Uncertainty is responsible for what would, in the absence of entrepreneurship, be a failure to perceive the future in a manner sufficiently realistic to permit action. Entrepreneurship, so to speak, pushes aside to some extent the swirling fogs of uncertainty, permitting meaningful action. It is this function of entrepreneurship that must be kept in view when we study the market process. The uncertainty that characterizes the environment within which market entrepreneurship plays its coordinative role must be fully recognized; without it there would be no need and no scope for entrepreneurship. But an understanding of what entrepreneurship accomplishes requires us to recognize not so much the extent to which uncertainty is the ineradicable feature of human existence but rather the extent to which both individual action and social coordination through the market can occur significantly despite the uncertainty of the future (and in spite also of the uncertainty-analogue that would, in the absence of the arbitrageur, fog up even the single-period market).

Further Reflections on Uncertainty and Alertness

Thus we can see how those writers who have denied that the pure entrepreneurial role involves the bearing of uncertainty were both correct and yet at least partly irrelevant. Both J.A. Schumpeter[34] and J.B. Clark insisted that only the capitalist bears the hazards of business; the pure entrepreneur has, by definition, nothing to lose.[35] No doubt all this is true, as far as it goes, But what is important about linking the entrepreneur with the phenomenon of uncertainty is not that it is the entrepreneur who accepts the disutilities associated with the assumption of the hazards of business in an uncertain world. What is important is that the entrepreneur, motivated by the lure of pure profits, attempts to pierce through these uncertainties and endeavors to see the truth that will permit profitable action on his part.

A number of economists may be altogether unwilling to accept the notion of alertness with respect to uncertain future. In fact many may wish to reject the very formulation we have employed to schematize the uncertainty of the future. For us uncertainty meant the essential freedom with which the envisaged future may diverge from the realized future. Entrepreneurial alertness means the ability to impose constraints on that freedom, so that the entrepreneur's vision of the future may indeed overlap, to some significant extent, with that future that he is attempting to see. But many will be unwilling to treat the future as something to be seen at all. "The present is uniquely determined. It can be seen by the eye-witness. . . . What is the future but the void? To call it the future is to concede the presumption that it is already 'existent' and merely waiting to appear. If that is so, if the world is determinist, then it seems idle to speak of choice."[36] Similarly many are unwilling to see the entrepreneur as "alert to opportunities" if this terminology implies that future opportunities already "exist" and are merely waiting to be grasped. "Entrepreneurial projects are not waiting to be sought out so much as to be thought up."[37]

What perhaps needs to be emphasized once again is that in using phrases such as "grasping future opportunities," "seeing the future correctly or incorrectly," or the "divergence between the envisaged future and the realized future," we do not wish to imply any determinacy regarding the future. No doubt, to say that one sees the future (with greater or lesser accuracy) is to employ a metaphor. No doubt the future that one "sees" is a future that may in fact be constructed significantly by one's action, which is supposed to be informed by that very vision. But surely these metaphors are useful and instructive. To dream realistically in a way that inspires successful, creative action is to "see correctly" as compared to the fantasies that inspire absurd ventures or the cold water poured by the unduly timid pessimist that stunts all efforts at improvement. "The future," we have learned, "is unknowable, though not unimaginable."[38] To acknowledge the unknowability of the future is to acknowledge the essential indeterminacy and uncertainty surrounding human existence. But surely in doing so we need not consign human existence to wholly uncoordinated chaos. To speak of entrepreneurial vision is to draw attention, by use of metaphor, to the formidable and benign coordinative powers of the human imagination. Austrian economists have, in principled fashion, refused to see the world as wholly knowable, as suited to interpretation by models of equilibrium from which uncertainty has been exhausted. It would be most unfortunate if, in pursuing this refusal, economists were to fall into a no-less-serious kind of error. This error would be the failure to understand how entrepreneurial individual action, and the systematic market forces set in motion by freedom for entrepreneurial discovery and innovation, harness the human imagination to achieve no less a result than the liberation of mankind from the chaos of complete mutual ignorance. Mises's concept of human action and his analysis of the role of entrepreneurial market processes surely remain, in this regard, unique and as yet insufficiently appreciated contributions to the profound understanding of human society.

Notes

1. L. von Mises, *Human Action* (New Haven: Yale University, 1949), p. 253.

2. Ibid., p. 288.

3. Ibid., p. 255.

4. Ibid., p. 254.

5. Ibid., p. 105.

6. I.M. Kirzner, *Competition and Entrepreneurship* (Chicago: University of Chicago, 1973), pp. 86–87.

7. Ibid., chap. 2. See also I.M. Kirzner, *Perception, Opportunity, and Profit* (Chicago: University of Chicago, 1979), chap. 10.

8. F.A. Hayek, *Individualism and Economic Order* (London: Rout-ledege and Kegan Paul, 1949), p. 42.

9. Kirzner, *Competition and Entrepreneurship,* pp. 86–87. (Italics in original.)

10. Such activity was subsumed under arbitrage by pointing out the formal similarity between (1) buying and selling in different markets today and (2) buying and selling in different markets at different dates. (See Kirzner, *Competition and Entrepreneurship,* pp. 85–86.)

11. Henry Hazlitt, review of *Competition and Entrepreneurship,* in *Freeman* (December 1974):759. Similar concerns seem to be expressed in a review of *Competition and Entrepreneurship* by Percy L. Greaves, Jr. in *Wertfrei* (Spring 1974): especially pp. 18–19.

12. See unpublished paper by Murray N. Rothbard, "Professor Hébert on Entrepreneurship," pp. 1–2. Reprinted with permission.

13. Ibid., p. 7.

14. L.H. White, "Entrepreneurship, Imagination, and the Question of Equilibrium," unpublished paper (1976). See also L.H. White, "Entrepreneurial Price Adjustment" (Paper presented at Southern Economic Association meetings Washington, D.C., November, 1978), p. 36, n. 3.

15. J. High, review article on *Perception, Opportunity and Profit* in *Austrian Economics Newsletter* (Spring 1980):14.

16. High's criticisms of my references to uncertainty as a characteristic of the entrepreneurial environment focus most specifically on what he believes to be my use of uncertainty to "serve as the distinguishing characteristic between entrepreneurship and luck." (Ibid.) Here there seems to be a definite misunderstanding of my position. So far from the presence of the uncertainty surrounding entrepreneurship being what separates entrepreneurial profit from the lucky windfall, almost the exact reverse is the case. What marks entrepreneurial profit as different from the lucky windfall is that the former was, despite the (inevitable) uncertainty that might have discouraged the entrepreneur, in fact deliberately pursued. Where luck confers gain may well reflect the circumstance that the uncertainty of this gain deterred the actor from even dreaming of winning it. High's reading apparently resulted from his understanding a passage that he cites (from Kirzner, *Perception, Opportunity and Profit,* pp. 159–160) to represent the case of a purely lucky gain. In fact the passage cited does not refer to luck at all. If one knows that one's labor can convert low-valued leisure into high-valued apples, the apples one so gains through one's hard work does not constitute a lucky windfall. The point of the cited passages is that Menger's law shows how there is no value gain at all derived from that labor, since one would already have attached the higher value of the ends to the available means. Our discussion in this chapter, however, proceeds on the assumption that High's unhappiness at my treatment of uncertainty in entrepreneurship

does not rest solely on the validity of the way in which I distinguish entrepreneurial profits from windfall gains.

17. Mises, *Human Action,* p. 253.

18. See Kirzner, *Competition and Entrepreneurship,* pp. 32–35. See also Kirzner, *Perception, Opportunity and Profit,* pp. 166–168.

19. G.L.S. Shackle, *Epistemics and Economics* (Cambridge: Cambridge University, 1972), p. 136. (Italics in original.)

20. Ibid., p. 351.

21. See also Kirzner, *The Economic Point of View* (Princeton: Van Nostrand, 1960), p. 167.

22. See also Kirzner, *Perception, Opportunity and Profit,* chap. 9.

23. F.H. Knight, *Risk, Uncertainty and Profit* (New York: Houghton Mifflin, 1921), p. 268.

24. Mises, *Human Action,* p. 105.

25. See Kirzner, *Perception, Opportunity and Profit,* chap. 10, especially pp. 158–164.

26. Ibid., p. 162.

27. Idid., p. 163.

28. See, for example, Kirzner, *Competition and Entrepreneurship,* p. 39.

29. See note 15 of this chapter.

30. B.J. Loasby, *Choice, Complexity and Ignorance* (Cambridge: Cambridge University, 1976), p. 5.

31. Knight, *Risk, Uncertainty and Profit,* p. 199.

32. Our discussion proceeds in terms of the market for a single commodity. It could be couched, without altering the essentials in any respect, in more general terms. See also the subsequent section of this chapter.

33. The three pairs of statements may be viewed as additions to the two lists of twelve statements developing the analogy between the individual and the market, provided in Kirzner, *Perception, Opportunity and Profit,* chap. 10, pp. 170–172, 173–175.

34. J.A. Schumpeter, *The Theory of Economic Development* (Cambridge, Mass.: Harvard University, 1934), p. 137; J.A. Schumpeter, *History of Economic Analysis* (Oxford: Oxford University, 1954), p. 556. See also S.M. Kanbur, "A Note on Risk Taking, Entrepreneurship and Schumpeter," *History of Political Economy* 12 (Winter 1980):489–498.

35. J.B. Clark, "Insurance and Business Profit," *Quarterly Journal of Economics* 7 (October 1892):46 (cited in Knight, *Risk, Uncertainty and Profit,* p. 38.)

36. Shackle, *Epistemics and Economics,* p. 122.

37. White, "Entrepreneurship, Imagination," p. 7.

38. L.M. Lachmann, "From Mises to Shackle: An Essay," *Journal of Economic Literature* 14 (March 1976):59.

13 Alertness and Judgment: Comment on Kirzner

Jack High

Entrepreneurship Past

For nearly twenty years, Israel Kirzner has elaborated the differences between economics as a science of maximizing and economics as a science of human action. At the heart of his undertaking lies the idea of entrepreneurship. Entrepreneurship is that part of human consciousness that is alert to opportunities for gain. Alertness, according to Kirzner, is the defining characteristic of entrepreneurship.[1]

Among other things, Kirzner has shown us:

that human action is a broader notion than maximizing, in that action encompasses not only maximizing but also entrepreneurship, which identifies the ends-means framework within which maximizing takes place.[2]

that entrepreneurship enables us to capture pure profit, by discovering previously overlooked facts that enable us to satisfy our wants more fully[3]

that entrepreneurship sets in motion a competitive market process, by discovering and acting on opportunities for arbitrage.[4]

that the market process set in motion by entrepreneurship equilibrates the market in the sense of coordinating previously discoordinate plans.[5]

Kirzner's work on the nature of economic theory has taken its inspiration from the writings of Ludwig von Mises. Yet, in comparing their views, we see a difference worth noting. Kirzner has, until chapter 12 of this book, given only cursory attention to uncertainty. This is worthy of remark because Mises defines entrepreneurship in terms of uncertainty. For Mises, "The term entrepreneur as used by catallactic theory means: acting man exclusively seen from the aspect of the uncertainty inherent in every action."[6] How has Kirzner been able to capture such a large part of Mises's entrepreneur, while dropping the defining characteristic of entrepreneurship? Answering this question will shed light on Kirzner's present treatment of uncertainty.

Kirzner could drop uncertainty and still retain a large part of Misesian entrepreneurship by implicitly relying on a distinction between ignorance that causes uncertainty and ignorance that does not. Uncertainty is a mental state in which we know only some of the influences that will determine the course of events.[7] Uncertainty can only be caused by ignorance, and the task of entrepreneurship, as seen by Mises, is to deal with this ignorance by anticipating the future as well as we can.

However, for analytical purposes we can speak of ignorance that causes uncertainty and ignorance that does not. A man may not know everything, but what he does know, he knows certainly. In particular, although he may be ignorant of many things, a person knows that if he sets out to accomplish goal A by means B, he can in fact do so. By employing the distinction between ignorance that does and ignorance that does not create uncertainty, we can derive the salient features of Kirzner's entrepreneurial system:

> A person knows with certainty the ends-means framework within which he maximizes. But he is ignorant of particular facts that, if he knew them, would extend his framework and enable him to satisfy his wants better. Alertness to these facts (which we assume him to know with certainty once he has identified them) is the meaning of entrepreneurship.

> A person's ignorance of some facts may be the result of his failure to notice what was there to be noticed. The failure to notice these facts is an economic error, and correcting our errors (by being alert) enables us to capture profit.

> In a market, noticing previously overlooked price discrepancies enables a person to arbitrage. This sets in motion a competitive market process.

> By removing people's ignorance of their opportunities, entrepreneurship brings people's plans into greater coordination. Entrepreneurship equilibrates the market.

Mises defines entrepreneurship in terms of uncertainty and uncertainty in terms of ignorance. The function of entrepreneurship is to deal with uncertainty, which means to deal with ignorance. Kirzner (implicitly, and for expository purposes only) distinguishes between ignorance that creates uncertainty and ignorance that does not. By setting aside the complication of uncertainty and focusing on the second kind of ignorance, Kirzner is able to define entrepreneurship and develop a theory of market process that is in many respects similar to that of Mises. The common link in the two systems is that entrepreneurship removes ignorance. This is worth stressing—when

Kirzner introduces uncertainty into his theory, he sees it as something that provides additional scope for the exercise of entrepreneurship, not as something that changes the fundamental nature of entrepreneurship.

Entrepreneurship Present

Kirzner brings uncertainty into his theory by emphasizing the forward-looking nature of human consciousness. One of the tasks of consciousness is to form an accurate picture of those events on which action is to be predicted. Our consciousness gives us no guarantee that our projections of the future will correspond to the actual future. The possibility that the actual future will diverge from our projected future is what Kirzner means by uncertainty.[8]

Since successful action depends on an accurate picture of future events, we try to form as accurate a picture of the future as possible: "We call this motivated propensity of man to formulate an image of the future—man's alertness."[9]

Kirzner's present conception of entrepreneurship differs from his past conception. The present conception is more broad and includes "those aspects of imagination and creativity through which the individual may himself *ensure* that his envisaged future will be realized."[10] The reason for this broader conception may be seen if we reflect on the difference between ignorance that creates uncertainty and ignorance that does not.

When ignorance does not create uncertainty, we move from ignorance to certain knowledge in a single step. Removing ignorance consists of noticing something new, and, once we notice it, we know all the implications for action. We see that we can get a higher price for our good than we previously thought, and we know exactly what to do—we quit selling at the low price and start selling at the high price. But when ignorance creates uncertainty, noticing something new may mean noticing a possible course of action. Even if we do notice a new fact, something of which we are certain, this new fact may only suggest ways in which the future might unfold. Once we allow for ignorance that creates uncertainty, we also have to allow for those mental operations that try to see through to the future—hence the expanded meaning of entrepreneurship.

Although Kirzner recognizes that his new conception of entrepreneurship introduces "substantial modification into the way we must imagine entrepreneurship to be exercised concretely,"[11] he still stresses the similarity between the two conceptions. Stressing the similarity is valuable for two reasons.

Under the old conception, the entrepreneur was not a passive reactor to market conditions; rather, the entrepreneur actively sought out opportunities. Under the new conception, the entrepreneur is not a passive bearer of uncertainty; rather he seeks out opportunities to reduce uncertainty. The entrepreneur tries to "peer through the fog," as Kirzner says. This is a valuable insight, and one that we are apt to overlook if we focus on the entrepreneur as the bearer of uncertainty. Certainly this is a prominent aspect of entrepreneurship as conceived by Mises.[12]

Under the old conception, the entrepreneur equilibrated the market in the sense that entrepreneurial activity brought about movement toward a single market price. Under the new conception, the entrepreneur coordinates present and future actions. This activity is vital to a market system, where production plans can span years, where innovation continually occurs, and where a low value is placed on economic custom. Both the division of labor and the extent of the market are influenced by power of entrepreneurship to coordinate present actions with future actions.

Entrepreneurship as Alertness

Although stressing the similarity between Kirzner's past view of entrepreneurship and his present view does have its value, it also has its drawbacks. For one thing, using the term *alertness* to encompass all those mental processes by which we derive possible futures from present states is an exceptional use of the term. Moreover, using alertness this way is especially likely to mislead where we have previously used the term in a narrower and more normal way.

In the *Art of Conjecture*, Bertrand de Jouvenel has suggested that we call this set of mental processes "proference." He says, "The action of going from present data to an assertion about the future is *sui generis;* it lacks a name, and so I propose to call it 'proference'; this suggests the action of carrying forward and will serve us more or less adequately."[13]

If we are to look on entrepreneurship as foreseeing the future, then *entrepreneurship* and *proference* are identical terms. However, entrepreneurship usually implies anticipating the future. The entrepreneur does not idly gaze into the future, as a scientist might; he tries to discern those aspects of the future, on which he can act, that will influence his well-being. Entrepreneurship is that subset of proference that is motivated by gain and on which action is based.[14]

Alertness is an important part of proference, generally, and of entrepreneurship in particular. If we are "at the lookout" for those elements in the present environment that will influence the future, our actions will be more likely to correspond to the reality that eventually unfolds. We might also wish to speak of the alertness to possible outcomes, but now we are no longer speaking of direct perception. We are now speaking of mental constructions, of different ways in which we conceive present influences working themselves out. But alertness, even in this broader sense, is not enough to explain action. A person who has alertly conceived a number of ways in which the future might unfold must also choose which of those images will guide his action. He must exercise his judgment. Judgment is an indispensable part of entrepreneurship.

In one way, Kirzner's analysis of entrepreneurship submerges the part played by judgment, and, in another way, his analysis bypasses it. Judgment, according to the *Oxford English Dictionary* is the "formation of an opinion or notion concerning something by exercising the mind upon it." Judgment influences action in two ways.

First, judgment assigns relevance to all the known causative factors of an unknown outcome.[15] That is, once we have identified those elements in the present that we think will influence the course of the future, we have to weigh mentally the relative strengths of these influences. The relevance that we assign to the various causal factors will influence which outcomes that we regard as likely. Judgment is one of the mental operations of entrepreneurship.

If we discuss entrepreneurship without uncertainty, we have no need to consider judgment. Entrepreneurship means alertness to opportunities, and once we have spotted the opportunity, we know exactly what to do and exactly what the outcome of our action will be. There is nothing to judge. However, if we bring in uncertainty, we do need to consider judgment; judgment helps us formulate our picture of the future. By continuing to call entrepreneurship alertness, which previously required no judgment, Kirzner submerged the role that judgment plays in entrepreneurial activity.

Judgment influences action in a second way. Once we have formulated our picture of possible futures and of how we can respond to various situations, we must decide on a particular course of action. We must form an opinion of how we should act.

Again, this kind of mental operation is unnecessary when ignorance does not cause uncertainty. Alertness removes ignorance, expands our ends-means framework, and, since we know that framework with certainty, enables us to maximize. Although alertness can, once uncertainty is introduced, lessen uncertainty, as Kirzner has pointed out, alertness cannot obviate the need for judgment as long as uncertainty is present.

Entrepreneurship á la Mises or á la Kirzner

The inclusion of judgment in entrepreneurship is very much in keeping with entrepreneurship as elaborated by Mises. Mises discussed judgment under the heading of the "understanding of the historical sciences," but he recognizes that "understanding" also applies to the future.

The task of understanding is to "appraise the effects and the intensity of the effects brought about by an action; it must deal with the relevance of each motive and each action."[16] Understanding is called on to evaluate the unique and individual features of a historical episode. This evaluation is required because there are no constant functional relationships in the human sciences. Even if we are able to enumerate all the causal factors at work in a particular situation, we still have the task of assigning relevance to each of these factors.[17]

Although Mises discusses understanding in the context of assigning relevance to the causes of historical outcomes, he recognizes that the same kind of mental activity is required to assess uncertain future outcomes. He notes that "Understanding is not a privilege of the historians. It is everybody's business. Everybody uses understanding in dealing with the uncertainty of future events to which he must adjust his own actions. The distinctive reasoning of the speculator is an understanding of the relevance of the various factors determining future events. . . . Acting man looks, as it were, with the eyes of a historian into the future."[18]

The inclusion of judgment as part of entrepreneurship differentiates Mises's view of the market process from Kirzner's. Kirzner has emphasized that entrepreneurship is the discovery of profit opportunities and that profits are vital to the market process. He has not particularly emphasized the role of losses in the market process.

In his earlier work, Kirzner had no need to emphasize the role of losses, because he had set uncertainty aside. In chapter 12 he does not mention them. This may be because his view on entrepreneurship excludes entrepreneurial loss. The entrepreneur discovers profit opportunities. To engage in this task, he needs no ownership of resources. For Kirzner, "ownership and entrepreneurship are to be viewed as completely separate functions."[19] If entrepreneurship is completely separate from ownership, is it meaningful to speak of entrepreneurial loss? Can losses fall on the entrepreneur, or must they fall on the resource owner?

If we include judgment as part of the entrepreneurial decision, then we can attribute loss to entrepreneurship. It will still be true, as Kirzner emphasizes, that people will be alert to possible profit opportunities. But where there is uncertainty, these opportunities are only possibilities. The decision to pursue a possible opportunity can result in a loss because of a faulty entrepreneurial judgment.

Mises clearly believed in the idea of entrepreneurial loss. "There is a simple rule of thumb," he says, "to tell entrepreneurs from non-entrepreneurs. The entrepreneurs are those on whom the incidence of losses on the capital employed falls."[20] Moreover, Mises condemned the idea of dealing with profit "without simultaneously dealing with its corollary, loss," and he assigned entrepreneurial loss an important role in the functioning of the social order.[21] "A social order based on private control of the means of production cannot work without entrepreneurial loss."[22]

Mises's views on entrepreneurial loss stem directly from his inclusion of judgment in entrepreneurship. For Mises, "It is the entrepreneurial decision that creates either profit or loss."[23] "What makes profit emerge is the fact that the entrepreneur who judges the future prices of the products more correctly than other people do buys some or all of the factors of production at prices which, seen from the point of view of the future state of the market, are too low. . . . On the 'other hand, the entrepreneur who misjudges the future prices of the products allows for the factors of production prices which, seen from the point of view of the future state of market, are too high."[24]

Summary

In his past work, Kirzner has defined entrepreneurship and described its effects in the market without considering uncertainty to any great extent. Once he considers uncertainty, Kirzner changes his definition of entrepreneurship. Earlier in his work it meant alertness to opportunities; now it means the motivated propensity to formulate an accurate image of the future, an image on which we can base our action. This latter definition is also referred to as man's alertness.

Kirzner sees uncertainty as the freedom of the actual future to diverge from our image of the future. This freedom provided additional scope for the exercise of alertness but leaves the essential nature of entrepreneurship and its primary function—coordinating market activity—unchanged.

Kirzner's emphasis on the similarity between his past and present views does serve a valuable function. His emphasis draws attention to the ability of entrepreneurship to reduce uncertainty and to coordinate present with future actions.

However, his emphasis on the similarity of his past and present views has led Kirzner still to look on entrepreneurship as alertness, and alertness does not (in normal usage) encompass the mental activity of judgment. Alertness is the mental quality of being on the lookout for something new; judgment is the mental process of assigning relevance to those things we already know. In an uncertain world, judgment influences the images we form of the world, and it chooses among courses of action whose outcomes are not known.

Judgment is a part of entrepreneurship as conceived by Mises, and it influenced his view of the market. Mises thought that entrepreneurial profit and loss should be treated together. He thought that profit resulted from superior foresight and judgment and that loss resulted from inferior foresight and judgment. The emphasis that Mises placed on judgment and entrepreneurial loss differentiates his view of the market process from that of Kirzner.

Notes

1. See Israel Kirzner, *Competition and Entrepreneurship* (Chicago: University of Chicago, 1973), pp. 15–16.

2. Ibid., p. 33.

3. Israel Kirzner, *Perception, Opportunity, and Profit* (Chicago: University of Chicago, 1979), p. 132.

4. Ibid., pp. 29–30.

5. Ibid., pp. 3–7.

6. Ludwig von Mises, *Human Action* (Chicago: Henry Regnery Co., 1966), p. 253.

7. Ibid., p. 110.

8. See chapter 12, p. 151.

9. See chapter 12, p. 149.

10. Ibid., p. 151.

11. See chapter 12, p. 154.

12. "The only source from which an entrepreneur's profits stem is his ability to anticipate better than other people the future demand of the consumers." Mises, *Human Action*, p. 290.

13. Bertrand de Jouvenel, *The Art of Conjecture* (New York: Basic Books, 1967), p. 59.

14. This corresponds to Kirzner's "motivated propensity" to see the future.

15. Compare Mises, *Human Action*, p. 56.

16. Ibid., p. 55.

17. Ibid., pp. 56–57.

18. Ibid., p. 58.

19. Kirzner, *Competition and Entrepreneurship*, p. 47.

20. Ludwig von Mises, "Profit and Loss," in *Planning for Freedom* (South Holland, Ill.: Libertarian Press, 1962), p. 112.

21. Mises, *Human Action*, p. 298.

22. Mises, "Profit and Loss," p. 149.

23. Ibid., p. 120.

24. Ibid., p. 109.

14 The Development of the Misesian Theory of Interventionism

Donald C. Lavoie

The aim of this chapter is to describe the evolution of the Misesian theory of internationalism from its first articulations by Ludwig von Mises to its modern reformulation by Murray N. Rothbard. The main focus will be on an emerging typology of interventionism according to which various government actions can be classified and their economic effects analyzed. It will be argued that Mises's theory of interventionism has undergone substantive changes, by both Mises and Rothbard, and further that these changes can be called extensions and improvements. The changes are extensions of the scope of the concept of interventionism to an increasing variety of categories of government policy to which the original form of argument was applicable. They can be called improvements because it is only this more comprehensive concept of interventionism that can adequately fit into the analytical role that Mises tried to make it play in his overall theory of economic policy.[1]

Origins of the Theory: Price Control

The earliest discussion by Mises of interventionism was a short section of his *Theory of Money and Credit* (1912) on "The Regulation of Prices by Authoritarian Decree" in which can be found in embryo the main features—both strengths and weaknesses—of his later and more developed analysis. The strengths, in this writer's view, are (1) his detailed account of the "phases" of action and reaction as spontaneous market forces respond to and frustrate attempts by the government to intervene into the market (in this case, control prices) (1912, pp. 245–249) and (2) his placement of the critique of interventionism into the wider context of the analysis of comparative economic systems, in particular his familiar statement that "there is no middle way" between capitalism and socialism (1912, p. 247). The major weakness of his critique of interventionism, I will argue, is his narrow focus on only some particular types of intervention (in this case only price control) even though the basic logic of his theory is much more general.

Since the purpose of this section in the 1912 book was limited to the relevance of price controls to monetary theory, a better starting point for examining the origins of Mises's theory of interventionism might be his more extensive paper on the "Theory of Price Controls" (1923). Here Mises offers his more detailed analysis of the "phases" of government action and market reaction, which constitutes the heart of his critique of interventionism.

Mises does not claim complete originality for his theory. As he pointed out in the first paragraph of this essay, the fundamental idea on which his critique of interventionism is based came from the demonstrations by the physiocrats and the classical economists that market prices are not arbitrary but determined by the conditions of supply and demand in the market. From this follows the classical economists' critique of price controls as "superfluous, useless, and harmful."

> It is superfluous because built-in forces are at work that limit the arbitrariness of the exchanging parties. It is useless because the government objective of lower prices cannot be achieved by controls. And it is harmful because it deters production and consumption from those uses that, from the consumer's viewpoint, are most important (1923, p. 140).

Clearly Mises saw himself as merely elaborating on this basic insight in classical economics that attempts to set prices by decree were inappropriate means to the ends sought. Mises added the following to this classical critique of interventionism: (1) He placed it in a wider context by relating it to the alternative economic systems of capitalism and socialism. (2) He presented a lucid step-by-step analysis of how market forces react to interventionist policy in such a way as to frustrate it at every turn.

The classical economists had formulated their criticism of price controls before the ascendancy of Marxian socialism and its advocacy not of the control over prices but of the complete abolition of the price system. The Marxist insisted that the market order is not the only option available to society but that central planning could undertake deliberately the functions performed spontaneously by the market. The choice is not laissez faire versus the interventionism that had been discredited by the classical economists. The choice is private versus common ownership of the means of production. As Mises points out, the doctrines of Marxism contain "the beginnings of this perception" that state intervention into a private property order is fundamentally incapable of achieving the redistributionary goals of the socialist movement (1923, p. 140).

It is one of Mises's significant contributions that he was able to place the critique of interventionism in the wider context of the study of comparative economic systems. Whereas to classical economists the critique of interventionism comprised the whole of their case for the classical liberal policy of laissez faire, to Mises it was but one component of a three-part argument.

1. We have three main types of economic order to choose among: socialism, capitalism, or interventionism.[2] Such other systems, such as syndicalism, which lack any kind of ordering mechanism, cannot be treated as a serious option for society. We could rely on the unhampered market as the ordering mechanism of the economy; we could use government policy to intervene in that mechanism; or we could select the Marxian alternative of central planning as a deliberate ordering mechanism and entirely dispense with the market. No viable fourth option has ever been formulated.

2. Of these three, socialism must be rejected for any technologically advanced society. As Mises's "calculation argument" showed, the economic order is too complex to be susceptible to deliberate control in the form of comprehensive central planning.[3] Market prices act as what he called "aids to the mind" for decentralized decision makers; these aids permit them to utilize far more knowledge than any one human mind could assimilate on its own. Thus the market system cannot be entirely abolished without reducing society's production processes to a very primitive level. The private property system cannot be replaced. All that remains is the possibility that it be regulated by some form of intervention.

3. But interventionism is itself not a viable option; either attempts to implement it must fail because of reactions by spontaneous market forces, or it must be carried further and more extensively until it is indistinguishable from socialism.

The bulk of Mises's 1923 essay on price controls is devoted to a discussion of how spontaneous market forces react to attempts at controlling prices in such a way as to lead interventionists either to expand their control until private property exists in name only, and thus its knowledge-generating function is subverted, or to accept defeat and cease intervening altogether. The point is not that interventionism is impossible but rather that a coherent, workable economic order founded on a principled application of interventionist policy is impossible. Isolated acts of intervention invariably result in responses by private owners and entrepreneurs, which in turn call forth more extensive policies of intervention.

Thus, for example, the government places a ceiling on the price of milk lower than that which the market would dictate, leading milk suppliers to respond by withholding milk from the market to await the lifting of the ceiling. This in turn leads milk buyers to look for and bid up the price of substitutes. The government counters by ordering milk suppliers to sell at the decreed price, but this disrupts the operation of the price-rationing mechanism, leading to arbitrary distribution of milk to those buyers "who come first" or "have personal connections." The government's attempts to regulate distribution do not eliminate the queues or the corruption and in any case only affect the distribution of the already available supply of milk. The existing inventories will soon be depleted, since milk production "no longer covers its cost," so the government will have to compel milk producers to supply their product even at a loss or to place ceilings on the factors of production such as cows and milking machines, whose costs now exceed the revenues permitted milk producers (1923, p. 145).

In this way the attempt to make the first control over a single price work necessitates the imposition of more extensive controls until, if the policy is pursued, there is nothing left of private ownership. Mises specifically refers to the war economy (from World War I) as an illustration of these fairly predictable "phases" of increasing interventionism: "at first price control, then forced sales, then rationing, then regulation of production and distribution, and, finally, attempts at central planning of all production and distribution" (1923, p. 146).[4]

These two related aspects of Mises's theory of interventionism, his placement of the critique of intervention into the wider context of comparative economic systems and his analysis of the phases of increasing intervention and market response, continued as the main themes of his later discussions of the subject. And in this writer's view these main themes have never been answered and still constitute the primary strengths of the Misesian theory of interventionism.

But just as the 1923 essay contained the essential strengths of the Misesian theory of interventionism, it equally reflects the main weakness of that theory, a weakness that Mises alleviated but never entirely eliminated in his later writings. Although the basic logic of his detailed analysis of interventionism is quite general, Mises persisted in applying it rather narrowly, in this case only to price controls. This was unfortunate not only because it prevented Mises from analyzing other types of intervention whose consequences were also subject to his critique, but more crucially, this narrow focus seriously weakened his broader argument concerning comparative economic systems. It was Mises's stated objective, even in 1923, to "reject all intervention as superfluous, useless, and harmful," and this is logically required if his argument for choosing among capitalism, socialism, and interventionism is to be complete (1923, p. 140). But, in fact, as the title of his 1923 essay makes clear, he was providing a detailed case against only one type of intervention, price control, leaving untouched the plethora of other forms of interventionist tools.[5] Thus this is not merely a complaint about other things we would all like Mises to have done. It represents a serious gap in his argument. That price controls cannot work is simply not sufficient for proving that there is no middle way between capitalism and socialism.

Broadening the Theory: Price Control and Production Restrictions

Mises's first attempt to present a general theory of interventionism, his 1926 essay "Interventionism," represents a clear advancement over his previous work. Here Mises offers a definition of interventionism that appears general enough to encompass a wide variety of types of government interference into the market order, and thus it is more appropriate to his contention that "there is no middle of the road" between capitalism and socialism (1926, p. 26). "Intervention is a limited order by a social authority forcing the owners of the means of production and entrepreneurs to employ their means in a different manner than they otherwise would" (1926, p. 20). The use of the phrase "limited order," Mises explains, is intended to distinguish interventionism from socialism, which aims at "directing the whole economy and replacing the profit motive of individuals with obedience as the driving force of human action" (1926, p. 20). Thus it might appear from this definition that any government policy, beyond that necessary for the preservation of private property and short of complete control over the means of production, qualifies as interventionism.

Yet Mises draws back from such an interpretation of his definition and proceeds to explicitly narrow its scope. First he excludes "partial socialization" from the category of interventionism. "Nationalization of a railroad constitutes no intervention; but a decree that orders an enterprise to charge lower freight rates than it otherwise would is intervention" (1926, p. 19). Actually this limitation can be reconciled with his quoted definition, since the nationalization of a railroad is not a "limited order" to private owners of railroads but a complete confiscation of their property. But this should argue for a still more general definition of interventionism, because in his critique of socialism Mises excluded partial socialization from his definition of socialism.[6] If the nationalization of a railroad is neither intervention nor socialism, nor, certainly, laissez faire capitalism, then perhaps it is the "middle way." The whole thrust of Mises's economic writings seems more consistent with the inclusion of nationalization of industries within the category of intervention into the market order.

The exclusion of government subsidies and of at least some forms of taxation from Mises's 1926 concept of interventionism is just as explicit—and just as disturbing—as his barring of nationalization from the concept. And there is a complete omission of the various types of macroeconomic interventionism such as monetary expansion and credit manipulation from his discussion (with the exception of a remark that government cannot enrich mankind by printing money). His 1926 categories of interventionism do not readily incorporate any of these kinds of policy, although they all involve the use of force, they all temporarily induce market participants to employ their resources in a manner different from the way they otherwise would, and they all invariably result in a spontaneous market reaction that at least partially frustrates the policy. Although there may be sufficient differences between, on the one hand, price control and product restrictions and, on the other, taxes, subsidies, or monetary expansion to warrant making them different types of intervention, it would seem to be inconsistent with Mises's overall perspective to omit the latter type altogether.

Mises insists that "government measures that use market means, that is, seek to influence demand and supply through changes of market factors, are not included in this concept of intervention" (1926, pp. 19-20).[7] When the government offers a subsidy that supplies milk to destitute mothers, he says, "there is no intervention" (1926, p. 20). Of course Mises is free to define intervention as narrowly as he wants, but doing so leaves a gap in his critique of the "middle way." He does not explain why an economic system in which the state taxed half of all incomes, and then used "market means" to purchase consumption goods from private owners, does not constitute a workable compromise between capitalism and socialism.

In a footnote Mises acknowledges that "there may be some doubt about the suitability of . . . interference by taxation which consists of expropriation of some wealth or income" as a category of intervention, and ndeed Mises was to add a separate category for confiscatory and redistributionary taxation in his later work. But Mises gives two reasons in 1926 for excluding taxation as a separate classification of interventionism. First, he says that the effects of such measures may in part be identical to those of another category that he does include, production restrictions.[8] Although this may be admitted, it is also true that taxation is different enough from other forms of intervention to justify separate analysis. Second, and less plausibly, he contends that taxation in part consists of "influencing the distribution of production income without restricting production itself." This statement I find in fundamental conflict with the whole Misesian analysis of the market order. Mises always emphatically argued that distribution in the market system is inextricably connected to the production process. There is no separate process of the production of goods that is followed by their distribution, rather the distribution of incomes is an integral part of the single process of capitalist production. As Mises phrased it, "under capitalism incomes emerge as the result of market transactions which are indissolubly linked up with production" (1922, p. 151).[9] One cannot arbitrarily redistribute incomes without drastically disturbing the process of production in the market. Thus the notion of taxes that somehow influence production income without disturbing production itself is difficult to reconcile with Mises's own depiction of the process of production under capitalism.

Despite these somewhat artificial restrictions of the scope of his concept of intervention, Mises does extend the idea to cover two main types of intervention: "restrictions of production" and "interference with the structure of prices" (1926, p. 20). Thus we see here a definite advance over his earlier treatments, which seemed to implicitly identify interventionism with price control, and we have for the first time a rudimentary typology of interventionism.

Although Mises does not offer as detailed an analysis of production restrictions as he had of price controls, his three pages on the former mention "protective tariffs," "class restrictions of trade and occupation" such as licenses, and labor legislation (1926, pp. 21-22). He offers no detailed analysis of the effects of these measures, but he does present a concise general statement of such effects.

> All production restrictions directly hamper some production inasmuch as they prevent certain employment opportunities that are open to the goods of higher order (land, capital, labor). By its very nature, a government decree that "it be" cannot create anything that has not been created before (1926, pp. 22-23).

All forms of production restrictions close off options that might have been available to entrepreneurs and capitalists, and thus are bound to reduce the number, variety, and value of new opportunities that otherwise would have been discovered. Since it is the discovery of such new opportunities for improving products and services that is the driving force of the market process, "we cannot calculate how much better those products and services would be today, without the expenditure of additional labor, if the hustle and bustle of government were not aiming (inadvertently, to be sure) at making things worse" (1926, p. 33). Since in Mises's system the market is viewed not as a mechanism for allocating known means to given ends but rather as what Hayek calls a "discovery procedure," we can never know what will fail to be discovered when we hamper that procedure.[10]

A More General Theory: The Inclusion of Taxation and Macrointervention

The outlines of a general Austrian theory of interventionism were already evident in Mises's 1926 essay, but his extensive discussion of "The Hampered Market Economy" in *Human Action* (1949) constitutes Mises's most comprehensive analysis of interventionism. One of the most serious limitations of his earlier presentations, the exclusion of at least some kinds of taxation from the category of intervention, is largely rectified. Furthermore Mises now explicitly includes a section on "Currency and Credit Manipulation," including foreign exchange control and legal tender laws, as varieties of intervention. Not only does Mises broaden the scope of interventionism to these new areas, he also provides a more substantive analysis of the general nature of interventionism. Despite these important revisions there is still room for improvement in the theory of interventionism as Mises left it, particularly as regards the nature of partial socialization and government expenditures.[11]

Mises begins his discussion of "Interference by Taxation" by conceiving of an ideal tax as one that is neutral rather than one that is just. A neutral tax, were it achievable, "would not divert the operation of the market from the lines in which it would develop in the absence of any taxation" (1949, p. 730). But after establishing this as the ideal Mises proceeds to point out that such a tax could only be possible "in the imaginary construction of the evenly rotating economy" under conditions of "perfect income equality" and that, since the "changing economy is entirely different from this imaginary construction," in the real world "no tax can be neutral" (1949, p. 731)[12] Thus Mises now treats taxation as a category of interventionism, which he nontheless still defines as he had in 1926 as any government policy that "forces the entrepreneurs and capitalists to employ some of the factors of production in a way different from what they would have resorted to if they were only obeying the dictates of the market" (1949, pp. 714–715).

Many of the deleterious effects of taxation are examined by Mises in his chapter on "Confiscation and Redistribution." The close resemblance of this critique of interference with the market by taxation to his critique of other forms of intervention are evident. The argument here as elsewhere is not that the market yields the best imaginable results—in this case some optimal distribution of wealth—but rather that (1) the market process is absolutely necessary for the preservation or expansion of any technologically advanced economy and (2) the intervention at issue—in this case taxation—seriously impedes, and if carried far enough completely undermines, the operation of this process. Not only does intervention sabotage the market mechanism, but the market by responding to the intervention equally sabotages it. Thus attempts to achieve a preconceived ideal distribution of wealth through taxes will not only reduce the total available for distribution but will also be continually undone by the redistributionary processes inherent in the workings of the market.

Mises's writings had from the very first treated government manipulation of the supply of money and credit as a harmful interference with the workings of the market process. Thus his explicit inclusion of a chapter in 1949 on these policies as instruments of interventionism is more a clarification of the broadened scope of the concept of intervention than it is a change in his views on the effects of such policies.[13]

Since both taxation and monetary expansion are now accepted by Mises as forms of interventionism, evidently there is no longer the loophole cited earlier concerning government expenditures. If there is no way government can obtain revenues without intervening into and thereby hampering the market, then there is no room for a "middle way" policy that is neither laissez faire capitalism nor socialism but that employs selective subsidies to improve on the operation of capitalism. The government cannot spend resources in its favored spheres of activity without forcibly withdrawing them from other spheres that are more highly valued by the consumers. As Mises puts it, "government does not have the power to encourage one branch of production except by curtailing other branches (1949, p. 737). Thus in contrast to his statement in 1926, "If government buys milk in the market in order to sell it inexpensively to destitute mothers or even to distribute it without charge, or if government subsidizes educational institutions" there *is* intervention (1926, p. 20).

Even so, Mises's treatment of taxation and subsidies is so one-sided as to leave unanalyzed a whole class of economic consequences on the expenditure side. When the government taxes and then spends, the distortions it imposes on the market are not confined to those revealed by a study of the incidence of the taxes per se. Rather the net effect of the government policy should contrast the government's use of resources with those uses the taxpayers would have made of them in the absence of the taxes. This should involve an analysis of the incidence of the government's spending as well as its taxing. The government intervenes when it collects its revenues and then intervenes again when it spends them on milk for destitute mothers or whatever instead of on what the taxpayers would have preferred. By focusing exclusively on the taxation side of the government budget, Mises's theory of interventionism still fails to cope fully with the economic impact of government expenditures.

Rothbard's Typology of Interventionism

The final form of Mises's theory of interventionism constitutes more an unordered list of types of government interference into the market than an actual typology. Rothbard's contributions to the Misesian theory of interventionism are his establishment of definite categories of intervention (into which the kinds of intervention Mises analyzed can be meaningfully classified), his further subdivisions and analysis of taxation (which Mises had included but said little about), his inclusionof government expenditure, and nationalization (which Mises had excluded altogether).

Rothbard's typology derives from the fact that in the free market the complex of voluntary relationships that develops can be reduced to a series of exchanges between two individuals, or autonomous actions by individuals. Thus a very natural way of classifying various forms of violent interference into the market is to distinguish them on the basis of how they impinge on these paired relationships and autonomous activities of the market.

An intervention that solely restricts an individual's autonomous activities Rothbard calls an "autistic intervention." When the government forces an individual to engage in a coerced exchange with it, this is called a "binary intervention." And when the government interferes with the otherwise voluntary relationship between a pair of individuals, Rothbard calls this a "triangular intervention."

Most of the interventionist policies to which Mises gave serious attention come under the category of triangular intervention, the interference with pairs of otherwise voluntary transactors in the market. Indeed Rothbard's two-way subdivision of triangular intervention bears great resemblance to Mises's 1926 classification of intervention: price control and product control (either by prohibition or by grant of monopoly privilege). The other two types of intervention Mises listed in 1949, taxation and monetary and credit expenditure, constitute the three subcategories of Rothbard's binary intervention. Autistic intervention, since it refers to isolated actions of an individual outside of the exchange nexus, does not pose any significant problems that are amenable to economic analysis.

Some clarification is in order concerning these categories as Rothbard uses them. First, although *binary intervention* is formally defined as a situation "where the intervener forces the subject to make an exchange or gift to the former," the category is used to cover cases that do not readily fit this definition (1962, p. 767). In particular Rothbard designates not only taxation, which clearly fits this definition, but also government expenditure, monetary expansion, and credit expansion as binary interventions.[14] In the case of government expenditure it is difficult to see how, by handing out a subsidy, the government is forcing the subject to make an exchange or gift to the intervener. Rather it seems that the government is completing a coerced transfer of wealth from one subject to another, which was begun when the taxes were collected. Similarly monetary and credit expansion involve not simple transfers of wealth from one subject to the intervener but rather a whole series of unpredictable transfers from those who happen to receive the new money relatively late in the inflation process to those—including but not confined to government—who get to spend the money relatively early. Perhaps a reformulation of the definition of binary intervention, to make it specifically include coerced transfers of wealth to others individuals as well as to the intervener, would help to clarify this.

A second caveat concerning Rothbard's typology is that the categories, as he admits, are not mutually exclusive. Some government policies such as tariffs can be put under both binary and triangular classifications, and "acts of binary intervention have definite triangular repercussions" (1970, p. 11). This may present serious difficulties in classifying some government policies and may even raise doubts about the cogency of the distinction between binary and triangular intervention. However, in the absence of a better typology, Rothbard's seems to be fully adequate for the task at hand: facilitating the systematic study of the economic effects of all forms of government intervention into the market order. For the purpose of carrying out this study it is not so important whether a license restriction that imposes a fee as a condition to enter an industry is analyzed as a triangular type because it is a form of product control or as a binary type because it is a form of taxation. For practical purposes it might be sufficient to simply decide on the basis of whether the primary purpose of the intervention is to manipulate production or prices directly (triangular) or to raise revenues or redistribute wealth, which would have indirect effects on production and prices (binary).

In addition to the articulation of a typology, the main contributions of Rothbard's analysis are in his examinations of the two subcategories of binary intervention that Mises had minimized or neglected: taxation and government expenditure.[15] By offering a more detailed study of the effects of taxation, and by explicitly including government expenditure as a form of intervention, Rothbard has substantively advanced the Misesian theory.

Although Mises distinguished among three "classes" of taxation, these classifications are not very satisfactory, nor was his analysis of any of them very detailed.[16] Rothbard provides a more helpful distinction between taxes on income and taxes on accumulated wealth and then further subdivides each of these according to type of income or wealth (1962; 1970). This procedure permits him to engage in a much more systematic analysis of the different economic effects associated with a wide variety of tax policies, from sales and excise taxes to taxes on wages, corporate income, profits, capital gains, gifts, and property.

I have argued that the main limitations of Mises's 1949 theory of interventionism was its failure to include nationalization and government expenditure as forms of intervention. As the description of Rothbard's typology of interventionism has shown, he assigned an important analytical role to the category of government spending. In addition, Rothbard was able to cope with nationalization both under this government expenditure category as well as under the rubric of "Grants of Monopolistic Privilege." Just as Rothbard had usefully broken taxation into analytical subcategories he also subdivides government expenditures into "transfer" and "resource-using" expenditures. The latter involve circumstances where the intervener determines the direction of spending of the forcibly collected revenues, and the former consist of circumstances where beneficiaries designated by the intervener spend the revenues.

In Rothbard's theory, then, the government subsidy to milk consumers that Mises had excluded is treated as interventionism of the binary, government-expenditures category and, within this, under the transfer-payments subcategory. The other government policy I have criticized Mises for excluding, the nationalization of an industry, is a bit more complicated but can readily fit into Rothbard's categories and can perhaps serve as an illustration of the analytical utility of these categories. First the act of nationalization itself entails the confiscation of the property of all the capitalists in that industry, clearly a form of binary intervention analogous to a lump-sum tax. Next the operation of the industry by a government bureau involves a second binary intervention of the resource-using government-expenditures variety. Then if the bureau runs a deficit further binary taxation interventions may be required. And in many cases the government may find it necessary to exclude legally potential new entrants into the industry from competing with the nationalized bureau, constituting an additional triangular intervention in the form of product control via a grant of monopoly privilege.

Conclusion

The basic form of argument that Mises employed in critique of price control has found an increasingly general application to a wide variety of government policies. In an economy that is founded on private property, voluntary exchange, and the market process, attempts to violently manipulate the outcomes of this process lead to reactions that the intervener can neither specifically predict nor effectively prevent. Efforts to make the initial intervention work as designed must take the form of ever-wider and more obtrusive interventions, which are in further conflict with the workings of the market mechanism. In the end the interventionists must either extend their activities to the point where the process has been completely sabotaged or they must abandon their quest to control the market. Any "middle way" between these extremes may, of course, be advocated but would consist in a series of haphazard shocks to the economic system, scarcely any more deserving of the label "policy" than it would be to call throwing a monkey wrench into a complex piece of machinery "engineering." And of the two extremes the policy that abandons the market process altogether must—for reasons Mises presented in his critique of socialism—also abandon the benefits of a technologically advanced economy.

The proliferation of new forms of government interference into the market is certain to present many new challenges for the analyst in the future. Rothbard's extensive applications of the Misesian theory were far from exhaustive when he wrote them, and numerous interventionist innovations that require further study have since appeared. But I believe all these will prove susceptible to the Misesian critique of interventionism and that this susceptibility is enhanced by the extensions of the scope of the theory that Mises and Rothbard have made and, in particular, to the inventions by the latter of a general typology into which any interventionist policy can be classified.

Notes

1. I have limited the focus of this chapter to the scope of the concept of interventionism because I believe that the main substance of the Misesian

theory of interventionism has not undergone any important change by Mises or his students. Only the scope—the range of application—of the argument has evolved over time, while the essence of the argument has remained the same and is firmly rooted in Mises's theory of the market process.

2. In this chapter I will loosely refer to society's "options" or "choices" among economic systems, despite the fact that strictly speaking, of course, societies do not choose their economic systems or anything else for that matter. An economic system is not consciously chosen but rather evolves under economic and ideological influences.

3. See Mises (1922). The chronological order in which Mises formulated these three steps of argument was (1), (3), and then (2), as is illustrated by the quoted comments about interventionism in Mises (1912), written before he had articulated the calculation argument. However the order used here is more convenient for explaining the logical place of the critique of interventionism in Mises's system of thought.

4. But of course there is nothing inevitable in this sequence of increasing government control over economic life. A change in ideology that favors abandoning this trend can quickly reverse its direction, as Mises hoped would one day happen. See John Hagel (1975).

5. In the 1920s price control was probably the most popular form of interventionism advocated, but this is no longer the case.

6. See Mises (1922, p. 119): "nationalized and municipalized undertakings within an otherwise capitalist system are not Socialism."

7. The use of the market means to accomplish interventionist goals is not a clearcut way to distinguish Mises's price and product control from other government policies. Any violent intervention into the market relies on the market as a necessary surrounding environment and at the same time employs nonmarket means to alter the direction in which this environment would have otherwise developed.

8. Mises, both in 1926 and in 1949, wanted to include some taxation such as tariffs under his production-restriction category.

9. See also Mises (1949, p. 800): ". . . in the market economy this alleged dualism of two independent processes, that of production and that of distribution, does not exist. There is only one process going on. Goods are not first produced and then distributed. There is no such thing as an appropriation of portions out of a stock of ownerless goods. The products come into existence as somebody's property. If one wants to distribute them, one must first confiscate them." Incidentally, this statement seems to argue against Mises's 1926 dichotomy between taxation (as at least sometimes restrictive) and subsidization (as never restrictive). Rather these two policies should be viewed as connected aspects of the same redistributionary type of intervention.

10. On this discovery-hindering aspect of interventionism see Kirzner

(1978). This essay also offers a fascinating argument that relates Mises's critique of interventionism to his calculation argument against socialism.

11. I have not been able to find any discussion by Mises that retracts his 1926 exclusion of nationalization from the concept of interventionism.

12. In a recent paper Rothbard seemed to suggest that Mises thought a neutral tax was achievable in the real world. This may have been true of the Mises of 1926, but I cannot see how the Mises of 1949 can be so interpreted.

13. Mises had in 1929 intended to include a chapter on the manipulation of credit in his original German edition of *A Critique of Interventionism,* which suggests that he already considered macroeconomic policy as a category of intervention (1977, p. 153).

14. Rothbard's reason for including monetary and credit expansion under the binary category is that "creating new money is, anyway, a form of taxation" (1962, p. 794). It could plausibly be included under the triangular category also, on the grounds that eroding the value of the monetary unit undermines all the outstanding contracts that have been made in terms of that unit, thus intervening with pairs of transactors.

15. Rothbard claims that "writers on political economy have recognized only the [triangular] type as intervention" (1970, p. 10). Although I would agree that most writers, including Mises, have neglected government expenditure and have offered very little analysis of taxation, Mises did (at least by 1949) specifically recognize taxation and monetary and credit manipulation as forms of intervention.

16. Mises tried to distinguish among three "classes" of tax intervention: (1) taxes that aim "at totally suppressing or at restricting the production of definite commodities," (2) taxes that expropriate income and wealth "entirely." The last of these he dismisses as "merely a means for the realization of Socialism," and the first he subsumes under the production-restrictions category (1949, pp. 734–735). Only his second class of tax intervention, "confiscatory measures," receives separate attention (chap. 33).

References

Hagel, John, III. 1975. From laissez-faire to Zwangswirtschaft: the dynamics of interventionism (presented at the June 1975 Symposium on Austrian Economics).

Kirzner, Israel M. 1978. The perils of regulation: market-process approach. *Law and Economics Center: Occasional Paper* (Coral Gables, Fla.: University of Miami School of Law, 1978).

Mises, Ludwig von. 1912. *The theory of money and credit,* trans. H.E. Batson. Irvington-on-Hudson, N.Y.: Foundation for Economic Education, 1971.

————. 1922. *Socialism: an economic and sociological analysis,* trans. J. Kahane. London: Jonathan Cape, 1936.

————. 1923. Theory of price controls,'' in Mises (1977).

————. 1926. Interventionism, in Mises (1977).

————. 1949. *Human action: a treatise on economics. London: William Hodge, 1949.*

————. *1977. A critique of interventionism.* New Rochelle, N.Y.: Arlington House, 1977.

Rothbard, Murray N. 1962. *Man, economy, and state: a treatise on economic principles.* Los Angeles: Nash, 1962.

————. 1970. *Power and market: government and the economy.* Menlo Park, Calif.: Institute for Humane Studies, 1970.

15 Interventionism: Comment on Lavoie

Murray N. Rothbard

I was delighted to read Professor Lavoie's chapter. As far as I know, he is the first person to mention, let alone stress, the importance of my own contributions to the typology of government intervention. This makes Lavoie, in my own biased view at least, an unusually perceptive economist.

My development of the three categories of intervention—autistic, binary, and triangular—stemmed from unhappiness at the way in which economists were analyzing intervention. Even Mises, so systematic in every other area, treated various forms of government intervention on a piece-by-piece, ad hoc basis. Hence I sought a systematic way of categorizing and analyzing different forms of intervention.

It then became clear that free-market economists who opposed government intervention generally confined their opposition to what I have called "triangular" intervention: that is, government interference in exchanges between pairs of subjects. But, for some reason, when the government itself compelled someone to make an "exchange" with it, this was somehow omitted from the discussion. Yet, it was clear to me that this "binary" intervention was at least as much a coerced diversion from the voluntary activities of the market as the more conventional triangular variety—that, in short, taxation is fully as much an act of intervention as, say, price control.

On Don Lavoie's criticisms, I concede his point that it is incomplete to simply define binary intervention as the intervener, for example, the government, compelling someone to transfer something to itself. As Lavoie points out, this would cover taxation but not government expenditures financed by taxation. I agree with Lavoie that government expenditures should be treated as the completed result of a coerced transfer beginning with taxation, and the definition of binary intervention needs reformulation accordingly. In my defense, however, I would point out that in practice, in *Power and Market,* especially in treating government subsidies, this is precisely what I did. Expenditures were treated as completing coercion levied on taxpayers. Second, as Lavoie points out, specific acts of government intervention can overlap both the binary and triangular categories. The categories, however, are still helpful in analyzing and distinguishing between the various consequences.

I will go beyond Lavoie in self-criticism and underline my own unhappiness with the subdivision of government expenditures between "resource using" and "transfer payments." This distinction, of course, is not my own creation. The problem is that all government expenditures whatsoever are transfer payments, the only difference being whether a group of people calling themselves "government" acquire the money and the resources or whether other groups acquire the money and the resources *from* the government. Despite this problem, however, I still believe it is useful to distinguish between expenditures in which the government uses the resources and those where the government functions as a conduit for others.

Also, more needs to be done on monetary inflation as binary intervention. I believe Lavoie is correct in focusing on the transfers from the late to the early receivers of the new money. The crucial point is government money creation as a species of counterfeiting, in which resources are fraudulently—and therefore coercively—siphoned off from producers to the gainers from the counterfeiting operation.

Returning to the idea of government expenditures as the completion of a coercive act beginning with taxation, let us assume that $A, B, C, \ldots$ and so on are taxed a total of $10 billion and that the $10 billion are transferred to $X, Y, Z, \ldots$ and so on. The major point of taxation is precisely to transfer resources from one set of people to another, the recipients including the government itself among others. But suppose that the $10 billion, after being collected, are destroyed in a great bonfire. In that case, $A, B, C, \ldots$ would still lose the $10 billion, and they would lose the same amount of resources. Since the money supply would fall, everyone except $A, B, C, \ldots$ would gain proportionately from the general deflation. Clearly, such instances are rare; in all other cases, expenditures are necessary to complete the coercive transaction and the transfer of resources.

To move on to broader concerns, let us ponder the implications of our new approach for the free-market economist. For the economist now finds that, in addition to the almost conventional attacks he may make on price controls or grants of monopoly privilege, binary intervention is just as much an intervention and perhaps just as reprehensible as the more familiar triangular categories. But if he is to oppose all binary intervention, too, the free-market economist must oppose all actions of the government whatsoever, since almost all such acts involve taxation and certainly all involve expenditures. And this would mean that the government, including the one under which he is forced to live, ineluctably takes on the praxeological status of an organization of banditti. Sociologically, the economist might even find himself a maverick or even a pariah among his fellow free-market economists, let alone in the profession as a whole.

Fortunately, the consistent free-market economist has the consolation of knowing that one of the fathers of our discipline, J.B. Say, held many similar views. Thus, in rebutting the argument that taxes are harmless because they are recirculated into the economy by the state, Say quotes with approval Robert Hamilton who compared such impudence with the "forcible entry of a robber into a merchant's house, who should take away his money, and tell him he did him no injury, for the money, or part of it, would be employed in purchasing the commodities he dealt in, upon which he would receive a profit." Say then comments that "the encouragement afforded by the public expenditure is precisely analogous." Say then goes on to define taxation as: "the transfer of a portion of the national products from the hands of individuals to those of the government, for the purpose of meeting the public consumption of expenditure. . . . It is virtually a burden imposed upon individuals . . . by the ruling power . . . for the purpose of supplying the consumption it may think proper to make at their expense. . . ."[1] Say's hard-hitting politicoeconomic conclusion was eminently consistent with our current analysis. He declared that "the best scheme of finance is, to spend as little as possible; and the best tax is always the lightest."[2]

But even in the seemingly uncomplicated area of triangular intervention, there are deeper implications than might at first appear. If a free-market economist, for example, declares that A and B should be allowed to exchange goods or services without hindrance, then what if A or B are themselves interveners or participants in intervention? In short, if A has a horse and B a cow, and the economist is to advocate free and unhampered exchange between them, then suppose that A had stolen the horse from C a few weeks earlier? In that case, A was a previous intervener in the market and should himself at the very least be forced to give the horse back to C. Although it is true that this action will disrupt possible exchanges of property between A and B, it also restores the possibility of exchanges between B and C, or between C and someone else.

To put it another way: when free-market economists advocate free exchanges, they are saying that A and B, B and C, D and E, and all other possible pairs of people should be allowed to exchange their products freely. But exchanges are concretely transfers of property titles. In our previous example, if a horse is exchanged for a cow, then a property title in a horse is being exchanged for a title in a cow. But to say that A and B should be free to exchange property titles implies immediately that both property titles are valid, that is, that A and B legitimately own their property. For if, as we have seen, A has stolen his horse from C, this means that the government, if that is the justice-pursuing agency, cannot simply abstain from intervening in A's property title. For if theft is to be illegal, C is the true owner rather than A, and A's alleged property must be seized by the government and handed over to C, the legitimate owner.

We cannot, then, even talk about the free market without also talking about property titles. But, more than that, we cannot talk about the free market or about property without committing ourselves to *some* theory of justice in property titles, some way of deciding between, say, *A*'s and *C*'s competing claims to the same horse. Unless the decision is purely arbitrary, it can only be on the basis of some theory of justice in property.

The consistent free-market economist is now in parlous shape. He is close to concluding not only that government itself is illegitimate but also that the free market implies some theory of justice in property rights. But this means that he is likely to be a pariah, not only for his political stance but also for believing that applied economics cannot keep separate and watertight the realms of fact and value. In both these areas the free-market economist must find himself differing from, even while standing on the shoulders of, Ludwig von Mises. But he has the consolation of knowing that the same Mises, in never shirking the task of following the truth no matter where it might lead, is ever his inspiration and guide.

Notes

1. Jean-Baptiste Say, *A Treatise on Political Economy,* 6th ed. (Philadelphia: Claxton, Remsen, and Haffelfinger, 1880), pp. 413, 446; quoted in Murray N. Rothbard, "The Myth of Neutral Taxation," *The Cato Journal* 1 (Fall 1981):551–552.

2. Say, *Treatise,* p. 449; Rothbard, "Myth," p. 554.

16 Monopoly in Theory and Practice

Gerald P. O'Driscoll, Jr.

In dealing with every case of monopoly prices one must first of all raise the question of what obstacles restrain people from challenging the monopolists. —Ludwig von Mises

The Theoretical Issue

The central theoretical issue to be solved by any monopoly theory is the entry problem. If monopoly yields a net revenue or surplus, then why does entry of new firms not occur? The profitability of monopoly should ensure its own demise. However it characterizes monopoly and whatever else it does, a theory must confront this issue.

My point can be quickly restated by aid of figure 16–1, a familiar graph. A single producer confronts the entire demand for a good and accordingly charges a price, $\bar{P}$ and an output, $\bar{Q}$. On the assumption that price discrimination is absent, all the familiar conditions of monopoly are present (for example, average revenue exceeds marginal cost). It is commonplace that attaining a monopoly does not automatically confer supranormal returns. No one would seek a monopoly position, however, unless he expected to earn returns in excess of revenues foregone. Why then do others not follow suit or imitate the first rent seeker, thus breaking down the monopoly and competing away that monopoly rent?

A second, related question faced by monopoly theories is how to deal with the deadweight loss created by setting price above marginal cost of production. This loss represents an unexploited profit opportunity. The existence of persistent, unexploited profit opportunities is inconsistent with the standard assumptions of economic theory. Further, as I will argue, standard (neoclassical) monopoly theory implies that there is an unexploited

I would like to thank especially Richard Langlois and Mario Rizzo for their insightful comments and assistance at crucial junctures. The comments of Israel Kirzner, Bruno Stein, and Lawrence H. White were each helpful on key points. I benefited from discussion by participants at the Liberty Fund conference in honor of the 100th anniversary of Ludwig von Mises's birth.

Part of the research for this chapter was supported by a grant from the Scaife Family Charitable Trusts. That support is gratefully acknowledged.

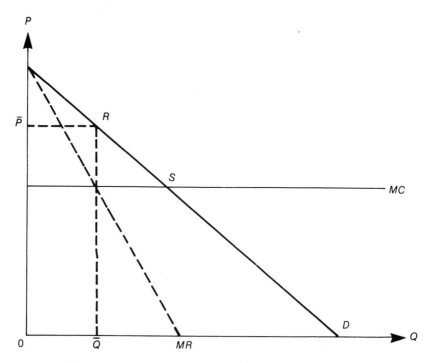

Figure 16-1. Equilibrium for Neoclassical Monopolist

surplus on the margin in "equilibrium" for a monopolist. This implication is inconsistent with the assumptions of general economic theory. Something needs to be changed.

In this chapter, I shall adopt a historical approach in examining the options open to theorists. This approach helps place in perspective standard approaches to monopoly analysis, as well as revealing at least two avenues of theoretical development that in retrospect appear superior to the current road we are traveling. One of these approaches is far more consistent with the modern property-rights approach adopted extensively in other areas of economics than is neoclassical monopoly theory.

The second alternative was suggested by Carl Menger but, surprisingly, was not developed by later Austrian economists. Modern Austrians divide in their development of monopoly theory. Some, such as Ludwig von Mises and Israel Kirzner, present a variant of the neoclassical theory. Others, such as Murray Rothbard and Dominic Armentano, present a distinctive theory with roots deep in the history of economics and with strong affinity to the common-law treatment of monopoly. Their theory is not, however, the outcome or development of any particular Austrian insight. To anticipate a conclusion, a distinctively Austrian theory of monopoly remains to be written.

Monopoly in Law

Concept and Practice

In Anglo-Saxon thought, *monopoly* is a legal and social concept predating its use and specialized meaning in economics. The term arose not as a scientific abstraction but as a description of certain concrete, objectionable policies. By the eighteenth century, monopoly had a definite meaning in law and in political discourse. This meaning was introduced into modern political economy by Adam Smith. Eventually, usage and meaning changed, and monopoly became a scientific term. In a linguistic turning of the tables, this specialized usage influenced subsequent legal and political thinking about monopoly.

The process just outlined has not been wholly salutary. It is doubtful if the modern economic concept of monopoly is fruitful or otherwise superior to the clear meaning evolved in English common law. Even if it were true that the modern economic concept of monopoly is theoretically useful or informative, severe problems with applying it to public-policy questions would remain. Indeed, in this chapter I argue that economists now have little useful to say about public policy toward monopoly because of the way in which the concept has evolved in economics. Before being able to demonstrate convincingly these points, I must turn to the historical development of the monopoly concept and monopoly theory.

The Common Law

According to Sir Edward Coke:

> a monopoly is an institution, or allowance by the king, by his grant, commission, or otherwise, to any person or persons, bodies politique, or corporate, of or for the sole buying, selling, making, working, or using any thing, whereby any person or persons, bodies politique, or corporate, are sought to be restrained of any freedom or liberty that they had before, or hindered in their lawful trade.[1]

He was joined in this view by William Blackstone, who defined monopoly as "a license or privilege allowed by the king for the sole buying and selling, making, working, or using of any thing whatsoever; whereby the subject in general is restrained from that liberty of manufacturing or trading which he had before.''[2] Not surprisingly, the common-law view was absorbed into American jurisprudence. In the *Charles River Bridge* case, the U.S. Supreme Court defined monopoly as ''the withdrawal of that which is a common right from the community and vesting it in one or more individuals, to the exclusion of all others.''[3]

Although Coke's claim that monopoly was void at common law has been questioned, there is little doubt that his definition and characterization of monopoly accurately reflected a view that predominated by the end of the eighteenth century.[4] Condemnation of letters patent, as restraints on freedom to trade and to produce, attained wide currency as liberal ideals flourished and political economy developed.

Blackstone perceived English common law to be grounded in Saxon law and custom. In his *Commentaries,* Blackstone pursued a purified legal code, cleansed of alien intrusions and recrudescences.[5] Many monopolies granted to corporations and bodies politic resulted from the Norman conquest.[6] Characterizing these as restraints on ''that liberty of manufacturing or trading which (the subject) had before'' fits with Blackstone's view of English law and society. Not monopolies, but the ancient rights of man were custom from time immemorial.

The system of granting letters patent to court favorites reached its heyday under Elizabeth. In a notorious case, Elizabeth's grant of a playing-card monopoly to her groom, Darcy, was struck down by the Court of King's Bench.[7] Eventually, with the Statute of Monopolies of 1624, Parliament asserted itself against royal prerogatives. But this case cannot be viewed as an early precursor to the Sherman Act or even as an antimonopoly statute.[8] The law decided a constitutional issue, whereby Parliament asserted its right over the Crown's to grant monopolies. ''By whom and for whom'' were the issues, not monopoly as such.[9]

The Stuarts raised to high art the granting of monopolies for revenue. They thereby did violence to Parliament's prerogatives in at least two respects. First, they reasserted the Crown's claim to grant monopolies to its favorites as opposed to those of Parliament. Second, they circumvented Parliament on revenue collection. The outcome of that struggle is history.

Consistent, general hostility to monopoly grants and privileges only developed later. Indeed, what is frequently taken to be a precursor of antimonopoly sentiment and policy more often evidenced the dominance of the opposite view. Common and statutory law on forestalling, engrossing, and regrating evolved in a climate of overt hostility to markets. These laws disappeared only with the ascendancy of promarket feelings and policies. These laws were part of a general policy of detailed economic regulation, which attained its zenith in the middle ages with the guild system. The direct effect and intent of these laws was to prevent speculation and provision of middlemen services in food-stuffs.[10] They also protected the monopoly grants made to private owners of town markets. In this, the laws were virtually the enforcement mechanism for these grants. In prohibiting purchases outside legally sanctioned markets, laws against forestalling, regrating, and engrossing enriched the monopolist owners of markets. William Letwin cites the case of the Prior of Coventry (1308), who sued several individuals selling outside his market, averring that he thereby "lost stallage, terrage, and cottage, etc., wrongfully and to his damage."[11]

Medieval attitudes and policies hostile to competition are not precursors of eighteenth-century attacks on monopoly. The former buttressed a system of monopoly, aptly described by Sir John Culpepper in his characterization of English monopolies:

> Like the frogs of Egypt they have gotten possession of our dwellings, and we have scarce a room free from them. They sup in our cup; they dip in our dish; they sit by our fires. We find them in the dye fat, wash bowl and powdering tub. They share with the butler in his box; they will not bait us a pin. We may not buy our clothes without their brokerage. These are the leeches that have sucked the Commonwealth so hard that it is almost hectical.[12]

As is generally recognized, the laws on forestalling, regrating, and engrossing fell into disuse and were repealed with the rise of the commercial society and of liberal or laissez faire economic thinking.[13] Even those authors who argue that these laws restrained monopolistic practices recognize that they stood in the way of modern competitive, society.[14] Being part of feudal and monopolistic regulation of the economy, the laws were an impediment to the development of markets. It is anomalous to argue that the laws were precursors of modern antitrust policy.[15]

Monopoly in Economics

Classical Political Economy

In the *Wealth of Nations,* Adam Smith set down a continuous barrage of arguments and invective against the state's exercise of its police powers over the economy. The concept of monopoly as a privilege, violating the natural liberty of citizens, was congenial to Smith's goal. After pointing out that monopolists undersupply effectual demand and raise price and their profits above the natural level,[16] Smith contrasted the "price of monopoly" and the "price of free competition": "The one is upon every occasion the highest which can be squeezed out of the buyers, or which, it is supposed, they will consent to give: The other is the lowest which the sellers can commonly afford to take, and at the same time continue their business."[17]

As will be seen, all the major elements of classical and neoclassical monopoly theories are present in Smith. In a preponderant number of cases, however, Smith employed one clear monopoly concept—that of an exclusive government grant excluding would-be competitors. His extensive discussions of monopolies over colonial trade clearly support my thesis. At one point, he makes an analogy between a temporary monopoly over foreign trade and the "monopoly of a new machine . . . granted to its inventor, and that of a new book to its author."[18] In each case, the source of monopoly is a special government privilege granted to certain individuals restricting the natural liberty of other citizens.

It is revealing what Smith did not consider to be a source of monopoly. Ignorance of profit opportunities or trade secrets each result in market price being above natural price, a condition that "may sometimes last for many years thereafter."[19] These were "particular accidents" raising price above cost of production. Monopoly was treated as a distinct category, resulting from different sources and being more pernicious in its effects.

Land is not a clear exception to my theses, for the Ricardian view that landownership confers monopoly is not yet fully developed in the *Wealth of Nations*. In his discussion, "Of the Natural and Market Price of Commodities," Smith considers land but places it in the category of trade secrets rather than "a monopoly granted to an individual or trading company." Some goods require "singularity of soil and situation." These produce a land rent "paid above its natural rate: These commodities may be sold at prices above their natural prices" for whole centuries."[20] Again, there is a distinction between temporary scarcity prices and high prices because of government intervention through the creation of monopolies.

In analyzing rent, Smith does consider land as a monopoly. But he here refers to local monopolies, which will be broken down by transportation improvements and extensions of markets. His point is to show once again how business uses state power to insure monopoly, when competition would otherwise prevail. He recounted how landlords in counties adjacent to London petitioned Parliament against turnpike extensions to remoter counties.[21] They wished to preserve their high locational rents. This is a case of monopoly involving governmental support.

In dealing with taxation of land rent, Smith seemingly equates the scarcity price of superior land with monopoly price. But note his phrasing: "when the ordinary price of any particular produce of land is *at what may be called a monopoly price,* a tax upon it necessarily reduces the rent and profit of the land which grows it."[22] He seems to be suggesting an analogy between scarcity and monopoly price. For the purpose there at issue, they were treated similarly, for taxation has similar effects on their component parts. As Smith clearly noted in previous discussions, the sources or causes of monopoly, on the one hand, and natural scarcities, on the other hand, are quite different.

Smith does switch his analogy to equating scarcity and monopoly price in the rent-taxation case. Such a switch in concepts is consistent with Smith's eclecticism in analysis and in use of concepts.[23] Nowhere is this eclecticism more evident than in his treatment of land, whose rent sometimes is and sometimes is not a cost of production.

To repeat, in the preponderance of cases, Smith viewed monopoly as a government restriction on competition in trade and manufacturing.

Smith adopted a property-rights theory of monopoly, which he treated as a legal-political problem. The form of legal institutions, the pattern of property rights, and the impact of public policy determined whether market forces would tend to establish prices at their "natural" level. If the government did not take positive steps to stay these market forces, then they would be operative in every market. "Particular accidents" might intervene to abate competitive market forces, but their presence would always be felt. Monopoly meant the active suppression of market forces by government fiat. Monopoly was not something that just happened on the market without the influence of exogenous disturbances. Thus, for Smith, self-interest and the appropriate property rights and legal institutions ensured competition. Only government could create monopoly, for no other institution has the ability to exclude potential entrants attracted by above-normal returns. Its control over the political-legal apparatus makes the state essentially different from any other social institution.

Even where Smith saw intervening causes staying the movement of prices down to costs, he saw these as typically unimportant in practice. Of trade secrets, he observed that: "secrets of this kind, however, it must be acknowledged, can seldom be long kept; and the extraordinary profit can last very little longer than they are kept."[24] The Ricardians would make more of land monopoly, but this latter concept just did not play an important part in the *Wealth of Nations.*

Thus Smith implicitly answered the central question posed at the beginning of this chapter. Above-normal profits would be competed away in a private-property-rights system with open markets. Free entry and private greed insured this. No form of monopoly, save perhaps that of specialized land, is a natural market phenomenon.

David Ricardo moved economics away from a property-rights approach to monopoly and competition. Monopolized goods were those in absolutely inelastic supply. Monopoly value, unlike competitive value, was determined by demand and supply rather than by costs. Works of art and products of superior land (for example, great wines) were Ricardo's paradigm case of monopoly. Specialized land earns a monopoly return because the quantity of its output is not augmentable. According to Ricardo, in such cases there is no competition among sellers. For the products of such land, "their price is limited only by the extent and power and will of the producers."[25] What in Smith was a special case, an exception, became the paradigm in Ricardo.

The Ricardian shift redirected attention away from government and public policy as the source of monopoly to a quest for divisions in market organizations inherent in the type of good or in the economy's parameters. As was so often true, Ricardo desired an institutionless explanation of a phenomenon.

Nassau Senior both generalized Ricardo's monopoly concept and provided a much more systematic treatment of the topic. According to Senior, "equal competition" occurs when all can compete "with equal advantages," that is, when production is at constant cost. Whenever natural resources are used in production, however, there will be increasing cost. In modern terms, there will be economic rent. For Senior, who extended Ricardo's preoccupation with rent and income distribution, the existence of rent created distinct theoretical and practical problems. "A commodity thus produced is called the subject of a *monopoly; and* the person who has appropriated such a natural agent, a *monopolist.*"[26]

Senior adduced four types of monopoly, including scale economies, patented processes, naturally scarce goods, and "THE GREAT MONOPOLY OF LAND."[27] Special attention is paid to land, which is no longer just Ricardo's French vineyards, but all land. For Senior, monopoly occurs whenever production yields a surplus over cost, that is, a surplus over wages of labor and abstinence. Unlike Smith, Senior did not see even minimal land rent as being part of cost.

Three points must be made about the Ricardian monopoly theory. First, it focuses on supply or cost conditions, not demand or demand elasticity. The level of demand does affect the size of the monopoly surplus. The elasticity of demand simply does not enter into the picture. With their concern over distribution and the size and growth of rent, Ricardians were led to categorize markets on the basis of cost conditions.

Second, in Ricardian analysis, monopoly exists if a surplus (economic rent) exists. In neoclassical monopoly theory, monopoly is one possible source of rent.

Third, whatever else its merits or justification in terms of a research program, the Ricardian concept of monopoly redirected economists' attention. Smith's property-rights approach on this and other topics was eclipsed. Neoclassical economists eventually took up the problem of a generalized rent concept and the laws of cost. Thus twentieth-century economists adopted the pose of discussing monopoly in an institutionless context. Government is only brought in as a sort of deus ex machina, to solve a spontaneous monopoly problem arising on unregulated markets. It was not even noted that the Ricardian formulation trivialized the central question of this chapter. Entry does not occur in a Ricardian monopoly because, *ex hypothesi,* cost conditions make entry unprofitable. Neoclassical economists reformulated monopoly in terms of demand rather than cost factors. But the entry problem remained unsolved and tended not even to be raised forcefully until recent times.

The Neoclassicals

Modern monopoly theory is certainly constructed from Marshallian elements, but this is not Alfred Marshall's theory. In the *Principles,* Marshall postulated that *monopoly value* occurs whenever "a single person or association of persons has the power of fixing either the amount of a commodity that is offered for sale or the price at which it is offered."[28] This statement about monopoly price is consistent with a wide variety of monopoly theories, including either the Smithian or Ricardian theories. Marshall's own views are not entirely clear in the *Principles.* We do know that he felt that an individual confronting a downward-sloping demand curve was consistent with competition.[29]

There is evidence that Marshall thought of competition and monopoly in Smithian terms. He prefered defining competition as "Economic Freedom." His examples of monopoly all involved legal monopolies, although they tended also to involve scale economies (for example, gas works).[30]

Thus as late as Marshall's *Principles* (the turn of the century), we do not yet have neoclassical monopoly theory. Nonetheless, key theoretical elements had been developed, such as the analysis of price elasticity and marginal revenue. From this, it would not be a great leap to pick up on Smith's suggestion that monopolists exploit demand curves. This, of course, would mean dropping some Ricardian baggage, something the neoclassicals were generally eager to do.

Yet the origins of neoclassical monopoly theory have proved elusive. It has even been suggested that what we have today is a flawed attempt at reconstructing what earlier writers meant in their discussions of monopoly.[31] New elements were introduced into monopoly discussions at the turn of the century. In American economics, which gained new importance in this era, those economists educated at German universities played a prominent role in this process—Richard T. Ely is exemplary in this respect.

As modern economics evolved, land ceased playing the special role it had in Ricardian economics. Nonetheless, one Ricardian legacy persisted. This was the idea that some goods are inherently produced under monopolistic and others under competitive conditions. The rationale for this supposed natural division changed. Ely concisely articulated the new view.

In the new view, technology and not land was the key factor. Natural monopoly acquired great importance, both in theory and in political discussions of utility consolidation and regulation. Ely described a natural monopoly as "a pursuit . . . excluded from the steady, constant pressure of competition."[32] Increasing returns were the necessary condition. Not only did Ely view natural monopoly as an important problem in itself, but he also argued that other monopolies ("artificial monopolies") depended for their existence on a "tie" to a natural monopoly. Tariffs and other protective legislation help foster artificial monopolies, but tariff reform would not eliminate them.[33] Ely thus generalized an idea prevalent in the literature on railway economics: railroad-rate discrimination, the product of natural monopoly, created industrial monopoly in otherwise competitive industries.

Ely's theory viewed monopoly as a spontaneous market phenomenon. His theory did have an answer to this chapter's central question. Accepting that natural monopolies exist, we can explain why competition could not be a permanent condition. In fact, Ely was worried that mistaken legislators would seek to foster competition in such situations. Attempts to do so would lead to competitive "waste" and "bring about commercial crises and stagnation in business."[34]

In Ely's time, economists were gaining new political and social importance. Ely was conscious of this process and exploited it in propounding his views. Much of his writing addressed topical public-policy questions of the day in newspapers and magazines, such as *Harper's* (in which he had a column at one point). Breaking with longstanding American tradition, Congress turned to professional experts, such as economists, in framing legislation and policy. Ely couched his theories to fit these realities.

Like many of his colleagues, Ely had acquired a naive and uncritical faith in government's ability to solve social problems, particularly at the local and state level. This accorded well with the "civic" movements that accompanied the Progressive tide in the early twentieth century. Ely continually held up continental examples of government ownership of utilities and railways as superior to American practice. Unfortunately, Ely's passionately held convictions colored his analyses and that of subsequent analysts influenced by him. Ely was convinced that as a matter of fact utilities and railways were natural monopolies. He was equally convinced that government ownership is superior to regulated private monopoly. (To quote him today on the wonders of the public post office versus private telegraph companies would be merely embarassing.)

Ely and others professed to be factually oriented, as opposed to the older generation of theoretical economists, whom they viewed as biased in favor of laissez faire. Yet Ely's conviction of a widespread natural-monopoly problem was largely unsupported by facts testing that conviction. What we know today suggests that he was in error in almost all his contentions. Utilities sought state regulation rather than had it foisted upon them. They did so because they operated in a competitive environment. Major utilities sought refuge from competition. State utility regulation raised rates and profits and created an untold number of utility "empires."[35] Whatever might have been true once, U.S. railways were not natural monopolies by Ely's time. Rather, they were a maturing cartel on the verge of a fifty-year decline from which they may only now be recovering.[36]

Ely's legacy is a heart-felt conviction among economists that the natural-monopoly problem is a real one and justifies classic economic regulation. An equally important legacy is theorizing about monopoly without reference to political or legal realities. The long process of separating monopoly theory from any economic analysis of law and politics resulted in a series of policy misdiagnoses, whose effects still linger in the guise of legislated monopolies and exploited technologies. Much has been learned about the history and practice of railroad regulation. The full story of utility regulation remains to be written.[37]

Natural monopoly occupies an important place in neoclassical monopoly theory, although not the central place accorded by Ely. Neoclassical monopoly theory evolved based on elasticity of demand and substitution. Pure monopoly is a situation of one seller facing the entire-industry demand. The situation depends on there being no producers of "close substitutes."[38]

The theory lacks any defensible, coherent answer to the entry question. Monopoly is postulated without being explained.[39] Over the years, a series of ad hoc hypotheses have been adduced to supplement neoclassical monopoly theory and to explain how an "open-market monopolist"—a single firm with no legal authority to exclude competitors—would maintain his superior position in a profitable industry. Most of these hypotheses can be subsumed under the category of barriers to entry to predatory practices. It is impossible to deal in detail with these hypotheses in this chapter. These hypotheses have been sharply criticized in recent years, and, apparently, their erstwhile adherents are increasingly abandoning them.[40]

Barrier-to-entry theories typically have two general failings. They tend to identify real scarcities—such as capital—as a "barrier." Second, they fail to demonstrate that new firms face costs not faced by existing firms when they were entering the industry. If consumers place value on stability or on established firms, then this value must be treated as any other good. The question then concerns whether entering firms are somehow impeded from making the investment previously made by established firms.

Predatory-pricing theories overlook the fact that virtually all such hypothetical schemes (real-world examples being difficult to document) cost the predator more than the victim. Further, having "disciplined" one set of competitors would render a predator less rather than more fit for future predation.

We have now come full circle and must confront current monopoly theory with the original question. If monopoly is profitable, why does it not attract entry? Property-rights theorists argue that entry will occur. A profitable open-market monopoly is not a stable situation and hence is not one to concern either the economist or the policymaker. The property-rights tradition is to concentrate on the many and varied ways in which governments create, foster, and maintain monopoly. There are legal monopolies enough to occupy fully any applied economist concerned with monopoly. As I have argued, however, non-property-rights theorists tend to overlook such monopolies. Or, being truly uninformed about the legal and political mechanisms used by would-be monopolists, they will seek other explanations. Barrier-to-entry models are one example of this futile search.

Standard neoclassical analysis has no answer to the entry question because, on its own terms, there is no answer. Modern economic theory accepts the self-interest assumption of Smith in the guise of a rationality postulate. This postulate, joined with the assumption of open markets, makes nonsense out of monopoly theory. Nor does the latter explain why the monopolist does not expand output. Graphical analysis purporting to illustrate monopolistic equilibrium (see figure 16-1) really demonstrates something quite different. The analysis reveals unexploited profit opportunities for the monopolist. These profits could be appropriated by price discrimination. It will not do to suggest that price discrimination is too costly. For this answer means that the marginal cost curve does not cut the demand curve at S, but at R. The incremental cost of selling an additional unit must include all costs—production, marketing, transportation, and transaction costs. The long debate over selling and advertising costs in monopolistic competition surely revealed the arbitrariness of excluding some costs from analysis. All sorts of welfare losses and inefficiencies can be contrived by this exclusion procedure.

In figure 16-1, either there is no monopoly or there is no equilibrium. With the assumed cost conditions, a monopolist will price discriminate. At the margin, price will equal marginal cost. No welfare loss will exist. If the cost conditions are accurate, $\bar{Q}$ is not an equilibrium output. If $\bar{Q}$ is the equilibrium output, cost conditions are other than what is shown.

If, for some reason, the monopolist does not price discriminate, then other firms would enter to exploit the potential for mutually advantageous trade. Failure of other firms to enter would evidence some cost of trading not included in the analysis. Either that, or a new entry barrier must be conjured up.

Subjectivist considerations help us to reformulate the analysis of monopolistic price determination in a manner more consistent with standard economic assumptions. Assume for the moment that costs of price discriminating are prohibitive and that for reasons of analytic convenience, these costs (that is, transactions costs of price discriminating) are excluded from the analysis. From a subjectivist perspective, however, cost must always be related to a concrete decision. The cost of a decision must be the cost to the decision maker. It is the value foregone, as seen by a decision maker, that influences choice.[41] We must look afresh, then, at the monopolist's decision. Referring to figure 16-2, we see that the decision to expand output from Q to $Q + \Delta Q$ results in a loss of revenue, $Q(\Delta P)$. The loss is usually

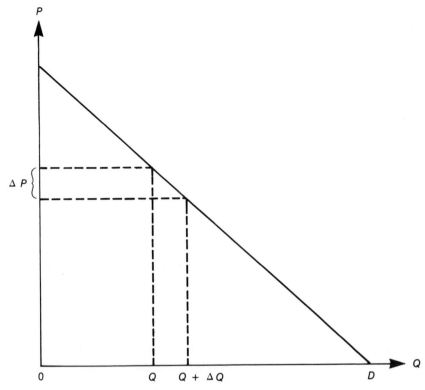

Figure 16-2. Demand Curve of Monopolist

captured by noting that marginal revenue falls faster than does average revenue. Yet this prospective loss is part of the monopolist's cost of selling an additional unit, ΔQ. So the firm's subjective opportunity cost of supplying an additional unit is $MC + (-Q\frac{dP}{dQ})$. Equilibrium is then given by: $MC - Q\frac{dP}{dQ} = P(Q)$. This is, of course, just a rearrangement of the standard first-order conditions for a monopolist ($MC = P(Q) + Q\frac{dP}{dQ}$). But, as shown in figure 16-3, the difference in results is significant. Equilibrium price and output are necessarily the same in the two cases. But in the amended analysis, expected cost and price are equal. Subjectively perceived opportunities foregone are just balanced by the price received for the marginal unit. In this analysis, only the average-revenue and reformulated

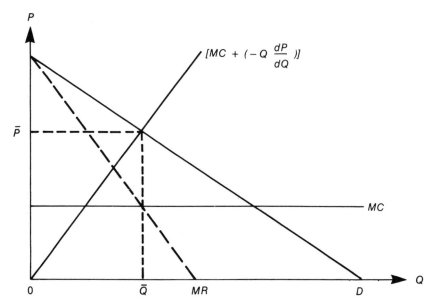

Figure 16-3. Subjectivist View of Price Searcher

marginal-cost curves are relevant; marginal revenue and ordinary marginal cost are shown for purposes of comparison. The subjectivizing of the monopolist's decision produces a result according with classical intuition: in open markets, price is driven to costs. Only by reformulating costs, however, does one obtain this classical result.

I am arguing for consideration of costs from the producer's viewpoint, not costs as they would appear to an ideal observer doubling as benign economic despot. The contrast between standard monopoly analysis and the amended analysis suggested here is, of course, an instance of the difference between a social and an individualistic or subjective cost theory. A subjectivist approach to cost theory views cost from the decision maker's perspective.

Indeed, cost has no meaning apart from a decision; there are no disembodied costs. If there were an omniscient observer of the economy he would doubtless allocate resources differently than would 200 million separate decision makers. If the observer owned all resources, then he might allocate them as orthodox welfare theory suggests that he do: $P = MC$ (in the standard sense). What we need, however, is not an economic theory for an omniscient observer owning all resources but motivated only for the public good; we need an economic theory of decentralized economies. The former situation conforms to the idealized construct of politicians acting solely for the public good. At that level, it has been driven from the textbooks by public-choice theorists. But social-cost analysis persists in monopoly theory and elsewhere.

Compelling a resource owner to produce at some point other than at this profit-maximizing level of output is not compelling him to produce "at cost." Economic costs relate to a decision of an economic agent to allocate his resources in one way rather than in another way. He who has not made the decision cannot bear the costs—foregone benefits—of that decision, for those benefits were never his to forego. A directive to an agent to produce at such-and-such a level cannot accurately be described as compelling the agent to produce at his cost of production—nor would he be producing at society's costs. In the former case, the purpose of the directive is to countervene the agent's own valuation of foregone benefits, that is, to ignore costs as he perceives and experiences them. In the second instance, there is no entity, society, making a decision for which there are costs. Even were one to hypostatize society as a decision maker, one must recognize that costs are not independent of who the decision maker is, what the property rights are, or how knowledge is made available. Thus there is no given cost structure on the basis of which welfare statements can be made.

The implications of a subjectivist approach to costs are many, and one is of immediate concern. The theoretical case against a single producer in an open market is attenuated if not eliminated. The producer operates where his cost of producing an additional unit would exceed his benefits. It is of course true that if institutions and property rights were other than what they are assumed to be, the producer and his benefits and costs would differ. It is also true that other individuals may have reasons to prefer that the producer behave differently. If they have the political power to enforce their views, then production decisions will be altered. In the former case, a law and economics approach could make a comparative-institution analysis. In the latter case, a public-choice approach might be useful in analyzing and predicting outcomes. If, however, analysis purports to describe decentralized decision making in a world of well-specified private-property rights, it cannot be the same analysis appropriate to a highly idealized and stylized socialist economy. Standard monopoly theory (and welfare theory generally) attempts to be both and accordingly fails to be either.

To reiterate the main point, standard monopoly analysis defines cost and revenue not as they appear to decision makers within the system but as they would appear to an ideal observer outside the system. The switch in perspective from the individual to the social level is what enables the economist to discover a deadweight loss, which, in terms of the analysis, represents an unexploited profit opportunity. The profit opportunity is not exploited in the real world because it does not exist. Its existence in economic models results from a methodological gambit. The gambit consists in switching from an individualistic or subjectivist analysis to collectivist or social analysis. The purported loss would exist and could thus be eliminated only in the hypothetical world of the benign despot owning all resources but concerned only with consumers' wants. This methodological sleight-of-hand aside, the standard analysis ignores the fact that costs are not the same when the level of decision making is changed.[42]

In analyzing monopoly, I have avoided dealing with oligopoly, collusion, or "shared monopoly" of any kind. As a practical matter, far more intellectual effort is devoted to cases of monopoly power than to pure monopoly. The case of pure monopoly is, however, theoretically more fundamental. If theory cannot explain how a single firm would exclude entrants, it perforce will not be successful in explaining how oligopolists or cartellists would exclude entrants. With multiple producers there are the additional problems of divided interests, duplicity, and cheating. If monopoly theory crumbles, a fortiori, so does oligopoly theory.

The Austrian School

Mises and Kirzner

Where do the members of the modern Austrian School fit in this monopoly taxonomy? None adopt the Ricardian approach. But they divide between endorsing a variant of neoclassical monopoly theory and adhering to a property-rights view.[43] None has followed Carl Menger's approach, which has the best claim to being distinctively Austrian.

For Ludwig von Mises, monopoly exists when "the whole supply of the monopolized commodity is controlled by a single seller or a group of sellers acting in concert."[44] Monopoly is condemned for violating consumer sovereignty:

> Monopoly prices are consequential only because they are the outcome of a conduct of business defying the supremacy of the consumers and substituting the private interests of the monopolist for those of the public. They are the only instance in the operation of a market economy in which the distinction between production for profit and production for use could to some extent be made. . . .[45]

Israel Kirzner has argued that the entrepreneurial function is essentially competitive and requires no resources to pursue. As a consequence, monopoly can only arise if some necessary input is completely controlled by one person—a monopolist: "Without access to oranges, entry into the production of orange juice *is* blocked."[46] Absent government intervention, "monopoly . . . means for us the position of a producer whose exclusive control over necessary inputs blocks competitive entry into the production of his products."[47]

Kirzner claims to be elucidating Mises's theory, and there is general agreement between the two theorists. Mises does consider a number of specific types of monopoly not considered explicitly by Kirzner. But these could undoubtedly fit into the latter's analyses.[48] On one question there is significant difference between Kirzner's and Mises's treatment. Kirzner scarcely mentions government intervention as a source of monopoly. Merely theoretical possibilities aside, Mises considered government a progenitor of monopoly.

> The monopoly problem mankind has to face today is not an outgrowth of the operation of the market economy. It is a product of purposive action on the part of governments. It is not one of the evils inherent in capitalism as the demagogues trumpet. It is, on the contrary, the fruit of policies hostile to capitalism and intent upon sabotaging and destroying its operation.[49]

In emphasizing the practical importance of government intervention, Mises perhaps straddles the two approaches with which we are concerned. Mises does raise the problem of resource monopoly, which Kirzner develops into his general theory of monopoly. Kirzner goes to great length distinguishing his monopoly theory from the static neoclassical version. He emphasizes that his is a theory couched not in terms of equilibrium conditions, but in terms of monopoly's blockage of the competitive process. He also argues the significance of focusing on the input instead of the output markets.[50]

Is the Mises-Kirzner theory different in a relevant way from the standard neoclassical analysis? Apparently not. First, resource monopoly is one source of neoclassical monopoly. Second, the Mises-Kirzner theory is no more successful at answering the entry question than is neoclassical theory. In Kirzner's formulation, it is also internally inconsistent.

Kirzner's entrepreneur owns no resources. Therefore, he is always in a position of a would-be orange-juice producer in Alaska—his inputs are elsewhere. By Kirzner's logic, all entrepreneurs would be blocked from seizing profit opportunities, since resources are owned by others (capitalists). In fact, even in the situation suggested by Kirzner—all oranges are owned by one orange-baron—no entrepreneur would be blocked from entering the orange-juice market. *Ex hypothesi,* our entrepreneurs face a profit opportunity. This presumably means they are high-valued users of oranges. The orange baron could do no better in the market than to sell to eager orange squeezers. If, in fact, there were a monopoly return to be earned, the owner of oranges would be indifferent at what stage he collected the return. Unless Kirzner subscribes to some kind of leverage theory of monopoly, he must recognize that the orange baron has no particular desire to move into producing juice.[51]

The Coase theorem can be appropriately applied to Kirzner's orange-juice example. Transaction costs aside (and they are not the issue in Kirzner's example), it does not matter who initially owns the necessary resources to produce orange juice. Property titles will be exchanged so that these resources are transfered to the highest-valued user.

Kirzner essentially denies his own thesis. He assumes that an entrepreneur spots a profitable opportunity in the orange-juice market. In Kirzner's own analysis, this must mean the entrepreneur spots an arbitrage opportunity. He can buy inputs at a low price and resell output at a high price. Kirzner cannot then assert that the monopolist will not sell at the low price. That assertion is simply a denial of the original assumption. There was simply no profit opportunity in the first place.

To pursue his argument, Kirzner must define an input (as opposed to substitute inputs). Kirzner suggests that the shape of the demand curve for the product has no bearing on whether someone is a monopolist. But Kirzner cannot even define an input apart from the demand elasticity for that input. He has merely pushed all the difficulties of neoclassical theory back to the input market. He not only must answer all the questions and difficulties raised by standard theory, but he also must deal with the particular ones raised by the peculiarities of his own analysis.

There is yet a further difficulty with Kirzner's analysis. For him, monopoly derives from ownership of an input without which some valueable good cannot be produced. It must then be the case that there is no substitute for this input, and the input itself cannot be reproduced. This highly specialized case strains one's imagination for a real-world example. Oranges and orange juice will not do. Perhaps Cournot's mineral spring would work. In any case, Kirzner does not have what could be recognized as a general theory of monopoly.[52]

Menger

Most pieces of theoretical analysis in modern Austrian economics can be traced to an idea or theory of Carl Menger. This is not true for monopoly theory, although his analysis in this area accords well with his general approach to economic and social questions. This approach has been adopted in other areas by later Austrians.

As is well known, Menger was the most concerned with the origin and progress of social institutions. Menger traced the evolution of markets from "bilateral monopoly," to multiparty trade, and only then to large-scale competitive markets. Monopoly is primary, and only with time does the growth of markets make competition possible. Menger outlined the process of market evolution.[53]

Menger describes the "exceptional position of a monopolist as his ability to choose either the quantity of the good to be traded or the terms of trade."[54] Menger linked the question of price elasticity of demand to a monopolist's profit-maximizing behavior, but he did not formally state the precise nature of this link.[55] In terms of his concept of a static monopoly or his statement of monopoly power, Menger would be only one among many who supplied building blocks for modern monopoly theory. What makes Menger's analysis distinctive is his insistence on treating monopoly and competition dynamically.

In terms of Menger's analysis, it would make little sense to ask whether a market is monopolistic or competitive. All markets begin with monopoly and move toward being more and more competitive. The sensible Mengerian question would be to ask at what point a given market is in this natural evolutionary process. Widespread monopoly in an economy would be indicative of an early stage in economic development and a low level of demand. Competition is limited by the extent of the market.

Menger's concept of monopoly is thus different from either the neoclassical or the property-rights views. I would suggest, however, that Menger's analysis is a fruitful way of conceptualizing the rise and development of markets. It certainly fits in with the general Austrian evolutionary approach to institutions, such as law and money. The property-rights view can certainly be accommodated within Menger's framework. Legal monopolies represent a freezing of market development at one stage in an evolutionary process. Menger felt, however, that the property-rights view is too narrow a concept of monopoly. He insisted that:

> These are persons who, as a result of their property holdings, or due to special talents or circumstances, can market goods that it is physically or economically impossible for other economizing persons to supply competitively. And even where special circumstances of these types are not present, there is often no social barrier to the emergence of monopolists. Every artisan who establishes himself in a locality in which there is no other person of his particular occupation, and every merchant, physician, or attorney, who settles in a locality where no one previously exercised his trade or calling, is a monopolist in a certain sense, since the goods he offers to society in trade can, at least in numerous instances, be had only from him.[56]

Menger's theory deals directly with the question posed to other monopoly theories. Market forces do break down monopoly. The monopolist's very method of exploiting his power—undersupplying the market—is the source of his own demise. More and more potential buyers will remain unsatisfied as the economy grows and demand increases. The "economic progress of civilization" leads to competition. ". . . The need for competition itself calls for competition, provided there are no social or other barriers in the way."[57] Moreover, Menger was sanguine about the effects of entry by a single competitor. With as few as two competitors, the practical scope for either one controlling price or output is all but removed.[58]

Two observations on Menger's analysis should be made. First, Menger emphatically did not believe that competition would ever be "perfect," as that concept is used today. He denied that any good has a unique price at which it can be bought and sold.[59] Indeed, Menger based his theory of money on the varying illiquidity of real goods. Second, Menger's analysis leaves no scope for an independent policy on monopoly. Governments should refrain from interfering with competitive market forces. Save for general policies aiding economic growth, governments have no real power to improve on market forces.

It is somewhat curious that subsequent generations of Austrians did not use Menger's analysis as a departure point for their own theories. One partial explanation suggests itself. By Mises's generation, the younger Austrians were more directly influenced by Eugen von Böhm-Bawerk and Friedrich von Wieser. In other areas where the latter diverged from Menger, such as capital theory, it was their approach and not Menger's that predominated. This process may have been at work in the area of monopoly.

Rothbard and Armentano

Rothbard and Armentano have adopted the property-rights view. Each has persevered in arguing for this approach to monopoly. Rothbard goes directly back to the common-law concept, quoting Lord Coke.[60] He also relies on American political economists of the nineteenth century. Although well acquainted with the Ricardians, the Americans tended to pursue the new science autonomously. American political economy was much less influenced by Ricardianism than was its British counterpart. The Americans' views on monopoly were thus much more consistent with eighteenth-century British legal and political thinking than was the Ricardian approach. Moreover, a number of these American writers were extremely influential, writing popular texts on political economy. This group included Francis Wayland, Francis A. Walker, and Arthur Latham Perry. Perry wrote a textbook that had twenty-one editions. He described monopoly as "a restriction imposed by government upon the sale of certain services."[61]

Although legislated monopolies were much less prevalent in America than in Britain, the antimonopoly spirit was stronger in America. Hostility and attention to government intervention persisted longer in American political economy. In addition, in a nation of "free land," the Ricardian obsession with land rent could not be taken seriously as the core of a monopoly theory.

We have seen that the tradition espoused by Rothbard and Armentano has deep historical roots. As I have made clear, the common-law view has much to recommend it. It is a view rooted in a British and American political tradition, however, not in the earlier Austrian school. The view is compatible with Menger's analysis (although "monopoly" is used equivocally in the two approaches). But it represents a distinct conceptualization of the monopoly problem.

Policy and Theory: A Synthesis

Surely few would argue that monopoly is a concept of any interest independent of policy implications. Except as an exercise to illustrate the use of calculus in economics, the pure theory of monopoly would be of little interest if it had no applications. The resource-monopoly position of Mises and Kirzner suffers not only from theoretical difficulties as outlined but also from a lack of applicability. Although resource monopoly is a favorite of textbook writers, they are short on examples that are not hypothetical or of a local and temporary nature. A true resource monopolist is a rarer bird than a genuine natural monopoly.[62]

There really is no good historical reason for modern Austrians to continue to adhere to a variant of neoclassical monopoly theory. The variant is not superior to the more general theory. The former suffers from all the problems of the latter, plus its own peculiar weaknesses. The problems with the neoclassical monopoly theory are being increasingly recognized, particularly when extended to shared monopoly or oligopoly. Most applications of the theory to public-policy questions are currently being rethought. Deregulation is proceeding apace and even antitrust policy is being reconsidered. I am suggesting, then, that orthodox monopoly analysis is problematical from a theoretical perspective and an abject failure as a way of thinking about public policy. It is time to abandon it.

Austrians especially have good reason to reconsider Menger's approach. It is original and distinctive. It offers a different approach to thinking about markets. Much work remains to be done in developing and extending it.

But the property-rights approach has perhaps the best claim to economists' attention. First, there is a long tradition in law and in economics to draw on. Second, economists have increasingly adopted a property-rights approach to other public-policy issues. Third, the approach is ideally suited to deal with the concrete policy issues of monopoly and cartelization. Once again, like the frogs of Egypt, the products of government intervention are among us. Deregulation has only barely begun to deal with them. If economists have any useful social role to play, it is surely in addressing the effects of governmental intervention in markets.

Notes

1. Sir Edward Coke, *The Third Part of the Institutes of the Laws of England* (London: E.&R. Brooke, 1797), p. 181.

2. William Blackstone, *Commentaries on the Laws of England,* bk. 4 (London: T. Codell and W. Davies, 1803), p. 159. Blackstone and Coke are cited in Hans Thorelli, *The Federal Antitrust Policy: Origination of an American Tradition* (Baltimore: Johns Hopkins, 1954), pp. 14–15n.

3. II Peters 567. Cited in A. Leo Weil's address to the *Chicago Conference on Trusts* (Chicago: Civic Federation of Chicago, 1900), p. 86.

4. See William Letwin, *Law and Economic Policy in America: The Evolution of the Sherman Antitrust Act* (New York: Random House, 1965), pp. 19–32.

5. See Richard A. Posner, "Blackstone and Bentham," *Journal of Law and Economics* 19 (October 1976):582–585.

6. Thus the *Abbot of Westminster* dealt with a patent granted by William the Conquerer. See Letwin, *Law and Economic Policy,* pp. 35–36.

7. In *Darcy* v. *Allen.* See Letwin, *Law and Economic Policy,* pp. 27–29.

8. As is done in Thorelli, *Federal Antitrust Policy,* pp. 25–26; and in some antitrust law texts, such as Louis B. Schwartz and John J. Flynn, *Antitrust and Regulatory Alternatives* (Mineola, N.Y.: Foundation), pp. 1–2.

9. This point is argued persuasively in Letwin, *Law and Economic Policy,* pp. 31–32. Letwin takes note of Parliament's "inconsistency, which symbolized Parliament's willingness to have monopolies, provided Parliament alone granted them. . . . Only a few years after Darcy's monopoly of playing cards was judged void at common law, the same monopoly was given, under authority of the Statute of Monopolies, to the Company of Card Makers." Ibid., p. 32; footnote reference omitted.

10. As well as in certain other enumerated goods, ibid., pp. 32–36.

11. Ibid., p. 36.

12. Quoted in Weil, *Chicago Conference,* p. 86.

13. See Letwin, *Law and Economic Policy,* pp. 36–39.

14. Hans Thorelli suggested that changes in economic conditions and in intellectual opinion made it "natural" that these laws would become outmoded. Thorelli, *Federal Antitrust Policy,* pp. 16–17. I do not find his argument convincing.

15. See Letwin, *Law and Economic Policy,* pp. 37–39.

16. Adam Smith, *The Wealth of Nations,* ed. Edwin Cannan (New York: Modern Library, 1937), p. 61.

17. Ibid.

18. Ibid., p. 712.

19. Ibid., p. 60.

20. Ibid., pp. 60–61. Note that Smith here treats rent as having a "natural" level, thus making rent part of production costs.

21. Ibid., pp. 147–148.

22. Ibid., p. 844; emphasis added to the original.

23. Compare Thomas Sowell, *Classical Economics Reconsidered* (Princeton, N.J.: Princeton University, 1974), pp. 81–82; and Thomas Sowell, "Adam Smith in Theory and Practice," in *Adam Smith and Modern Political Economy: Bicentennial Essays on the Wealth of Nations,* ed. Gerald P.O'Driscoll, Jr., (Ames, Iowa: Iowa State University Press, 1979), p. 11.

24. Smith, *Wealth of Nations,* p. 60.

25. David Ricardo, *The Works and Correspondence of David Ricardo,* vol. 1, *On the Principles of Political Economy and Taxation,* ed. Piero Sraffa (Cambridge: Cambridge University, 1951), p. 250.

26. Nassau William Senior, *An Outline of the Science of Political Economy* (1936; reprint ed., New York: Augustus M. Kelley, 1965), pp. 102–103.

27. Ibid., pp. 103–105; emphasis in the original.

28. Alfred Marshall, *Principles of Economics,* 9th ed., 2 vols, ed. C.W. Guillebaud (New York: Macmillan, 1961), 1:477.

29. See George J. Stigler, "Perfect Competition, Historically Contemplated, " reprinted in *Essays in the History of Economics* (Chicago: University of Chicago, Phoenix Books, 1965), pp. 251–253.

30. Marshall, *Principles of Economics,* pp. 484–485.

31. See Shorey Peterson, "Antitrust and the Classic Model," in *A.E.A. Readings in Industrial Organization,* ed. Hefelbower and Stocking (Homewood, Ill.: Richard D. Irwin, 1958), pp. 316–333.

32. Richard T. Ely, *Problems of To-Day: A Discussion of Protection Tariffs, Taxation, and Monopolies,* rev. ed. (New York: Thomas Y. Crowell, 1888), p. 117.

33. Ibid., pp. 201–202.

34. Ibid., p. 121.

35. An early study by Stigler and Friedland found no effect of regulation on utility rates. See George J. Stigler and Claire Friedland, "What Can Regulators Regulate? The Case of Electricity," *Journal of Law and Economics* 5 (October 1962):1–16. A later study found that the move to state regulation favored electric utilities. See Gregg A. Jarrell, "The Demand for

State Regulation of the Electric Utility Industry," *Journal of Law and Economics* 21 (October 1978):269–295.

Most convincing is the evidence of major utilities' actions seeking state regulations. Men such as Samuel Insull were persevering in their pursuit of regulation, which they saw as protecting them both against competition and from an increasingly hostile public. See Forest McDonald, *Insull* (Chicago: University of Chicago, 1962), especially pp. 113–128 and 177–187; compare with James Weinstein, *The Corporate Idea in the Liberal State: 1900–1918* (Boston: Beacon, 1968), pp. 24–26 and 33–35.

36. See George W. Hilton, "The Consistency of the Interstate Commerce Act," *Journal of Law and Economics* 9 (October 1966):87–113.

37. One classic example is R.H. Coase, "The Federal Communications Commission," *Journal of Law and Economics* 2 (October 1959):1–40. Many economists would not consider broadcasting a public utility, but it has been treated as such in public policy.

38. See, for example, the brief discussion in Fred R. Glahe and Dwight R. Lee, *Microeconomics: Theory and Applications* (New York: Harcourt Brace Jovanovich, 1981), pp. 287–288.

39. Compare Harold Demetz, "Two Systems of Belief about Monopoly," in *Industrial Concentration: The New Learning* ed. J. Fred Weston (Boston: Little, Brown, 1974), p. 166.

I only read this paper after nearly completing my chapter. Demsetz deals with oligopoly and collusion rather than with pure monopoly. On the relationship between monopoly and oligopoly, see later in this chapter.

40. For a recent summary of these criticisms, which suggests the demise of the older view, see Richard A. Posner, "The Chicago School of Antitrust Analysis," *University of Pennsylvania Law Review* 127 (April 1979):925–948.

41. On this general point, see James M. Buchanan, *Cost and Choice* (Chicago: Markham, 1969).

42. For further elaboration on subjectivist cost theory, see ibid. Also see James M. Buchanan and G.F. Thirlby, eds., *L.S.E. Essays on Cost* (London: Weidenfeld and Nicholson for the London School of Economics and Political Science, 1973).

In an unpublished paper, Thomas Hazlett adopts a property rights perspective to reach a similar conclusion. He does not, however, explicitly bring in the subjectivist analysis of this chapter. Hazlett, "Opportunity Costs, Rents, and Monopoly Output Restrictions" (photocopy: 1982).

43. For a summary of the debate among the Austrians by a partisan of the property-rights view, see D.T. Armentano, "A Critique of Neoclassical and Austrian Monopoly Theory," in *New Directions in Austrian Economics,* ed. Louis M. Spadaro (Kansas City: Sheed Andrews and McMeel, 1978), pp. 94–110.

44. Ludwig von Mises, *Human Action,* 3d ed. (Chicago: Henry Regnery, 1966), p. 358.

45. Ibid., p. 371.

46. Israel M. Kirzner, *Competition and Entrepreneurship* (Chicago: University of Chicago, 1973), p. 103.

47. Ibid.; footnote reference omitted.

48. See Mises, *Human Action,* pp. 369–377.

49. Ibid., p. 366; compare ibid., p. 361. Even when Mises discusses one of his specialized types of monopoly, "margin monopoly," he cites the case of government intervention as an example of it, ibid., p. 365.

50. Kirzner, *Competition and Entrepreneurship,* pp. 104–111, 111–112, 131–134, 205–211.

51. Kirzner asserts, but offers no argument to prove, that juice prouction would be more lucrative than orange sales, ibid., p. 110. It is impossible to evaluate this conclusion without access to the argument that produced it. It does run counter to the conclusions of standard analysis of vertical integration as a route to monopoly.

52. My thanks to Roger Garrison for driving home the similarity between Cournot's theory and Kirzner's analysis.

53. Carl Menger, *Principles of Economics,* trans. James Dingwall and Bert F. Hoselitz (New York: New York University, 1981), pp. 191–225.

54. Ibid., p. 211.

55. Ibid., pp. 214–216.

56. Ibid., p. 216.

57. Ibid., p. 217.

58. Ibid., pp. 222–224.

59. Ibid., pp. 191–193 and 236–285.

60. Murray N. Rothbard, *Man, Economy, and State,* 2 vols. (Princeton, N.J.: D. Van Nostrand, 1962), 2:591.

61. Arthur Latham Perry, *Elements of Political Economy,* 14th ed. (New York: Scribner, Armstrong, 1877), p. 115.

62. Anyone tempted to refer to the Alcoa case ought to examine D.T. Armentano, *The Myths of Antitrust* (New Rochelle, N.Y.: Arlington House, 1972), pp. 110–122, especially p. 113.

17 Monopoly Theory and Practice— Some Subjectivist Implications: Comment on O'Driscoll

E.C. Pasour, Jr.

Gerald O'Driscoll presented an excellent summary and critique of monopoly theory in chapter 16. Since our views on monopoly are quite similar, my comments are primarily intended to extend rather than to challenge his analysis. This chapter has three parts. First, non-property-rights views of monopoly are briefly discussed, and it is argued on subjectivist grounds that monopoly is best defined as a grant of government privilege. Second, the implications of subjectivism for price regulation are discussed. Third, the affinity of the property-rights view of monopoly to rent seeking is described, and *rent seeking* is held to be a more descriptive term than monopoly for the wide range of activities today where government interaction restricts competition.

O'Driscoll demonstrates that the view of monopoly as a grant of government privilege was important in English common law as well as in classical political economy. This view of monopoly (characterized by O'Driscoll as a property-rights approach) appears to be most consistent with the process view of the market. The central theoretical issue to be solved by any monopoly theory is nicely put in his chapter: "If monopoly yields a net revenue or surplus, then why does entry of new firms not occur"?[1] Monopoly power exists only when the seller can prevent entry of new sellers. The most (only?) effective way to legally restrict entry is by the use of government power. Only government, having a monopoly on legalized coercion, can create monopoly, since no other institution can legally exclude potential entrants.

Neoclassical and Austrian Theories

In the neoclassical theory of monopoly, as O'Driscoll suggests, monopoly tends to be merely postulated without being explained. A monopolist, by conventional definition, exists when the industry contains only a single

The author wishes to thank Marc A. Johnson for helpful comments and suggestions.

firm.[2] But this definition provides little help in identifying monopoly conditions. If goods and services are classified narrowly, "every seller is a monopolist, since no two sellers will ever be offering completely identical products."[3] On the other hand, buyers would have no alternatives only if demand were perfectly inelastic. However, since all goods have substitutes, no seller of a good or service is a monopolist in the sense of facing a perfectly inelastic demand curve. And, since the closeness of substitutes is a matter of degree, any demarcation of how inelastic product demand must be for the seller to be considered a monopolist must be arbitrary.

F.A. Hayek attempts to define monopoly on the basis of whether the seller of a particular product or service is able to coerce the buyer. He concludes that monopoly is a problem or that coercion occurs only where "a monopolist might control an essential commodity on which people are completely dependent" such as "the owner of a spring in an oasis."[4] Necessity implies that buyers are unaffected by price—that demand is perfectly inelastic. However, the perfectly inelastic demand curve is a "mythical creature," as just suggested, since all goods and services have substitutes.[5] Thus, the concept of "necessity" or "need" provides no guidance in defining monopoly.

Similar problems are faced in identifying monopoly production with resource monopoly.[6] No producer can have a resource monopoly, since there are always substitutes in the resource market just as there are in the product market. Consider the Kirzner example in which control of a necessary input, oranges, by one producer is said to give that producer a monopoly position in the production of orange juice.[7] Instead of merely assuming that there is a resource monopoly, however, it is helpful to ask how a producer under real-world conditions would obtain a resource monopoly. The orange example is instructive. Orange producers obtain higher prices through a government "marketing order," which controls the quantity, quality, and market flow, which legally prohibits a grower from making shipments above the shipment allotment. Indeed, there are a large number of marketing orders affecting oranges, grapefruit, lemons, cherries, lettuce, raisins, milk, and other agricultural products in the United States today.

It is no accident that these supply-control programs in agriculture involve government sanctions. Cartel members have an economic incentive to "chisel" on agreements that, if widely honored, would result in a transfer to the group. Thus, in a group where the single individual's action makes little difference to the group as a whole, the "free rider" serves as an effective constraint against collusion to limit sales and increase price.[8] Consequently, an entrepreneur will not be able to obtain a "monopoly position" in oranges without the sanctions of government.[9] Moreover, oranges are not an exception: the important cartels we observe under real-world conditions arise as grants of government privilege.[10]

There is another problem with the resource-monopoly view of monopoly. As in the product market, if we define resources narrowly enough, every producer has a resource monopoly. Even if a necessary input is completely controlled by one person, however, competition is not blocked. Grandma Moses, for example, owned and controlled a necessary input in the production of her paintings, but few people would argue that she was a monopolist in any meaningful sense. There are many good substitutes for paintings of Grandma Moses just as there are for oranges produced in California, Florida, Mexico, or Spain.

Ultimately, we are faced with the problem of how to identify a monopoly. If, as in neoclassical theory, every firm is regarded as a monopoly that faces "a negatively sloping demand curve for its product," many sellers operating under highly competitive conditions, including the 10-year-old operator of a lemonade stand, will be classified as monopolists.[11] Similarly, if a monopoly is defined by control over a necessary input, producers operating under competitive conditions will be classified as monopolists.

How about the Carl Menger approach, which treats "monopoly and competition dynamically"?[12] Menger, as in neoclassical theory, identifies the monopolist as a sole seller.[13] Thus, his approach suffers the definitional problems already discussed. Moreover, it is not likely that any non-property-rights view of monopoly can overcome the problems encountered in attempting to distinguish between monopoly and competitive prices. In the free market, there are no observable human actions on the part of the seller that logically imply the existence of monopoly price. All businessmen attempt to maximize profit (monetary or psychic) and all produce less than they could have.[14] Thus, in the absence of legal barriers there is no way to distinguish a competitive price from a monopoly price. Even if sellers voluntarily collude and attempt to raise price, it may not be clear whether the price charged would be different in the absence of collusion. In view of uncertainty about present and future demand and supply conditions of oil, for example, are OPEC prices more accurately described as "competitive" or "cartel" prices?

Policy Implications—Economic Regulation

The monopoly concept, as O'Driscoll suggests, is of no interest independent of policy implications, and there is mounting evidence to support his conclusion that ". . . orthodox monopoly analysis is problematical from a theoretical perspective and an abject failure as a way of thinking about public policy."[15] S.C. Littlechild has shown that, in the equilibrium framework conventionally used to analyze monopoly, "all profit is due to monopoly, and necessarily implies a serious welfare loss."[16] Entrepreneurship, however, is a crucial element in the market process, and the extent of entrepreneurial activity is undoubtedly related to the rewards of entrepreneurship—profits. The conventional approach for measuring social costs fails to take into account the role of profits in innovation and increased coordination and provides a rationale for government intervention. This theory also diverts attention from the real source of monopoly—the government restrictions and regulations that enable certain groups of established firms to restrict competition.[17]

There are two important problems in price regulation of public utilities and other so-called natural monopolies. First, there is an incentive problem on the part of public decision makers, emphasized in the public-choice approach, caused by the separation of power and responsibility. In the market, the private decision maker takes the risks and reaps the rewards (or losses). In the words of Ludwig von Mises the private decision maker is "subject to the incorruptible judgment of an unbribable tribunal: the account of profit and loss."[18] Under public control, however, the entire community bears the costs and benefits associated with decisions made by bureaucrats. Public decision makers, like the rest of us, are aware of their own interests, and the self-interest of the bureaucrat is typically associated with "playing it safe." Thus, political failure, a divergence between an idealized policy and the way real-world political institutions actually operate, is a fact of life.[19]

There is a second and even more fundamental problem facing price regulators that is firmly rooted in subjectivism. The conventional neoclassical theory of monopoly regulation includes, among other alternatives, marginal-cost pricing under conditions of increasing and decreasing cost.[20] The discussion of marginal-cost pricing implies that the relevant data concerning costs and returns are given to the entrepreneur as well as to the regulator (or economic analyst).[21] When one takes into account the subjective nature of the entrepreneurial process, it becomes clear that diagrammatic comparisons of various regulatory procedures, as R.H. Coase suggests, are merely "blackboard economics."[22] The real world never contains an entity corresponding to the marginal-cost curve, since the amount of product that a firm will try to produce at any given price depends on many factors including length of run, technology, and expected input prices. Similarly, the real world never contains an actual entity corresponding to the demand curve for a particular product.[23] Moreover, demand conditions are not given to the decision maker but must be discovered through a process of trial and error. Thus, the most profitable price cannot be identified either by the producer or by the outside observer.[24] O'Driscoll mentions an important legacy of Richard Ely in theorizing about monopoly without reference to political or legal realities.[25] There was also a failure, then and now, in theorizing about monopoly to understand that the data that motivate entrepreneurial choice are subjective. As demonstrated by Mises and Hayek in the economic-calculation debate, regulators cannot simulate competition, and competitive prices can only be determined by having competition.[26]

What are the implications of the preceding discussion in cases of natural monopoly? "A natural monopoly exists when the optimum size for a firm in some area of production is so large that there is room for only one such firm on the market."[27] The natural-monopoly definition presupposes a problem by assuming that there are no good substitutes for the product involved. Since there are substitutes for all goods and services, any classification of what constitutes a natural monopoly must be arbitrary. Moreover, since the conventional wisdom that there is a widespread natural-monopoly problem is "largely unsupported by facts,"[28] it is not surprising that economic regulation is not achieving its stated objectives.[29] Where there are substantial economies of scale, competitive results can better be achieved by abolishing statutory monopoly rather than through futile attempts to simulate competition.

Monopoly versus Rent Seeking

Since classification under any non-property-rights definition of monopoly must be arbitrary, there are good reasons to define monopoly as a grant of special privilege by the state reserving a certain area of production for an individual or group. However, this view of monopoly also has limitations as a description of real-world activity. Since the recipient of a government privilege faces competition from sellers of substitute products, a seller protected by government can be considered as the sole seller only when the product is narrowly defined. In reality, the nature of the government privilege and the extent of restriction on competition varies widely. The benefit provided by the state may take various forms including direct subsidy, controls over substitutes and complements, and price fixing.[30] Thus, monopoly defined as the legal reservation of production to individuals or groups is not descriptive of much activity in the real world involving grants of special privilege by the state. The recent theory of rent seeking, describing the effects of attempts by individuals and groups to create income opportunities through political activity, is a more descriptive term for the wide range of activities today where the state is used to restrict competition.[31] The practice of rent seeking is very old, as O'Driscoll makes clear in citing Adam Smith's criticism of attempts by businessmen to use state power for their own ends.[32] Rent-seeking theory is helpful in explaining a wide range of transfer activities as well as state-conferred monopoly privileges.

Individuals and groups seek to increase wealth by profit-seeking and by rent-seeking activities.[33] Profit seeking under competitive market conditions leads to efficient resource use. Although groups organized competitively have an economic incentive to collude and restrict production as a means of increasing price and profits, profit seeking by voluntary organized group action is held in check by the free rider. Rent seeking through the political process (when successful), on the other hand, creates artificial scarcity causing fewer goods and services to be produced and to be sold at higher prices.

What contribution can economists make to public policy relating to monopoly? Attempts to measure competition cardinally are likely to be as unproductive as conventional social-costs measurements of monopoly.[34] Economists, however, can both emphasize the effects of regulation on the market process and describe the effects of various forms of state intervention in restricting entry and limiting competition.[35] Consider, for example, rent seeking in the real world of specialized inputs where the benefits accrue mainly to initial owners of specialized resources. A licensing of taxicabs, for example, yields windfall gains to the original license recipients. Later entrants required to purchase the right to operate face higher operating costs and receive little benefit from previously successful rent-seeking activity. However, later entrants also have an incentive to engage in rent-seeking activity to maintain the licensing system. Abolishing the monopoly privilege makes the license worthless and imposes a windfall loss on the licensed taxicab operator.[36] Thus, the greater is the success of rent seekers in obtaining wealth transfers and monopoly benefits, the greater is the loss if the government privilege is revoked and the more politically difficult it is to terminate the privilege.

Huge amounts of resources are devoted to obtaining and maintaining wealth transfers and monopoly advantages through rent seeking in the United States. Grants of government privilege, as suggested, vary widely in nature and in extent of benefit, including, to mention only a few, Chrysler federal-loan guarantees, marketing orders for oranges, tobacco and peanut production quotas, occupational licensing, restrictions on imports of Japanese autos and steel, education subsidies, labor cartels, transportation cartels, and the Post Office. When so many people are engaged in rent seeking, attempts to eliminate costly rent-seeking activities are likely to founder if approached piecemeal.[37] Even if there were a consensus as to the desirability of limiting rent-seeking and transfer activity, there is a "you first" problem associated with attempts to reduce government privilege—each group has an economic incentive to have other groups reduce their rent seeking while maintaining its own.[38] However, the costs of government intervention may eventually become sufficiently great as to make possible a constitutional change limiting the scope for rent-seeking behavior.[39]

In conclusion, since only the state can legally prevent entry, real-world monopoly problems invariably can be traced to government.[40] The emphasis of neoclassical theory on alternative procedures of the state to regulate monopolies is ironic in view of the widespread monopoly privileges sanctioned by the state. There is no consensus concerning the relationship between the concepts of rent seeking and monopoly involving grants of government privilege. However, both concepts should prove helpful to economists in their useful social role of "addressing the effects of governmental intervention in markets."[41] Moreover, a wider understanding of these effects is a necessary step in achieving the consensus that will be required to reinstate ". . . the wisdom of the Founding Fathers regarding the scope and power of government."[42]

Notes

1. See chapter 16, p. 189.

2. Jack Hirshleifer, *Price Theory and Applications,* 2d ed. (Englewood Cliffs, N.J.: Prentice Hall, 1980), p. 332.

3. Paul Heyne, *The Economic Way of Thinking,* 3d ed. (Chicago: Science Research Associates, 1980), p. 140.

4. F.A. Hayek, *The Constitution of Liberty* (Chicago: University of Chicago, 1960), p. 136.

5. Heyne, *Economic Way of Thinking,* p. 33.

6. "Clearly in the long run view, monopolistic control over production cannot be ascribed to firms as such, but only to the fortunate owners of unique resources." Israel M. Kirzner, "Divergent Approaches in Libertarian Economic Thought," *The Intercollegiate Review* 3 (January–February, 1967):108.

7. Israel M. Kirzner, *Competition and Entrepreneurship* (Chicago: University of Chicago, 1973), p. 103.

8. Mancur Olson, *The Logic of Collective Action* (Cambridge, Mass,: Harvard University, 1971).

9. The marketing order for oranges was originally established at the urging of Sunkist, a huge cooperative. In effect, the marketing order codified the cooperative's unsuccessful attempts in the 1920s and 1930s to regulate orange shipments on a voluntary basis. Ann Crittenden, "Fruit Growers' Control of Market Assailed." *New York Times,* 25 March 1981.

10. Mises agrees: "As a rule the state of affairs that makes the emergence of monopoly prices possible is brought about by government policies." Ludwig von Mises, *Human Action,* 3d ed. (Chicago: Henry Regnery, 1966), p. 361.

11. Milton Friedman, *Price Theory* (Chicago: Aldine, 1976), p. 126.

12. See chapter 16, p. 207.

13. Carl Menger, *Principles and Economics,* trans. James Dingwall and Bert F. Hoselitz (New York: New York University, 1981), p. 55.

14. Walter Block, "Austrian Monopoly Theory—A Critique," *Journal of Libertarian Studies* 1 (1977):271–279.

15. See chapter 16, p. 209.

16. S.C. Littlechild, "Misleading Calculations of the Social Costs of Monopoly Power," *The Economic Journal* 91 (June 1981):361.

17. It is ironic that the widely cited free-rider justification for government intervention fails to recognize the role of the state in shackling the free rider, who, in the absence of government sanctions, generally makes cartelization ineffective. E.C. Pasour, Jr., "The Free Rider as a Basis for Government Intervention," *Journal of Libertarian Studies* (forthcoming).

18. Ludwig von Mises, *Bureaucracy* (New Rochelle, N.Y.: Arlington House, 1969), p. 35.

19. James M. Buchanan et al., *The Economics of Politics,* IEA Readings 18 (London: Institute of Economic Affairs, 1978).

20. Hirshleifer, *Price Theory and Applications,* pp. 349–350.

21. E.C. Pasour, Jr., "Information: A Neglected Aspect of the Theory of Price Regulation," *Cato Journal* (forthcoming).

22. R.H. Coase, "The Theory of Public Utility Pricing and Its Application," *The Bell Journal of Economics* 1 (Spring 1970):49.

23. Leland B. Yeager, "*Methodenstreit* over Demand Curves," *Journal of Political Economy* 68 (February 1960):53–64.

24. Murray N. Rothbard, *Man, Economy and State* (Los Angeles: Nash, 1970), p. 605.

25. See chapter 16, p. 199.

26. Ludwig von Mises, *Socialism: An Economic and Sociological Analysis* (London: Jonathan Cape, 1959); F.A. Hayek, *Individualism and Economic Order* (Chicago: University of Chicago, 1948).

27. David Friedman, *The Machinery of Freedom* (New York: Harper Colophon, 1973), p. 41.

28. See chapter 16, p. 198.

29. Paul W. MacAvoy, *The Regulated Industries and the Economy* (New York: W.W. Norton, 1979), p. 79.

30. George J. Stigler, "The Theory of Economic Regulation," *The Bell Journal of Economics and Management Science* 2 (1971):3–21.

31. A number of the classic papers in the theory of rent seeking are included in James M. Buchanan, Robert D. Tollison, and Gordon Tullock, eds., *Toward a Theory of the Rent-Seeking Society* (College Station, Tex.: Texas A&M University, 1980).

32. See chapter 16, p. 194.

33. James M. Buchanan, "Rent Seeking and Profit Seeking" in Buchanan, Tollison, and Tullock, *Rent-Seeking Society.*

34. D.T. Armentano, "A Critique of Neoclassical and Austrian Monopoly Theory," in *New Directions in Austrian Economics,* ed. Louis M. Spadaro, (Kansas City: Sheed, Andrews and McMeel, 1978).

35. Israel M. Kirzner, *The Perils of Regulation: A Market-Process Approach* (Coral Gables, Fla.: Law and Economics Center, University of Miami School of Law, 1978).

36. Gordon Tullock, "The Transitional Gains Trap," in Buchanan, Tollison, and Tullock, *Rent-Seeking Society.*

37. James M. Buchanan, "Reform in the Rent-Seeking Society," pp. 359–367, in Buchanan, Tollison, and Tullock, *Rent-Seeking Society,* p. 365.

38. Terry L. Anderson and Peter J. Hill, *The Birth of a Transfer Society* (Stanford, Calif.: Hoover Institution Press, 1980).

39. James M. Buchanan, *Freedom in Constitutional Contract: Perspectives of a Political Economist* (College Station, Tex. and London: Texas A&M University, 1977).

40. Sudha R. Shenoy, "The Sources of Monopoly," *New Individualist Review* 4 (Spring 1966):41–44.

41. See chapter 16, p. 210.

42. Leland B. Yeager, "Economics and Principles," *Southern Economic Journal* 42 (1976):570.

18 Individual and Overall Viewpoints in Monetary Theory

Leland B. Yeager

The Need for a Clear Distinction

In or around 1951, while a graduate student at Columbia University, I was privileged to attend an extracurricular seminar on monetary theory conducted by Ludwig von Mises at Washington Square. The concepts that the seminar helped clarify for me included those of the demand for money and factors affecting it, the distinction between actual and demanded quantities of money, the services of or nonpecuniary yield on holdings of money, and diminishing marginal returns on those holdings.[1] Shortly after, I had occasion to ask my monetary-theory professor at Columbia a question presupposing the distinction between actual and demanded money holdings. Astonishingly, he was unfamiliar with that distinction and could make no sense of it. Every existing bit of money is held by someone, and held voluntarily, he said, so actual and demanded holdings not merely tend to become equal but are necessarily identical.

His error was a specific example of failure to grasp the distinction between individual and overall viewpoints. The importance of that distinction is the theme of this chapter: It seeks to illuminate both the fallacious and the fruitful interplay of viewpoints by bringing together examples of each.

In the demand-for-money example, the error lay in jumping from an aggregative fact to the supposed intentions of individuals. Of course all money belongs to somebody. Of course each holding is voluntary in the sense that the holder has accepted the money voluntarily and has not yet spent or otherwise disposed of it. But this fact does not necessarily mean that the holder is fully content with his cash balance, desiring neither to reduce or increase it. People will always accept payment in the routine medium of exchange whether they intend to continue holding it or instead intend to pass it on soon to someone else. Not every inpayment or outpayment represents a deliberate action to increase or reduce one's cash balance. The way that money functions in the economy, including the role of cash balances as buffers absorbing mismatchings of inpayments and outpayments, means that short-run changes in a person's actual cash balance need not reflect any change in his demand for an average cash balance over a span of time. Both for individual holders and for the aggregate of them, therefore, actual holdings of money are no exact measure of desired holdings.

To be sure, a macroeconomic process affecting prices (and usually affecting production and employment also) does tend to bring desired holdings into line with the actual quantity of money.[2] But understanding this process presupposes a firm grasp of the conceptual distinction between actual and desired quantities.

Individual-Experiments and Market-Experiments

The sound precept of methodological individualism does not call for rejecting the overall viewpoint in favor of the individual viewpoint. It calls, rather, for building bridges between the two, particularly by relating propositions about all economic phenomena, including the behavior of macroeconomic aggregates, to the perceptions and decisions of individuals.

One example of constructive interplay between the two viewpoints is the relation between individual-experiments and market-experiments, as distinguished by Don Patinkin.[3] In an individual-experiment one considers how some specified change would affect the choices of an individual or a set of individuals or even all members of the economic system considered in some particular capacity (such as actual or potential users of some commodity or as holders of money). It is legitimate in an individual-experiment to postulate alternative values even of some variable that cannot be a datum but rather is an endogenous variable from the standpoint of the economy as a whole. An example is the price of a particular competitively traded commodity. That price cannot simply change apart from underlying causes, apart from changes relatively exogenous to the market process, such as changes in tastes, resources, technology, institutions, and legislation. Still, it is legitimate to conduct the individual-experiment of inquiring, say, how purchases of the commodity desired by individuals or groups would respond to a price change, even though in a different (market-experiment) context that price change cannot simply be postulated by itself. The law of demand and law of supply (asserting downsloping demand curves and upsloping supply curves) are the two most familiar examples of results of individual-experiments. The law of supply and demand, describing how competitive pressures drive price toward the market-clearing level, is an example of the result of a market-experiment. So is an analysis of how equilibrium price and quantity traded would respond to a specified change in tastes, technology, or available resources affecting the demand for or supply of some commodity.

In monetary theory, an example of an individual-experiment is investigation of how the level of interest rates affects the quantity of money demanded (or, more comprehensively, investigation of the properties of the demand-for-money function). One cannot, however, legitimately try to investigate how the price level and real economic activity, say, would respond to a change in the level of interest rates, postulated by itself. In a market-experiment context, interest rates cannot simply change; their change must result from other changes, including changes exogenous to the market process. A legitimate market-experiment would specify these exogenous changes—perhaps technological developments affecting investment prospects and so the demand for loans—and would investigate their consequences, only one of which would be the interest-rate change. Another example of a market-experiment is investigation of the consequences of an exogenous increase or decrease in the quantity of money. It employs individual-experiment knowledge of the demand-for-money function and traces the consequences of the imbalance initially created between actual and desired holdings of money.

Fallacies of Composition

Probably the best known broad example of confusion of viewpoints is the fallacy of composition, unwarranted generalization from an individual to an overall viewpoint. (Recall the textbook example about standing on tiptoe to see a parade.) Often the fallacy consists of jumping from the result of an individual-experiment to the supposed result of a market-experiment without, of course, even distinguishing between the two types of experiment. The early Keynesian liquidity-preference theory of interest seems to be a case in point: from the inverse relation between the interest rate and desired holdings of money, an inverse relation between the actual money stock and the market-equilibrium interest rate was (invalidly) inferred. Another example is the blurring of distinctions between money and nearmoneys[4] on the grounds, apparently, that liquid assets in both categories are highly substitutable in the eyes of individual holders. Yet close similarity from the individual point of view does not entail close similarity in the ways that the medium of exchange and nearmoneys function in the economy as a whole, in the ways that the total quantities of each get determined, or in the ways that the two total quantities affect macroeconomic phenomena.[5] Explaining this point would require a chapter of its own; but, for a simple analogy, consider the close similarity for individual holders between gold coins and redeemable paper money under the historical gold standard, yet the great difference for the performance of the whole economy, especially at a time of balance-of-payments deficit, between having a monetary circulation composed mostly of gold coins and a circulation composed mostly of paper notes backed by only fractional gold reserves.

Some members of the rational-expectations school have recently asserted that increases in the money supply and in federal interest-bearing debt are essentially similar in causing price inflation. "Federal bonds are nothing more than an alternative form of currency—they are promises to deliver currency in the future. Like currency, these bonds are pieces of paper backed by nothing tangible; they are fiat paper." Since the government has no intention of ever retiring its debt, "there is little difference between currency and bonds; both are money." Any increase in the federal budget deficit, whether financed by issue of currency or of bonds, is therefore inflationary. "As is well understood, government can cause inflation by printing more money. It can also cause inflation by printing more bonds. Additions to the stock of money or bonds, by increasing the total amount of nominal wealth, increase private demands for goods and services. The increased demands, in turn, push up the prices of goods."[6] It would seem to follow from this argument that if government deficits are not to be avoided and are inflationary in any case, they might as well be financed in the simplest and cheapest way.[7]

The fallacy in these ideas rests, first of all, on the tacit assumption (reflected in the next-to-last of the sentences quoted) that money affects spending only by being part of its holders' wealth; the real-balance or cash-balance effect consists of nothing but a wealth effect. On this view, whether a good fairy gave a country's inhabitants $1 million worth of blankets (say) or $1 million of new money, spending on other goods and services would respond in the same way. Now, it is presumably true of an individual that his increased spending on goods and services would be unaffected by whether he received a gift of $1 million in cash or a gift of blankets sellable for $1 million after expenses. But it would be illegitimate to generalize from the irrelevance of the form of the gift for the individual to its supposed irrelevance for the behavior of the economy as a whole.

Yet a similar fallacy is committed in practically identifying bonds and money. No matter how wealthy the holders of bonds feel and how many goods and services their perceived wealth prompts them to buy, they can buy only by spending money. (Buying on credit merely delays but does not eliminate payment in money. A comprehensive system of offsetting debts against each other would make a big difference, but the discussion refers to actually existing institutions and practices.) On the warranted assumption that some relation exists between the flow of income and expenditure and desired holdings of the medium of exchange, the quantity of the latter in existence does pose some restraint on the flow of spending. Replacement of a substantial part of the money supply by bonds of equal value could hardly leave total spending unaffected.

When the government finances a deficit by issuing bonds, it finds willing buyers by offering the bonds at a lower price, in nominal terms, than the sum of their redemption price at maturity and interest payments in the meanwhile. In paying money for the bonds, the buyers forego other spending or lending. (If it is other lending that the bondbuyers forego, then the other persons to whom they would have made loans must either forego spending or else compete with still others for the limited supply of loanable funds. If the initial buyers want to cease holding the bonds, they cannot directly spend them on goods and services; rather, they, like the government in the first place, have to provide a price or interest inducement to others to take over the bonds.) Thus bond finance does not increase demands for goods and services and real resources—demands backed up by readiness to pay money—to the extent that the issue of money would have done. New money can be thrust into circulation by being directly spent on goods and services.

This is not to say that bond-financed deficits have no effect on spending. The textbooks explain how the rise in interest rates associated with bond finance will make people choose to hold smaller cash balances than otherwise in relation to income and expenditures; velocity will rise. On the other hand, insofar as people's desired money holdings are positively related to the total sizes of their wealth portfolios—if there is a wealth argument in the demand-for-money function—and insofar as government bonds count as part of the wealth of the private sector, issuing additional government bonds could tend to *increase* desired holdings of money. Conceivably, if not very plausibly, this wealth effect tending to *reduce* the velocity of the (unchanged) money supply could outweigh the above mentioned interest effect on velocity, resulting in *shrinkage* of total spending.[8] No such contractionary effect of a money-financed deficit is even conceivable (without utterly implausible assumptions).[9]

The notorious real-bills doctrine, dating from Adam Smith if not earlier and demolished by Henry Thornton in 1802,[10] keeps getting resurrected and reinvented with new twists. It got its name from the idea that bank lending, even the lending of money created in the process, would be noninflationary if accomplished by discounting short-term real bills, that is, bills of exchange arising from the production or marketing of real goods, as distinguished from mere finance or accommodation bills. The doctrine was also called the "needs-of-trade" theory on the grounds that if the expansion and contraction of money in connection with bank loans were linked to the production and marketing of goods, the quantity of money would be linked to the quantities of goods and thus to the needs of trade. If a bank loan enabled a manufacturer to buy raw materials and process them into goods for the market, the new goods would soon match the new money. Not the mere quantity of money but rather its quality—that is, the manner of its getting into circulation—was the supposed touchstone of sound policy.

Such qualitative regulation would gear the nominal quantity of money to the nominal value of goods rather than to their physical quantity. If prices should somehow happen to rise, then the nominal volume of lending and money issue supposedly justified by an unchanging physical volume of production would rise in step; monetary expansion in accordance with the doctrine would ratify and reinforce price inflation. A general decline of prices, conversely, would shrink the money supply and reinforce the deflation. Anchoring the money supply to a consequence of itself, namely the price level, means not anchoring it at all.

The real-bills doctrine has further fallacious aspects, but the one most relevant to this chapter is its invalid generalization from the individual to the overall point of view. Sure, a loan that expands the money supply may indeed enable the individual manufacturer (or retailer) to market goods that he could not otherwise have produced (or have acquired for his shelves). *His* production or marketing of goods may indeed be geared to his loan. But it does not follow that the total physical production and marketing of goods are geared to the total volume of loans. Real resources are scarce. Except perhaps in a seriously underemployed economy, lending newly created money to business does not so much bring additional productive resources into existence or into use as enable businessmen to bid more eagerly against each other for the resources available in any case.

Reverse Fallacies of Composition

What might be called the reverse fallacy of composition is the invalid supposition that what is true (or desirable) from an overall viewpoint is therefore true (or desirable) from an individual viewpoint as well. The idea sometimes turns up that the demand for money will tend to adapt itself to the actual quantity in a relatively painless way so that what would otherwise be a deficient money supply (at the going price level) will not constrain transactions, production, and employment after all. Faced with a shortage of coins in particular, people will cooperate to carry out their transactions anyway (the customer will give the retailer the extra dime or two cents needed to hold down the amount of change due). Similarly, George A. Akerlof suggests, people will cooperate to keep their transactions going when total money is in short supply.[11] They may adjust payments schedules or make more use of trade credits; financial institutions may devise new nearmoneys.

This optimistic argument is mistaken but instructive. A shortage specifically of coins is fairly obvious, and collaboration in coping with it works not only in the general interest but also in one's private interest (to keep one's own transaction going and to earn good will). An overall shortage of money is harder for individuals to diagnose. The disequilibrium does not show up on any particular market (whereas coins do have a market of their own in the sense that they exchange against money of other denominations); instead, the monetary disequilibrium shows itself obscurely as a generalized difficulty in selling things and earning incomes. Furthermore—and this is the most relevant point here—the fact that it would be in their common interest for people quite generally to employ money-economizing instruments and practices does not mean that it is in the interest of any individual to do so even before such expedients had already been generally adopted.

A similar point applies to proposals for adopting alternative money systems, such as reckoning in gold units or in units of constant purchasing power as calculated with a price index.[12] The government money might continue to circulate, but the amount changing hands in each particular transaction would be translated from the stable-value amount at the latest exchange rate or price index. Even if such a system would be in the general interest once firmly established, it might not be in the interest of individual transactors to go first in getting the system launched. Consider a bank. Would it be willing to accept deposits repayable in units of gold or of constant purchasing power before arranging to acquire assets similarly denominated? Would it find borrowers, for example, willing to commit themselves to repaying debt in gold or purchasing-power units before arranging to receive their revenues in such terms? Early users of the parallel money units would be exposing themselves to risk of adverse changes in the exchange rates of those units against the still-dominant government money. Inducements such as appropriately high or low interest rates might be found to make people bear such risks. The point remains, though, that the desirability of some change from the overall point of view does not imply that individuals will have reason to take the initiative in launching the change.

Further Confusions

The next examples defy easy classification under either the fallacy of composition or its reverse, although the reader may find trying to classify them instructive.

Writers on the Banking-school side of nineteenth-century British monetary controversies (including John Fullarton, Thomas Tooke, John Stuart Mill, and James Wilson) expounded a supposed "law of the reflux." An automatic process, they thought, would restrain issue of bank-created money in excess of the "wants of trade" or "needs of trade." Excessive note issues, in particular, would flow back to the issuing banks by way of deposits, repayments of loans, and, less significantly, demands for redemption in coin. (Banking-school writers emphasized the first two channels over the third.)[13] Sure, an individual bank trying to get too many notes into circulation (for example, by offering borrowers exceptionally easy terms) would find itself plagued and restrained by what we would nowadays call adverse clearing balances; but the same is not true of the system as a whole. If all banks were moving together in expanding their note and deposit issues, each would be acquiring more and more claims on the others as well as incurring more and more liabilities to them and so would be avoiding large adverse clearing balances. Furthermore, the effects of the monetary expansion on prices and nominal incomes would be increasing the quantities of money that the public demanded to hold. Apart, therefore, from redeemability requirements and prospects of exhaustion of specie reserves—and these circumstances are not at the core of the supposed law of the reflux—no check on inflationary overissue would operate after all. Determinacy of the money supply and price level presupposes some sort of real anchor or quantitative limitation, such as is provided by redeemability of bank money in base money of limited quantity.

The Yale School's "New View" of money and financial intermediation (in fact hardly new at all) confuses viewpoints in postulating a "natural economic limit" to the size of the money-creating system. Given their wealth and their asset preferences, says James Tobin, people will voluntarily hold additional demand deposits only if yields on alternative assets fall. This also means reduced yields on loans and investments available to the banks, making further lending and investing unprofitable for them beyond some point. In this respect the commercial-banking industry is not different in kind from any other system of financial intermediaries. Even without reserve requirements, the banking system's expansion "would be limited by the availability of assets at yields sufficient to compensate banks for the costs of attracting and holding the corresponding deposits."[14] As Basil Moore expresses the matter, the necessity facing banks, like all other business firms, "of operating at profit, combined with a downward sloping demand curve for bank loans and deposits, serves to restrict output expansion even in the absence of deposit control through reserve manipulation."[15]

This view slights some familiar contrasts. No obstacle on the demand-for-money side blocks lending and spending new bank demand deposits into existence. (Meeting reserve requirements, if they exist, and in any case maintaining redeemability of deposits in base money, operates on the supply-of-money side. These restraints are too familiar to distinguish any self-styled New View.) No one need be persuaded to invest in the routine medium of exchange before more of it can be created. Bankers do not need to find someone willing to hold it but only someone willing to accept it—if not a borrower, then someone selling a security from his portfolio, or a supplier of furniture or office equipment, or a bank employee. Once a person has accepted new money, he passes it along to others, if he does not want to hold it, instead of somehow making it go out of existence. It is hard to imagine why a bank might find it more profitable to hold reserves in excess of what the law and prudence call for than to buy riskless short-term securities with them. The New Viewers seem to be assuming, tacitly and mistakenly, that the individual bank is wary of bidding down yields on portfolio assets because it is concerned with maximizing not its own profits but those of the banking system as a whole.[16]

Even with regard to the banking system as a whole, something is wrong with the idea that a decline in yields obtainable will check expansion of loans and investments and deposits. That idea overlooks Knut Wicksell's cumulative process. As money expansion raises nominal incomes and prices, the dollar volume of loans demanded rises also, even at given interest rates. The great inflations of history discredit any notion of a natural limit to expansion of money and credit.

A recently popular version of the monetary theory of the balance of payments goes beyond merely recommending attention to the supply of and demand for domestic money holdings in an analysis of balance-of-payments disequilibrium and adjustment; it actually identifies a payments surplus under fixed exchange rates with the process of satisfying an excess demand for domestic money and identifies a deficit with the process of working off an excess supply of money.[17] Now, an association between money–supply-and-demand imbalance and payments disequilibrium is indeed a frequent case and perhaps even the typical case. Their outright identification, however, is fallacious, as could easily be shown by counterexamples (including the historical phenomenon of imported inflation). Actual changes in the money supply are misinterpreted as aggregates of deliberate and desired adjustments in the money holdings of individual holders.

This misinterpretation traces to failure to take due account of the functioning of money as the medium of exchange. It is true that a country's payments surplus or deficit, suitably defined, involves the residents' acquisition or relinquishment, respectively, of domestic money.[18] But these changes may not represent desired adjustments of money holdings. Because money is the routine medium of exchange, people will always accept it even when they do not, individually, desire to go on holding it. But new money does not automatically go out of circulation again just because it is undesired as additional holdings; rather, it touches off an expansionary or inflationary process that tends to make it all desired after all. Conversely, shrinkage of a country's money supply does not necessarily represent the deliberate and desired rundown of individual holdings. Instead, it could be the unintended consequence of money's routine use as the means of payment in a situation in which its domestic holders found purchases of goods and services and securities more attractive or more available than sales in transactions with parties other than themselves.

Suppose, for example, that the central bank, committing some colossal blunder, carries out a massive contractionary open-market operation. Private investors buy the securities being offered by the central bank because their low prices and high yields are attractive. These investors pay in money, of course, but probably *without* intending to get along thereafter with a cash balance smaller by that amount. Instead, each probably intends to replenish his cash balance by selling other securities or goods and services to somebody else. These intentions meet frustration, and the excess demand for money resulting from the contractionary open-market operation has disastrous macroeconomic consequences. Now suppose a different blunder with similar consequences: The central bank revalues the home currency upward, cutting in half the pegged home-currency price of foreign exchange. In consequence of all the related price changes, purchases of goods and services and securities abroad become much more attractive and available than sales abroad, the country runs a balance-of-payment deficit, and the home money supply shrinks, with painful deflationary consequences. In brief, by making foreign exchange such a bargain and selling it lavishly out of its reserves, the central bank takes out of circulation the domestic money received in payment. Yet this monetary contraction in no way represents an intentional rundown of private money holdings.

The theory reviewed rests, in short, on a confusion of viewpoints. Specifically, it mistakenly supposes that changes in a country's money supply associated with a balance-of-payment surplus or deficit must correspond (not just may correspond) to aggregates of desired changes in individual holdings.

Illuminating Interplay

Let us turn from castigating errors toward recognizing fruitful interaction between individual and overall viewpoints. A well-known example will serve as a start. How can the economist, observing the whole system of banks operating with fractional reserves, say that the system creates deposit money (when additional reserve funds or cuts in reserve requirements allow it to expand), while the individual banker can nevertheless maintain that he does not create any money at all but rather simply relends money deposited with him, and then not even its entire amount but only the excess over what he must set aside as reserves? What reconciles these contrasting views? Any undergraduate who has passed the money and banking course should know the answer, so I will not presume to repeat it here.[19]

In applying his regression theorem to the so-called circulatory problem, Ludwig von Mises was constructively bridging the two viewpoints. The problem is that money is demanded for its purchasing power: How many nominal units an individual demands to hold depends above all on the price level. Yet the price level is determined by the interplay of money's supply and demand. It is easy to show, as Patinkin has done, that there is no vicious circularity in these propositions.[20] A demand function for money holdings in which the purchasing power of the money units is the principal argument, together with the actual quantity of money, suffices to determine the equilibrium price level in the sense that demanded and actual quantities of money would be unequal at any other price level. This mathematical determinacy or noncircularity does not, however, render Mises's regression theorem otiose. Here, as in the analysis of the difference between near-moneys and the medium of exchange, it is necessary to pay attention not only to mathematical functions (such as demand functions for money and other assets) but also to the *functioning* of those assets in the economy and to the processes whereby individuals give effect to their demands for each. Patinkin was content with showing that there is no mathematical or logical inconsistency in imagining the individual-experiment that relates the quantity of money demanded to the purchasing power of the unit and then imagining the market-experiment of confronting that demand function with a definite supply of money to determine the equilibrium purchasing power. Mises, however, was mainly concerned with process, with who does what. We may agree that people demand a definite aggregate of holdings of nominal money at each of its conceivable alternative purchasing powers. But which one of the infinitely many alternative levels do people have in mind when they actually decide how much money to hold and try to conduct market transactions consistent with their decisions? Could a new pure fiat money be launched without any clue to its tentative initial value? (Fiat money, in contrast with other things, has no usefulness of its own for people to consider in deciding how much of it to demand.) Suppose the old money were declared invalid and each person were given x units of the new money and told nothing more than to start using it. How would anyone know what prices to ask and offer for things? Would not the launching of the new money be facilitated by some indication of its initial value? If the answer is "yes," Mises was right. He said, we recall, that the demand for money interacting with supply to determine money's value "today" is expressed in the light of money's value "yesterday," which was determined by supply and demand in the light of its value the day before, and so on back in history to the time when some commodity, valuable for its own usefulness, had not quite yet evolved into money. (To say that Mises was right is not to say that Patinkin is wrong, for they were dealing with subtly different questions. Patinkin may be faulted, though, for not pointing out this difference.)

It is important for clear theorizing to distinguish between money's services to society as a whole and its services to an individual holder. On the one hand, in other words, we perceive the advantages of having a monetary rather than a barter economy (advantages that extreme monetary instability undercuts). On the other hand we perceive the yield—subjective, intangible, and nonpecuniary, but genuine—that an individual holder receives on his cash balance, the yield that is one of the most fundamental concepts of monetary theory.[21]

Advantages of the first type enter into a public-goods aspect of money. Having a stable unit of account in which to conduct one's calculations and possibly to express one's claims and debts is advantageous even to people who do not hold that money and make and receive payments in it. A historical example will help make the point clear. Many business firms in Germany during the extreme inflation of the early 1920s reportedly took to figuring their costs and their selling prices in some relatively stable unit like the U.S. dollar or the Swiss franc, even though they continued receiving and making payments predominantly in German marks. They translated their stable-money prices into marks at the latest exchange rate at the time of sale. The very existence of the dollar and Swiss franc thus benefited Germans who might never have actually held or received or paid any dollars or francs.

A consideration like this bears on proposals (like that of Hayek, cited in note 12) for encouraging the competitive private issue of currencies. Each issuer would have his own unit (ducat, crown, florin, or whatever; the proposal does not envisage rival currencies all denominated in the same unit, such as a quantity of gold); and the different units would be free to fluctuate against each other. Each issuer would have an incentive, supposedly, to restrain his issues to keep the value of his unit stable, thereby attracting wider and wider circles of holders. Virtue would bring its own reward. The larger the real volume of his currency people would willingly hold, the larger the volume of loans the issuer could have outstanding and earning interest. Success in restraining his issue to the volume demanded at a stable value of his unit would itself strengthen that demand, which he could then profitably meet.

Because of the public-goods aspect, however—namely, the free availability of his money as a unit of accounting and calculation even to parties who held little or none of it—a well-behaved issuer could not collect compensation for all the advantages he was conferring on the public in general. The social benefits of his maintaining a stable money would not come fully to his attention. Here we recall the standard argument that the purely private provision of public goods falls short of the optimum, plausibly defined.

This point may not be welcome to those who are looking for monetary reform along private-enterprise lines. It may not be a quantitatively important point. But it is one that reformers should face. And it does illustrate the interplay of viewpoints that is the theme of this chapter.

Another sort of relation between viewpoints is that each individual's reasons for using and holding a particular money are strengthened to the extent that others are doing the same. This fact may be relevant to the question whether many or few private currencies or only one would survive in a regime of actual or potential competition. James Tobin has noted an analogy between money and language: "Both are means of communication. The use of a particular language or a particular money by one individual increases its value to other actual or potential users. Increasing returns to scale, in this sense, limits the number of languages or moneys in a society and indeed explains the tendency for one basic language or money to monopolize the field. Theory must give way to history in explaining which language and what money . . . are adopted in any given community." The analogy points to "arbitrariness and circularity" in a money's being accepted: acceptability enhances acceptability.[22] It also affords further insight into the aforementioned difficulties of launching competitive private moneys or a new stable unit to be used optionally in parallel with government money. Being one of the early users of a new unit would confer benefits on late-comers, if the reform could succeed, for which the early users could not collect compensation. They thus have inadequate incentives to provide what would be in part a public good.

In a different respect, switching to a new currency creates a public bad if it shrinks demand for holdings of the old one, whose value consequently fluctuates downward more sharply than otherwise. This problem of currency substitution might plague a system of competing private currencies even if it could somehow be successfully launched. According to the very logic of the scheme, holders of the different currencies, as well as the financial press, would be alert to signs of unsound management and incipient depreciation of any one of them. Its holders would dump it and fly into others. Sensitive responses of this sort would destabilize the exchange rates between the different currencies, upsetting transactions and calculations. Like bank runs (particularly in the days before deposit insurance), such runs from one currency to another would be harmful from an overall point of view, yet would result from individuals' efforts to protect themselves.

One should be careful, however, about applying such worries to the existing national currencies under floating exchange rates. Yet some writers connected with the rational-expectations school have argued that floating exchange rates are workable only when sensitive international capital transfers are throttled by government controls.[23] The worry seems to be that since fiat currencies lack any intrinsic value and have purchasing power thanks only to the demand for holdings of them in the context of limited supplies, people will make an all-or-nothing choice between one currency or another according to their perceived prospects of escaping inflation. With everyone alert to shift funds, no one can count on his own national currency continuing in general use.

Assessment of this worry requires a careful distinction of veiwpoints. If the choice of a general medium of exchange and unit of account were to be made collectively, then there might indeed be an all-or-nothing shift to the prospectively least inflation-plagued currency. But the choice is not made that way. In practice, the shift has to occur piecemeal. As long as one's fellow countrymen are still generally using the national currency, it is awkward and expensive for an individual or firm to try to initiate the shift. With money as with language, inertia tends to perpetuate an entrenched use. Continuing general use tends to maintain the nonpecuniary services that cash balances of the home currency yield. Furthermore, currencies cannot be compared in terms of a single (expected) rate of return on each (gain or loss of purchasing power being appropriately counted in or netted out). The service component of the yield depends at the margin on the size of the individual cash balance. If and as the individual cut his holding of the home currency, its subjectively appraised yield to him would rise at the margin and rise in relation to the marginal yield on holdings of foreign currency of similar real size. Inflation prospects may reduce the demand for holdings of the home currency, but those prospects would have to be bad indeed to eliminate the demand in an all-or-nothing choice.[24]

Questions about indexing are not unrelated to questions of parallel currencies and of shifts between currencies. Proponents recommend indexing as a way of coping with inflation. A warning is in order, though, against undue projection of advantages from the individual point of view to conclusions about overall feasibility. Clearly it would be convenient for the individual to be able to carry out his accounting and price and cost calculations, receive income, make contracts, accumulate savings, and incur debts all in constant-value units. From the overall point of view, however, parasitism would seem to be a problem. A price index serviceable for defining the constant-value unit and for making conversions between amounts in constant units and in current dollars must be compiled from prices determined by the interplay of market forces rather than from prices themselves mechanically calculated according to some formula. Indexing presupposes the prevalence of unindexed prices and wages and is parasitic on them. The more pervasively the index is applied, the more nearly meaningless it becomes in the sense that it is calculated from prices that are themselves calculated according to the index itself (or perhaps its level of a few months earlier).

Some Central Points of Macroeconomics

The distinction between viewpoints is vital to some central points of money-macro theory. Disequilibrium between actual and desired holdings of money, together with its macroeconomic consequences—in particular, recession or depression in the case of an excess demand for money—can persist for a long time because there is no specific money market on which a specific price of money adjusts to equilibrate supply and demand. Instead, equilibrating changes in the value of money have to take place through myriads of prices of individual goods and services and securities determined on separate though interlocking markets. Imbalance between supply and demand for a particular good or service typically affects not only its price but also its quantity traded and so its quantity produced. An excess demand for money can thus deflate not only prices but also real economic activity; and the less the deflationary impact is absorbed by prices, the more it must be absorbed by production and employment. (The familiar tautology $MV = PQ$ can be helpful in making this point.) Individual and collective rationality can diverge when interlocking wage and price decisions are made, as they realistically must be made, in a piecemeal, decentralized, unsynchronized manner. (The difficulties of maintaining monetary equilibrium through market-determined price-level adjustments form the basis, of course, of the ideal of avoiding monetary disequilibrium in the first place through suitable regulation of the money supply.)

In a depression (and in the absence of sensible monetary policy), it would be collectively rational to cut the general level of costs and wages and prices steeply enough to make the real value of the nominal money stock adequate for a full-employment volume of transactions and production. Nevertheless, the individual agent may not find it rational promptly to cut the particular price or wage for which he is responsible. Instead of initiating cuts in advance of other agents, he may well find it rational to wait for a better reading on the market situation. (The widespread practice of letting what may prove random mismatchings of supply and demand impinge initially on inventories reflects a justified belief that it would be irrational to try to keep supply and demand continuously in balance by prompt and frequent price adjustments.) Instead of going first, the individual agent may rationally wait to see whether cuts by others, intensifying the competition he faces or reducing his production costs or his cost of living, as the case may be, will make it advantageous for him to *follow* with a cut of his own. Here, as in the well-known example of the prisoners' dilemma, the individually rational and the collectively rational may well diverge. Taking the lead in downward price and wage adjustments is in the nature of a public good, and private incentives to supply it are weak.[25]

These observations about depression become relevant to present-day stagflation because of a close analogy holding between the stickiness of a price level and the momentum of an entrenched trend of prices and wages. Restraint on money-supply growth impinges not only on price inflation but also, and earlier, on production and employment. The momentum of wages and prices goes on for a while eroding the real value of the restrained nominal money supply. The momentum derives from the determination of interdependent prices in a piecemeal, unsynchronized manner as people attempt to catch up with past increases and to allow for expected future increases in costs and prices and wages other than their own. How can I, an individual businessman, be confident that restraint in my own pricing policy will be matched by restraint in my workers' wage demands and in my suppliers' and competitors' prices? Is it not sensible to continue allowing for past and future increases in all costs and prices that affect me until I get a better reading on how other people may or may not be modifying their price and wage behavior? Of course, if I and all other price setters and wage negotiators were to make our decisions jointly, then it would be in our collective interest to avoid the side effects of monetary restraint by practicing appropriate price and wage restraint. In fact, though, we make our decisions piecemeal, opening the way for divergence between collective and individual rationality.[26] This circumstance is not a defect of the market system but rather an inevitable consequence of the realities that any economic system must cope with, including the fact that inevitably dispersed knowledge can be effectively used only through decentralized decisions whose coordination can hardly be accomplished better than through market processes.

For reasons just implied, the degree of credibility and perceived resoluteness of an antiinflation policy affects how severe the withdrawal pangs will be. In two alternative situations with objectively the same monetary restraints, the policy will bite more strongly on prices and wages and its recessionary side-effects will be milder when the authorities are believed ready to tolerate such effects than when they are suspected of irresolution. It is not the purpose of this chapter, however, to pursue such policy issues. Enough has been said to illustrate how the distinction and interplay between individual and collective viewpoints is crucial to understanding the stickiness of price and wage levels and trends, the persistence of monetary disequilibrium, the phenomenon of stagflation, and the problems of stopping inflation.

Other Applications of the Distinction

Distinguishing between the two viewpoints is more familiar outside than within monetary theory. A mere reminder of a few examples will serve as a conclusion. The distinction is central in analysis of externalities and public goods and their relation to the incomplete specification and application of property rights and pricing. Consider the standard examples of oil capture and overfishing, as well as long waits in line at the King Tut exhibit or for gasoline during shortages. Anyone joining the rush for oil or fish or joining the line for the exhibit or for gasoline is imposing costs on others. Forbearance from joining would be a public good, and "correct" specification and application of property rights and "proper" pricing (as of tickets to the exhibit) would make this forbearance in the private interest of individuals also. (The quotation marks indicate that no premature policy recommendation is intended.) At a cocktail party, speaking in a loud voice is a private good but a public bad, contributing to the state of affairs that makes the shouting privately necessary. During an inflation, keeping one's own selling price or wage rate roughly in line with the general procession is something closely analogous. Divergence between individual and collective rationality is a pervasive fact of life, but this fact does not indict a price system. Rather, it exists because of the impossibility or impracticality of applying property rights and the logic of a price system to so many cases. The consequences of not being able to apply a price system in such cases testify, by the contrast they offer, to the advantages of a price system where it can work.

Concepts akin to those mentioned enter into the application of economics and methodological individualism to the analysis of government. They help explain how programs can get adopted piecemeal whose aggregate has an impact that runs counter to, and could have been expected to run counter to, the public interest in any plausible interpretation of the latter term. They help restrain sentimental exaggerations about how "the people" rule in a democracy and about the value of having affairs taken care of "democratically." They help one understand how democratic government adopts programs with an even less accurate confrontation of costs and benefits than the market process accomplishes even in exaggerated descriptions of market failure; they help explain, in particular, how the governmental decision process is biased toward hyperactivity. Attention to both individual and collective viewpoints reveals the narrowness and the piecemeal nature of so much governmental decision making. It serves for probing into the circumstances, incentives, and actions of the individual participants in this process—the "average voter" (who, as Anthony Downs explained, is "rationally ignorant" about most issues that his vote helps decide on), the special-interest voter, the legislator, the executive, the candidate, the bureaucrat, and the judge.

Ludwig von Mises was an early contributor of ideas in these fields. He appreciated the differences as well as the similarities between voting in political elections and voting with dollars in the marketplace. He contributed insights into the difference between bureaucratic and profit-oriented institutions and into the activities for which each type of institution had a comparative advantage.[27] In monetary theory his contributions were even more fundamental.

Notes

1. Other influences on my understanding around this time included Mises's *Human Action* (New Haven: Yale, 1949) and Edwin Cannan, "The Application of the Theoretical Apparatus of Supply and Demand to Units of Currency," *Economical Journal,* 1921, reprinted in American Economic Association, *Readings in Monetary Theory* (Philadelphia: Blakiston, 1951), pp. 3–12. W.H. Hutt's "The Yield on Money Held" (an absolutely fundamental contribution, in my opinion) appeared a few years later in the Mises *Festschrift,* Mary Sennholz, ed., *On Freedom and Free Entreprise* (Princeton, N.J.: Van Nostrand, 1956).

2. Both J.M. Keynes and Milton Friedman, separately, called the description of this process the "fundamental" or "most important" proposition of monetary theory. The demanded quantity that tends to be aligned with the actual quantity is expressed in nominal terms; with regard to the real (purchasing-power) quantity of money, the adjustment tends to work the other way around, the desired quantity pulling the actual quantity into line. The "fundamental proposition" referring to nominal quantities presupposes a floating exchange rate; for, with a fixed exchange rate, the demand for money can affect the actual quantity through the balance of payments.

3. *Money, Interest, and Prices,* 2d ed. (New York: Harper & Row, 1965), esp. pp. 11–12, 387–395.

4. As in the British Radcliffe Report of 1959; for citations and discussion, see my "Essential Properties of the Medium of Exchange," *Kyklos* 21, no. 1 (1968):45–69.

5. I am not forgetting that institutional changes may in fact now be blurring distinctions that formerly were real. That, however, is another story.

6. Preston J. Miller and Alan Struthers, Jr., "The Tax-Cut Illusion," Federal Reserve Bank of Minneapolis, *1979 Annual Report,* pp. 1–9 (preceded by an approving introduction by the Bank's president, Mark H. Willes), and Preston J. Miller, "Deficit Policies, Deficit Fallacies," Federal Reserve Bank of Minneapolis *Quarterly Review* 4 (Summer 1980):2–4. The quotations come from the *Report,* p. 2, and the *Review,* p. 2. In a footnote to the latter, Miller cites other authors who also, he says, perceive the essential similarity of bonds and money. Also see N.J. Simler's letter to the *Wall Street Journal,* 10 August 1981, p. 19.

7. John Bryant and Neil Wallace, "The Inefficiency of Interest-Bearing National Debt," *Journal of Political Economy* 87 (April 1979):365–381.

8. A mathematical formalization of this point, though available, would swell the discussion beyond what is appropriate here. For greater attention to the possibility in question than is usual in textbooks, see Thomas M. Havrilesky and John T. Boorman, *Monetary Macroeconomics* (Arlington Heights, Ill.: AHM Publishing, 1978), chap. 12 and passim.

For an example of a different notion about the relation between money and spending, namely, the erroneous assertion that the total money supply has no significant influence on aggregate spending because individual cash balances, being freely chosen, do not significantly influence spending by their individual holders, see James Tobin, "Asset Holdings and Spending Decisions," *American Economic Review* 42 (May 1952): especially, p. 115. G.M. Meier quotes this passage with approval in "Some Questions about Growth Economics: Comment," *American Economic Review* 44 (December 1954):936.

9. Another difference between the two types of finance is that bond finance can shift part of the "burden" of government deficit spending to future generations in a way that money finance cannot do. For resurrection of the proposition about burden-shifting, which for many years had wrongly been scorned as erroneous, see James M. Buchanan, *Public Principles of Public Debt* (Homewood, Ill.: Irwin, 1958). Buchanan pointed out what this chapter calls a confusion of viewpoints. The conventional wisdom that he attacked was proceeding directly from aggregate and material considerations (such as the fact that real resources cannot be shifted from the future into the present) to judgments about burdens supposedly borne or not borne by individuals in the current and future generations. It went wrong in adopting an insufficiently subjectivist (or even antisubjectivist) conception of burden and in focusing insufficiently on individual persons. The correctness of Buchanan's analysis now seems to be widely, although only tacitly, acknowledged in discussions of the difference between funded and pay-as-you-go programs of social-security financing.

10. *An Enquiry into the Nature and Effects of the Paper Credit of Great Britain,* ed. F.A. Hayek (1939; reprint ed., Fairfield, N.J.: Augustus M. Kelley, 1978), chaps. 2, 10. Also see Lloyd W. Mints, *A History of Banking Theory* (Chicago: University of Chicago Press, 1945), pp. 9–11, 25–30, and passim.

11. "The Questions of Coinage, Trade Credit, Financial Flows and Peanuts: A Flow-of-Funds Approach to the Demand for Money," Federal Reserve Bank of New York, Research Paper no. 7520, September 1975. A similar argument about money substitutes and a plastic demand for money had already been presented by Jean-Baptiste Say in *A Treatise on Political Economy,* trans. C.R. Prinsep (Philadelphia: Grigg & Elliot, 1836), pp. 133–134.

12. With modifications, the point also applies to Hayek's proposal for encouraging private moneys, whose issuers would compete for holders by achieving records of stability of the purchasing powers of their money units. See a later section of this chapter and F.A. Hayek, *The Denationalisation of Money,* 2d ed. (London: Institute of Economic Affairs, 1978).

13. Mints, *History of Banking Theory,* pp. 88–94, 134, 207. Mints describes the doctrine and regards it as wrong, but he does not make the confusion-of-viewpoints criticism. He comes close on page 26, however,

where he discusses Adam Smith's errors in connection with the real-bills doctrine and with supposed restraint on overissue of bank notes.

14. James Tobin, "Commercial Banks as Creators of 'Money,' " in *Banking and Monetary Studies,* ed. Deane Carson (Homewood, Ill.: Irwin, 1963), pp. 414, 416. Andrew D. Crockett forcefully echoes Tobin's general position in "The Euro-Currency Market: An Attempt to Clarify Some Basic Issues," *IMF Staff Papers* 23 (July 1976):375–386. For further citations and fuller discussion, see my "What Are Banks? in the *Atlantic Economic Journal* 6 (December 1978):1–14.

15. *An Introduction to the Theory of Finance* (New York: Free Press, 1968), pp. 168–169.

16. Paul F. Smith, "Concepts of Money and Commercial Banks," *Journal of Finance* 21 (December 1966):645–646; Rainer S. Masera, "Deposit Creation, Multiplication and the Euro-Dollar Market," in Ente per gli Studi Monetari, Bancari e Finanziari Luigi Einaudi, *Quaderni di Ricerche,* no. 11 (1973):151.

17. A monetary theory of floating exchange rates, in parallel, identifies a currency's exchange appreciation or depreciation as part of a process of correcting an imbalance between desired and actual holdings of domestic money. For documentation and fuller discussion, see Alan A. Rabin and Leland B. Yeager, "Monetary Approaches to the Balance of Payments and Exchange Rates," *Economic Perspectives* 1 (1979):173–201. My purpose here is not to explore the error in question fully but merely to cite it as still another example of confusion of viewpoints.

18. A surplus entails creating domestic money as the central bank buys up the country's net receipts of foreign exchange to keep the exchange rate fixed; a deficit entails shrinking domestic money as the central bank sells foreign exchange from its reserves to shore up the home currency's exchange rate. In some cases the central bank might be offsetting this creation or destruction of domestic money in its exchange-rate pegging with money destruction or creation in its domestic operations; but such monetary changes of domestic origin would give superficial support to the (mis) interpretation of the payments surplus or deficit as necessarily due to an excess demand for or supply of domestic money.

19. The correct explanation, in adequate detail, is commonly attributed to C.A. Phillips (*Bank Credit,* New York: Macmillan, 1920), but he had been anticipated by several others, including Herbert J. Davenport (*The Economics of Enterprise,* New York: Macmillan, 1913). See Mints, *History of Banking Theory,* pp. 113, 206, 257–258.

20. *Money, Interest, and Prices,* pp. 115–116. Compare Laurence S. Moss, "The Monetary Economics of Ludwig von Mises," in *The Economics of Ludwig von Mises,* ed. Laurence S. Moss (Kansas City: Sheed and Ward, 1976), pp. 13–49.

I am indebted to Roger W. Garrison for correcting my earlier inadequate appreciation of Mises's regression theorem. See his "The Austrian-Neoclassical Relation: A Study in Monetary Dynamics" (Ph.D. diss., University of Virginia, February 1981), pp. 77–81 in particular.

21. Compare J.R. Hicks, "The Two Triads," in his *Critical Essays in Monetary Theory* (Oxford: Clarendon Press, 1967), as well as the article by Hutt cited in footnote 1.

22. James Tobin, "Discussion," in *Models of Monetary Economies,* ed. John H. Kareken and Neil Wallace (Minneapolis: Federal Reserve Bank of Minneapolis, 1980), pp. 86–87.

23. John Kareken and Neil Wallace, "International Monetary Reform: The Feasible Alternatives," Federal Reserve Bank of Minneapolis *Quarterly Review* 2 (summer 1978):2–7. To explain away the absence of a flight away from the downward-floating Canadian dollar, Kareken and Wallace refer lamely to expectations that either the Canadian or the U.S. government would institute controls if such a flight got under way. Gottfried Haberler critically discusses this article in "Flexible-Exchange-Rate Theories and Controversies Once Again," in *Flexible Exchange Rates and the Balance of Payments: Essays in Memory of Egon Sohmen,* ed. John S. Chipman and Charles P. Kindleberger (Amsterdam: North-Holland, 1980), separately reprinted as Reprint no. 119 (Washington: American Enterprise Institute, January 1981).

24. Haberler, who characterizes Kareken and Wallace's paper as "an extraordinary example of how remorseless logicians can end up in Bedlam, if they get hold of the wrong assumptions," adds some further points: (1) Not everyone has the same expectations. (2) Only the cash, non-interest-bearing, portions of different countries' money stocks might be regarded as perfect substitutes for one another. Except in the most extreme inflations, interest-rate differentials would restrain any general rush from assets in one currency to assets in another. Even in the extreme circumstances of Germany in 1920–1923, the large-scale substitution of foreign for home money was slow to develop; and in present-day Brazil, where everyone expects the cruzeiro to keep on depreciating, no wholesale substitution of foreign for Brazilian money has occurred (although people would have found a way around the exchange controls if they had felt a strong urge to switch). Haberler, "Flexible-Exchange-Rate Theories," pp. 44–46.

25. Yet doctrines to the effect that markets are always or should be analyzed as always in equilibrium practically obliterate this distinction of viewpoints. Part of the trouble is their reasoning only in terms of the overall price level or price and wage levels, or distinguishing only between actual and expected average levels (or inflation rates), and not recognizing that these average levels are made up of and can change only by way of millions of separate prices and wages. Such doctrines seem to be gaining popularity

in parallel with the doctrine of rational expectations. I have discussed them in "Sticky Prices or Equilibrium Always?" a paper for the Western Economic Association meetings in San Francisco, 6 July 1981.

26. In these circumstances, price or wage restraint is a public good; it confers external benefits for which their creator cannot collect a privately adequate reward. Arthur Okun, among others, has recognized these externalities of pricing decisions; see his posthumously published *Prices and Quantities* (Washington, D.C.: Brookings Institution, 1981). Okun has also emphasized the role of the "invisible handshake" and of notions of fairness in the stickiness of levels or trends of prices and wages.

27. *Bureaucracy* (London: Hodge, 1945).

19 Ludwig von Mises and the Monetary Approach to the Balance of Payments: Comment on Yeager

Joseph T. Salerno

Leland Yeager offers an illuminating discussion of a serious problem that has historically plagued monetary theory and continues to do so to this day: the failure to clearly distinguish between the individual and the overall viewpoints in the analysis of monetary phenomena. I wish to emphasize particularly Yeager's insight that the source of this problem lies in the failure of monetary theorists to heed "the sound precept of methodological individualism," which dictates that bridges be constructed between the two viewpoints ". . . by relating propositions about all economic phenomena, including the behavior of macroeconomic aggregates, to the perceptions and decisions of individuals."[1] In detailing and critically analyzing the errors engendered by this confusion of viewpoints in monetary theory, Yeager has taught an elementary, although much needed, lesson in the principles of economic reasoning and the dire consequences of their neglect. I daresay this lesson would have been wholly unnecessary had economists attended more closely to the earlier lessons taught by Ludwig von Mises, certainly the foremost exponent and practitioner of methodological individualism in twentieth-century monetary theory.

Since I am in fundamental agreement with the thrust of Yeager's argument, I shall utilize one illustration in his discussion as a springboard to elucidating an especially neglected contribution to monetary theory made by Mises in his consistent application of methodological individualism to the explanation of monetary phenomena. In this connection, I wish to focus attention on Yeager's treatment of the modern monetary approach to the balance of payments. I propose to show, first, that the valid and vitally important insight upon which the monetary approach rests forms the basis of Mises's own elaboration of balance-of-payments theory and, second, that Mises's approach is not open to the objection raised by Yeager against the monetary approach precisely because Mises firmly adheres to the precept of methodological individualism. This enterprise, it may be noted, has important implications for the contemporary formulation of the

247

monetary approach as well as for doctrinal researches into its historical antecedents. On the doctrinal side, it is a matter of setting the record straight. In the recent spate of studies exploring the doctrinal roots of the monetary approach, Mises's contribution, with one minor exception, has been completely neglected.[2] From the standpoint of contemporary theory, one hopes that greater familiarity with Mises's contribution, which so strongly anticipates the monetary approach, will spark a rethinking of the monetary approach and its subsequent reformulation on sounder methodological foundations.

The fundamental insight of the monetary approach is that the balance of payments is essentially a monetary phenomenon. That is, the very concept of a balance of payments implies the existence of money; or, as one writer on the monetary approach puts it, "Indeed, it would be impossible to have a balance-of-payments surplus or deficit in a barter economy."[3] This being the case, when endeavoring to explain balance-of-payments phenomena attention must naturally be focused on the supply of and demand for the money commodity. The monetary approach consists in the rigorous delineation of the implications of this simple yet powerful insight for the analysis of balance-of-payments disequilibrium, adjustment, and policy. As I shall attempt to demonstrate, Mises fully anticipated the modern monetary approach in the explicit recognition of these implications.

To begin with, Mises grounds his balance-of-payments analysis on the basic insight that the balance of payments is a monetary concept. He states that, "If no other relations than those of barter exist between the inhabitants of two areas, then balances in favor of one party or the other cannot arise."[4] Mises thus conceives of money as the active element in the balance of payments and not as a residual or accomodating item that passively adjusts to the "real" flows of goods and capital:

> The surplus of the balance of payments that is not settled by the consignment of goods and services but by the transmission of money was long regarded as merely a consequence of the state of international trade. It is one of the great achievements of Classical political economy to have exposed the fundamental error in this view. It demonstrated that international movements of money are not consequences of the state of trade; that they constitute not the effect, but the cause, of a favorable or unfavourable trade-balance. The precious metals are distributed among individuals and hence among nations according to the extent and intensity of their demand for money.[5]

Mises applies his marginal-utility theory of money to the explanation of the principles governing the "natural" or equilibrium distribution of the world money stock among the various nations. In the case of a 100 percent specie standard, Mises states that:

the proposition is as true of money as of every other economic good, that its distribution among individual economic agents depends on its marginal utility . . . all economic goods, including of course money, tend to be distributed in such a way that a position of equilibrium among individuals is reached, when no further act of exchange that any individual could undertake would bring him any gain, any increase of subjective utility. In such a position of equilibrium, the total stock of money, just like the total stocks of commodities, is distributed among individuals according to the intensity with which they are able to express their demand for it in the market. Every displacement of the forces affecting the exchange-ratio between money and other economic goods [i.e., the supply and demand for money] brings about a corresponding change in this distribution, until a new position of equilibrium is reached.[6]

Mises goes on to conclude that the same principles that determine the distribution of money balances among persons also determine the distribution of national money stocks, since the national money stock is merely the sum of the money balances of the nation's residents.[7] In thus building up his explanation of the international distribution of money from his analysis of the interpersonal distribution of money from his analysis of the interpersonal distribution of money balances, Mises sets the stage for an analysis of balance-of-payments phenomena that conforms to the precept of methodological individualism.

Mises, like the later proponents of the monetary approach, envisages balance-of-payments disequilibrium as an integral phase in the process by which individual and hence national money holdings are adjusted to desired levels. Thus, for example, the development of an excess demand for money in a nation will result in a balance-of-payments surplus as market participants seek to augment their money balances by increasing their sales of goods and securities on the world market. The surplus and the corresponding inflow of the money commodity will automatically terminate when domestic money balances have reached desired levels and the excess demand has been satisfied. Conversely, a balance-of-payments deficit is part of the mechanism by which an excess supply of money is adjusted.

The role played by the balance of payments in the monetary-adjustment process is clearly spelled out by Mises in the following passage.

In a society in which commodity transactions are monetary transactions, every individual enterprise must always take care to have on hand a certain quantity of money. It must not permit its cash holding to fall below the definite sum considered necessary for carrying out its transactions. On the other hand, an enterprise will not permit its cash holding to exceed the necessary amount, for allowing that quantity of money to lie idle will lead to loss of interest. If it has too little money, it must reduce purchases or sell some wares. If it has too much money, then it must buy goods.

. . . In this way, every individual sees to it that he is not without money. Because everyone pursues his own interest in doing this, it is impossible for the free play of market forces to cause a drain of all money out of the city, a province or an entire country. . . .

If we had a pure gold standard, therefore, the government need not be the least concerned about the balance of payments. It could safely relinquish to the market responsibility for maintaining a sufficient quantity of gold within the country. Under the influence of free trade forces, precious metals would leave the country only if a surplus was on hand and they would always flow in if too little was available, in the same way that all other commodities are imported if in short supply and exported if in surplus.[8]

An implication of this view of the balance of payments as a phase in the monetary adjustment process is that international movements of money that do not reflect changes in the underlying monetary data can only be temporary phenomena. "Thus," writes Mises, "international movements of money, so far as they are not of a transient nature and consequently soon rendered ineffective by movements in the contrary direction, are always called forth by variations in demand for money."[9]

Although Mises therefore does regard the long-run causes of balance-of-payments disequilibrium as exclusively monetary in nature, he does not make the error, which Yeager attributes to the more radical, global-monetarist wing of the monetary approach, of identifying a balance-of-payments surplus with the process of satisfying an excess demand for domestic money or a deficit with the process of working off an excess supply of domestic money. Mises explicitly recognizes that changes occurring on the "real" side of the economy, for example, a decline in the foreign demand for a nation's exports, may well have a disequilibrating impact on the balance of payments, even in the absence of a change in the underlying conditions of monetary supply and demand. However, in Mises's view, such nonmonetary disturbances of balance-of-payments equilibrium are merely short-run phenomena. It is one of the functions of the balance-of-payments adjustment mechanism to reverse the disequilibrating flows of money that attend these disturbances and to restore thereby the equilibrium distribution of the world money stock, which is determined solely by the configuration of individual demands for money holdings.

If the state of the balance of payments is such that movements of money would have to occur from one country to the other, independently of any altered estimation of money on the part of their respective inhabitants, then operations are induced which reestablish equilibrium. Those persons who receive more money than they will need hasten to spend the surplus again as soon as possible, whether they buy production goods or consumption goods. On the other hand, those persons whose stock of money falls below the amount they will need will be obliged to increase their stock of money, either by restricting their purchases or by disposing of commodities in their possession. The price-variations, in the markets of the countries in question, that occur for these reasons give rise to transactions which must always re-establish the equilibrium of the balance of payments. A debit or credit balance of payments that is not dependent upon an alteration in the conditions of demand for money can only be transient.[10]

The foregoing passage illustrates the difference between Mises and the global monetarists, who deny the possibility that international flows of money can proceed from nonmonetary causes. Their denial is tantamount to claiming that all international movements of money are necessarily equilibrating, since they are undertaken solely in response to disequilibrium between national supplies of and demands for money. As Yeager has pointed out, this line of reasoning leads to the outright and fallacious identification of balance-of-payments surpluses and deficits with the process of adjusting national money stocks to desired levels.

It is not difficult to pinpoint the source from which this erroneous line of reasoning stems: it is the tendency of the monetary approach to depart from the sound precept of methodological individualism and to focus on the nation rather than the individual as the basic unit of analysis. In so doing, it has naturally, although quite illegitimately, applied to the nation analytical concepts and constructs that are appropriate only to the analysis of individual action. In particular, the monetary approach attempts to explain balance-of-payments phenomena by conceiving the nation in the manner of a household or firm that is consciously aiming at acquiring and maintaining an optimum level of money balances. The concept of what Ludwig Lachmann has called "the equilibrium of the household and of the firm" is then invoked to describe the actions which the nation-household must and will undertake in the service of this goal.[11] As Lachmann explains, the concept of household-firm equilibrium is implied in the very logic of choice.[12] An economic agent will always choose the course of action consistent with his goals and their ranking given his knowledge of available resources and of technology. His actions are, therefore, always equilibrating in the sense that they are always aimed at bringing about a (possibly only momentarily) preferred state of affairs.

In the context of the issues dealt with by the monetary approach, the implication of this analytical concept is that the nation will never alter the level of its stock of money unless it is dissatisfied with it, that is, unless there exists an excess supply of or demand for domestic money. A further implication is that all international movements of money will be equilibrating, the result of deliberate steps undertaken by nations to adjust their actual money balances to desired levels. National payments surpluses and deficits, then, are logically always associated with the adjustment of monetary disequilibrium. To argue that balance-of-payments disequilibria may arise, albeit temporarily, for reasons unrelated to monetary disequilibrium is to argue that the economic agent, in this case the nation, has taken leave of economic rationality. Why else acquire or rid oneself of money balances, if not as a deliberate act of choice aimed at securing a more preferred position? Thus the global monetarists are prepared to deny, for example, that a shift in relative demands from domestic to foreign products would create even a temporary deficit in the balance of payments in the absence of the development of an excess supply of domestic money.

The foregoing clearly illustrates the confusion that results when monetary theorists lapse into methodological holism and attempt to apply to hypostasized entities such as the nation concepts whose use is inappropriate outside the realm of individual action. The concept of household-firm equilibrium has meaning only within the framework of the logic of choice. And the logic of choice itself is meaningful only within the context of individual action.

Mises, on the other hand, by virtue of his thoroughgoing methodological individualism, maintains a firm grasp on the all-important distinction between the equilibrium of the individual actor and interindividual equilibrium in his balance-of-payments analysis. The difference between Mises's approach and the monetary approach in this respect may be illustrated with reference to their divergent analyses of the effects on the balance of payments of a change emanating from the "real" or "goods" side of the economy. Assuming an international pure specie currency and starting from a situation of monetary and balance-of-payments equilibrium, let us suppose that domestic consumers increase their expenditures on foreign imports and that this reflects increased valuations of foreign products relative to domestic products. Let us further assume that the demand for money balances remains unchanged for these individuals and that no other changes in the real or monetary data occur elsewhere in the system.

Under the conditions postulated, those proponents of the monetary approach who are inclined to identify balance-of-payments surpluses and deficits with the process of adjusting monetary disequilibrium would naturally deny any disequilibrating effect on the balance of payments, since the nation, by hypothesis, does not wish to alter its level of money balances but merely its mix of consumers' goods. The adjustment will thus proceed entirely in the goods sphere, with the nation simply increasing its exports of domestic products, which it now demands less urgently, to pay for the increased imports of the now more highly esteemed foreign products, while the level of its money balances remains unchanged.

For Mises, however, things are not simple, since the adjustment process does not consist of the mutually consistent choices and actions of a single macroeconomic agent. Rather, it involves a succession of configurations of mutually inconsistent individual equilibria representing numerous microeconomic agents who are induced by the price system to bring their individual actions into closer and closer coordination until a final interindividual equilibrium is effected.

As a consequence, in Mises's analysis, there will indeed emerge an initial balance-of-payments deficit and corresponding outflow of money for the nation in question as domestic consumers shift their expenditures from domestic products to foreign imports. Now, from the point of view of these individual domestic consumers, this outflow of money can certainly be characterized as "equilibrating" in the logic-of-choice sense, because it demonstrably facilitates their attainment of a more preferred position. Nevertheless, from the point of view of the economic system as a whole, far from serving to adjust a preexisting monetary disequilibrium, the flow of money under consideration disrupts the prevailing equilibrium in the interindividual distribution of money balances and is therefore ultimately self-reversing. Thus, the domestic producers of those goods for which demand has declined experience a shrinkage of their incomes, which threatens to leave them with insufficient money balances. On the other hand, the foreign producers, the demand for whose products have increased, experience an augmentation of their incomes and a consequent buildup of excess money balances. Without going into detail, suffice it to say that the steps undertaken by both groups to readjust their money balances to desired levels will initiate a balance-of-payments adjustment process by which the original, equilibrium distribution of money holdings among individuals and hence nations will be reestablished.

Mises thus arrives at the same long-run, comparative-static conclusion as the proponents of the monetary approach, to the effect that the change in question will not result in any alteration in national money stocks. However, his methodological focus on the individual economic agent leads him to analyze the dynamic microeconomic process by which the comparative-static, macroeconomic result emerges.

Before concluding, I wish to briefly note two other important respects in which Mises anticipated the monetary approach. The first involves the global perspective of the monetary approach, which contrasts so sharply with the narrowly national focus of closed-economy macro models typical of the various Keynesian approaches to the balance of payments. The monetary approach views the world economy as a unitary market with the various national commodity and capital submarkets fully integrated with one another and subject to the rule of the law of one price. As a consequence, arbitrage insures that a particular nation's prices and interest rates are rigidly determined by the forces of supply and demand prevailing on the world market.

The analytical importance of the global perspective, which has revolutionized modern balance-of-payments analysis, was grasped completely by Mises:

The mobility of capital goods, which nowadays is but little restricted by legislative provisions such as customs duties, or by other obstacles, has led to the formation of a homogeneous world capital market. In the loan markets of the countries that take part in international trade, the net rate of interest is no longer determined according to national, but according to international, considerations. Its level is settled, not by the natural rate of interest in the country, but by the natural rate of interest *anywhere*. . . . So long and in so far . . . as a nation participates in international trade, its market is only a part of the world market; prices are determined not nationally but internationally.[13]

I might add that Mises's individualist and subjectivist analytical focus enables him to deal more definitively than the writers on the monetary approach with the objection that the existence of internationally nontraded goods and services, for example, houses, haircuts, ice cream cones, severely limits the operation of the law of one price and thus undermines the unity of the world price level. The response of the proponents of the monetary approach, such as Jacob Frankel and Harry Johnson, is the empirical assertion that the elasticities of substitution between the classes of traded and nontraded goods approaches infinity in both consumption and production, a condition that places extremely narrow limits on the range of relative price changes between the two classes of goods.[14]

Mises, on the other hand, disposes of the objection theoretically.[15] His argument is based on the important insight that the location of a good in space is a factor conditioning its usefulness and, therefore, its subjective value to the individual economic agent. For this reason, technologically identical goods that occupy different positions in space are, in fact, different goods. To the extent that the overall valuations and demands of market participants for such physically identical goods differ according to their locations, there will naturally be no tendency for their prices to be equalized. Mises is able to conclude logically, therefore, that the existence of so-called nontraded goods whose prices tend to diverge internationally does not constitute a valid objection to the worldwide operation of the law of one price in the case of each and every good and the corollary tendency to complete equalization of the purchasing power of a unit of the world money.

A final respect in which Mises can be considered as a forerunner of the monetary approach is in his analysis of the causes and cures of a persistent balance-of-payments disequilibrium. For Mises and for the monetary approach, a chronic balance-of-payments deficit can only result from an inflationary monetary policy that continuously introduces excess money balances into the domestic economy via bank-credit creation. The deficit and the corresponding efflux of gold reflects the repeated attempts of domestic money holders to rid themselves of these excess balances, which are being recreated over and over again by the inflationary intervention of the monetary authority. The deficits will only be terminated when the inflationary monetary policy is brought to a halt or the stock of gold reserves is exhausted. Tariffs and other protectionist measures will fail to rectify the situation, since they do not address the fundamental cause of monetary disequilibrium.

The connection between inflationist and interventionist monetary policies and chronic balance-of-payments disequilibrium is delineated by Mises in the following passage:

> If the government introduces into trade quantities of inconvertible banknotes or government notes, then this must lead to a monetary depreciation. The value of the monetary unit declines. However, this depreciation in value can affect only the inconvertible notes. Gold money retains all, or almost all, of its value internationally. However, since the state—with its power to use the force of the law—declares the lower-valued monetary notes equal in purchasing power to the higher-valued gold money and forbids the gold money from being traded at a higher value than the paper notes, the gold coins must vanish from the market. They may disappear abroad. They may be melted down for use in domestic industry. Or they may be hoarded. . . .
>
> No special government intervention is needed to retain the precious metals in circulation within a country. It is enough for the state to renounce all attempts to relieve financial distress by resorting to the printing press. To uphold the currency, it need do no more than that. And it need do *only* that to accomplish this goal. All orders and prohibitions, all measures to limit foreign exchange transactions, etc., are completely useless and purposeless.[16]

In conclusion, Mises's contribution to balance-of-payments analysis should be hailed not only as a doctrinal milestone in the development of the monetary approach but, much more importantly, as a shining exemplar of methodological individualism in monetary theory.[17]

Notes

1. See chapter 18, p. 226.

2. The exception is Thomas M. Humphrey, "Dennis H. Robertson and the Monetary Approach to Exchange Rates," *Federal Reserve Bank of Richmond Economic Review* 66 (May/June 1980): 24, wherein Mises is briefly mentioned as one whose contributions to the monetary approach have been largely overlooked.

3. M.A. Akhtar, "Some Common Misconceptions about the Monetary Approach to International Adjustment," in *The Monetary Approach*

to International Adjustment, ed. Bluford H. Putnam and D. Sykes Wilford (New York: Praeger, 1978), p. 121.

4. Ludwig von Mises, *The Theory of Monetary and Credit,* new enl. ed., trans. H.E. Batson (Irvington-on-Hudson, N.Y.: Foundation for Economic Education, 1971), p. 182.

5. Ibid.

6. Ibid., pp. 183–184.

7. Ibid., p. 184.

8. Ludwig von Mises, *On the Manipulation of Money and Credit,* ed. Percy L. Greaves, Jr., trans. Bettina Bien Greaves (Dobbs Ferry, N.Y.: Free Market Books, 1978), pp. 53–54.

9. Mises, *Money and Credit,* p. 185.

10. Ibid., pp. 184–185.

11. Ludwig M. Lachmann, *Capital, Expectations, and the Market Process: Essays on the Theory of the Market Economy,* ed. Walter E. Grinder (Kansas City: Sheed Andrews and McMeel, 1977), p. 117.

12. Ibid., pp. 117, 189.

13. Mises, *Money and Credit,* pp. 374–375.

14. Jacob A. Frankel and Harry G. Johnson, "The Monetary Approach to the Balance of Payments: Essential Concepts and Historical Origins" in Jacob A. Frankel and Harry G. Johnson, eds., *The Monetary Approach to the Balance of Payments* (Toronto: University of Toronto, 1976), pp. 27–28.

15. Mises, *Money and Credit,* pp. 170–178.

16. Mises, *Manipulation of Money,* p. 55.

17. The limitation of space has prevented me from dealing with Mises's analysis of the exchange rate. Suffice it to say that his pathbreaking, pre-Casselian explanation of the purchasing-power-parity theory as well as his integration of expectations into the explanation of short-run exchange-rate movements is anticipatory of the monetary approach to the exchange rate. Moreover, his global perspective is brought to bear in his original yet neglected insight that the exchange rate between national currencies is to be explained on the same principles as the exchange rate between parallel currencies circulating in the same nation.

Index

About the Contributors

Stephan Boehm is a member of the faculty in the Department of Economics at the University of Graz, Austria.

James M. Buchanan is University Distinguished Professor of economics, and director of the Center for the Study of Public Choice at Virginia Polytechnic Institute and State University.

Roger W. Garrison is assistant professor of economics at Auburn University, Alabama.

Jack High is assistant professor of economics at George Mason University, Virginia.

Ludwig M. Lachmann is professor emeritus of economics at the University of Witwatersrand, South Africa, and visiting research professor of economics at New York University.

Richard N. Langlois is adjunct assistant professor of economics, and research assistant professor at the Center for Science and Technology Policy, New York University.

Donald C. Lavoie is assistant professor of economics at George Mason University, Virginia.

S.C. Littlechild is professor of commerce and head of the Department of Industrial Economics and Business Studies at University of Birmingham, England.

Brian J. Loasby is professor of management economics at University of Stirling, Scotland.

Gerald P. O'Driscoll, Jr. was associate professor of economics at New York University; beginning in 1983 he will be a senior economist at the Federal Reserve Bank of Dallas.

E.C. Pasour, Jr. is professor of economics at North Carolina State University.

261

Mario J. Rizzo is assistant professor of economics at New York University.

Murray N. Rothbard is professor of economics at New York Polytechnic Institute.

Joseph T. Salerno is assistant professor of economics at Rutgers University, Newark.

Karen I. Vaughn is associate professor of economics at George Mason University, Virginia.

Lawrence H. White is assistant professor of economics at New York University.

Leland B. Yeager is professor of economics at the University of Virginia.

About the Editor

Israel M. Kirzner received the Ph.D. in economics from New York University in 1957 and wrote his dissertation under the late Ludwig von Mises. He joined the faculty of New York University in the same year, and has been professor of economics since 1968. Professor Kirzner is the author of five books, including *The Economic Point of View* (1960), *Competition and Entrepreneurship* (1973), and *Perception, Opportunity and Profit* (1979). He has also authored many articles and contributions to published volumes. He founded the doctoral program in Austrian economics at New York University and organized the conference out of which the present volume emerged.